We the People

Edited by Bethany Poore

Notgrass
company

We the People

Edited by Bethany Poore

ISBN 978-1-60999-002-2

Published in the United States by Notgrass Company.

Notgrass Company
370 S. Lowe Avenue, Suite A
PMB 211
Cookeville, Tennessee 38501

1-800-211-8793
www.notgrass.com
books@notgrass.com

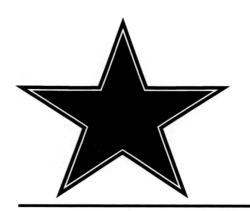

Table of Contents

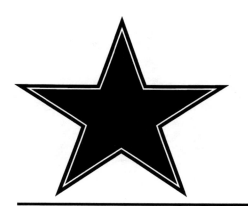

Introduction

These letters, stories, speeches, journals, memoirs, articles, poems, songs, and documents are building blocks of the history of America. They are called original sources because they were written on the spot, as history happened. To learn history, we look both to historians who come after to describe and interpret events and to the recorded words of the people that made the history themselves—the people who were there.

We are indebted to the people who preserved these original sources: archivists of the United States government, newspapers that filed and preserved past editions, families that saved letters and journals, librarians who did not throw away all the books that looked old and tattered, and museum curators who skillfully preserved important documents. Thousands of original source materials have been lost to floods and fires, careless handling, and the trash can. We should be thankful to the people who realize that history is important: that a letter, article, or speech that seems commonplace and unimportant now will someday be history, something for people like us to read in order to understand the past.

These readings will remind you that American history is the story of real people. Like you, each boy and girl, man and woman who lived, worked, learned, loved, ate, slept, and played here in the United States is part of the story of our country. Most of the people who wrote the story of history never got their names in a book.

The ordinary people we call the Pilgrims looked from their boat toward the shore of Massachusetts, not knowing how their new life was going to be. Native American families on the Plains celebrated their favorite holiday traditions and told stories. Founding Fathers like George Washington were once young boys who had to copy their school lessons into a notebook. John Jay, after he was the first Chief Justice of the Supreme Court, was an old man who had a loving family that came to visit him for Christmas. Travelers during the 1800s were thrilled to see the same places we get excited about today, like Niagara Falls and Yellowstone. Real husbands, fathers, and brothers bravely stood their ground at the Alamo, not knowing how it was going to turn out. Women just like your mother waited day after day for a letter from their husbands fighting in the Civil War. People across the country eagerly devoured the newspaper article describing their bachelor President's White House wedding. American housewives carefully followed the government's instructions to use less fat, sugar, and meat in their cooking so that millions of starving people in Europe would have enough after World War I. Young men from every walk of life serving in World War II soberly read the letter that their beloved General Eisenhower wrote to them before they made a brave and heroic invasion on D-Day. Grieving Americans looked to their President for words of comfort after seven astronauts perished as their space shuttle was taking off. And you, part of a movement to bring education back home, learn from your parents and other American history-makers. We're all everyday Americans, making American history—a few big events and lots of everyday life. As you learn the great story, may you be inspired to make a positive impact on the history of America. I hope you will enjoy getting acquainted with great Americans, the famous and the ordinary, in the pages of *We the People*.

Bethany Poore

We the People

contains these types of original sources:

Books & Stories

Newspaper Articles

Documents

Poems

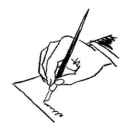
Journals, Memoirs, & Biographies

Speeches

Letters

Songs

America the Beautiful

Katharine Lee Bates, 1893

In 1893 Katharine Lee Bates took a trip to the top of Pike's Peak in Colorado and was inspired to write this poem about the beauty of America. It is usually sung to a tune written by Samuel A. Ward and has become one of America's most popular patriotic songs. The photo at the bottom shows Pike's Peak from a distance.

O beautiful for spacious skies,
    For amber waves of grain,
For purple mountain majesties
    Above the fruited plain!
America! America!
    God shed His grace on thee,
And crown thy good with brotherhood
    From sea to shining sea!

O beautiful for pilgrim feet,
    Whose stern, impassion'd stress
A thoroughfare for freedom beat
    Across the wilderness!
America! America!
    God mend thine ev'ry flaw,
Confirm thy soul in self-control,
    Thy liberty in law!

O beautiful for heroes prov'd
    In liberating strife,
Who more than self their country loved,
    And mercy more than life!
America! America!
    May God thy gold refine,
Till all success be nobleness,
    And ev'ry gain divine!

O beautiful for patriot dream
    That sees beyond the years
Thine alabaster cities gleam
    Undimmed by human tears!
America! America!
    God shed His grace on thee,
And crown thy good with brotherhood
    From sea to shining sea!

Indian Child Life, Part 1

Charles A. Eastman (Ohiyesa), 1913

Ohiyesa was a Native American of the Sioux tribe who lived from 1858 to 1939. He wrote several books for children so that "the children in our schools might read stories of real Indians by a real Indian." Ohiyesa told the story of his own boyhood in Indian Child Life, *published in 1913. His early childhood reflects the ways that the Sioux had lived for many years. Ohiyesa was called Hakadah in his early years. When he was older, he earned the name Ohiyesa, which means "the winner." Ohiyesa later took the English name Charles Alexander Eastman. He grew up to be a doctor as well as a writer. He worked to make life better for Native Americans in the United States.*

From Chapter 1, "The Pitiful Last"

I was so unfortunate as to be the youngest of five children who, soon after I was born, were left motherless. I had to bear the humiliating name "Hakādah," meaning "the pitiful last," until I should earn a more dignified and appropriate name. I was regarded as little more than a plaything by the rest of the children.

The babe was done up as usual in a movable cradle made from an oak board two and a half feet long and one and a half feet wide. On one side of it was nailed with brass-headed tacks the richly embroidered sack, which was open in front and laced up and down with buckskin strings. Over the arms of the infant was a wooden bow, the ends of which were firmly attached to the board, so that if the cradle should fall the child's head and face would be protected. On this bow were hung curious playthings—strings of artistically carved bones and hoofs of deer, which rattled when the little hands moved them.

In this upright cradle I lived, played, and slept the greater part of the time during the first few months of my life. Whether I was made to lean against a lodge pole or was suspended from a bough of a tree, while my grandmother cut wood, or whether I was carried on her back, or conveniently balanced by another child in a similar cradle hung on the opposite side of a pony, I was still in my oaken bed.

This grandmother, who had already lived through sixty years of hardships, was a wonder to the young maidens of the tribe. She showed no less enthusiasm over Hakadah than she had done when she held her first-born, the boy's father, in her arms. Every little attention that is due to a loved child she performed with much skill and devotion. She made all my scanty garments and my tiny moccasins with a great deal of taste. It was said by all that I could not have had more attention had my mother been living.

Indian Child Life, Part 2

Charles A. Eastman (Ohiyesa), 1913

Continued from Chapter 1, "The Pitiful Last"

Uncheedah (Grandmother) was a great singer. Sometimes, when Hakadah wakened too early in the morning, she would sing to him something like the following lullaby:

> Sleep, sleep, my boy, the Chippewas
> Are far away—are far away.
> Sleep, sleep, my boy; prepare to meet
> The foe by day—the foe by day!
> The cowards will not dare to fight
> Till morning break—till morning break.
> Sleep, sleep, my child, while still 'tis night;
> Then bravely wake—then bravely wake!

The Dakota women were wont to cut and bring their fuel from the woods and, in fact, to perform most of the drudgery of the camp. This of necessity fell to their lot because the men must follow the game during the day. Very often my grandmother carried me with her on these excursions; and while she worked it was her habit to suspend me from a wild grape vine or a springy bough, so that the least breeze would swing the cradle to and fro.

She has told me that when I had grown old enough to take notice, I was apparently capable of holding extended conversations in an unknown dialect with birds and red squirrels. Once I fell asleep in my cradle, suspended five or six feet from the ground, while Uncheedah was some distance away, gathering birch bark for a canoe. A squirrel had found it convenient to come upon the bow of my cradle and nibble his hickory nut, until he awoke me by dropping the crumbs of his meal. It was a common thing for birds to alight on my cradle in the woods.

Indian Child Life, Part 3

Charles A. Eastman (Ohiyesa), 1913

From Chapter 3, "An Indian Sugar Camp"

With the first March thaw the thoughts of the Indian women of my childhood days turned promptly to the annual sugar-making. This industry was chiefly followed by the old men and women and the children. The rest of the tribe went out upon the spring fur-hunt at this season, leaving us at home to make the sugar.

The first and most important of the necessary utensils were the huge iron and brass kettles for boiling. Everything else could be made, but these must be bought, begged or borrowed. A maple tree was felled and a log canoe hollowed out, into which the sap was to be gathered. Little troughs of basswood and birchen basins were also made to receive the sweet drops as they trickled from the tree. . . .

My grandmother did not confine herself to canoe-making. She also collected a good supply of fuel for the fires, for she would not have much time to gather wood when the sap began to flow. Presently the weather moderated and the snow began to melt. The month of April brought showers which carried most of it off into the Minnesota River. Now the women began to test the trees— moving leisurely among them, axe in hand, and striking a single quick blow, to see if the sap would appear. . . .

It is usual to make sugar from maples, but several other trees were also tapped by the Indians. From the birch and ash was made a dark-colored sugar, with a somewhat bitter taste, which was used for medicinal purposes. The box-elder yielded a beautiful white sugar, whose only fault was that there was never enough of it! . . .

Every pursuit has its trials and anxieties. My grandmother's special tribulations, during the sugaring season, were the upsetting and gnawing of holes in her birch-bark pans. The transgressors were the rabbit and squirrel tribes, and we little boys for once became useful, in shooting them with our bows and arrows. We hunted all over the sugar camp, until the little creatures were fairly driven out of the neighborhood. Occasionally one of my older brothers brought home a rabbit or two, and then we had a feast.

I remember on this occasion of our last sugar bush in Minnesota, that I stood one day outside of our hut and watched the approach of a visitor—a bent old man, his hair almost white, and carrying on his back a large bundle of red willow, or kinnikinick, which the Indians use for smoking. He threw down his load at the door and thus saluted us: "You have indeed perfect weather for sugar-making."

It was my great-grandfather, Cloud Man, whose original village was on the shores of Lakes Calhoun and Harriet, now in the suburbs of the city of Minneapolis. He was the first Sioux chief to welcome the Protestant missionaries among his people, and a well-known character in those pioneer days. He brought us word that some of the peaceful sugar-makers near us on the river had been attacked and murdered by roving Ojibways. This news disturbed us not a little, for we realized that we too might become the victims of an Ojibway war party. Therefore we all felt some uneasiness from this time until we returned heavy laden to our village.

Indian Child Life, Part 4

Charles A. Eastman (Ohiyesa), 1913

From Chapter 4, "Games and Sports"

Our sports were molded by the life and customs of our people; indeed, we practiced only what we expected to do when grown. Our games were feats with the bow and arrow, foot and pony races, wrestling, swimming and imitation of the customs and habits of our fathers. We had sham fights with mud balls and willow wands; we played lacrosse, made war upon bees, shot winter arrows (which were used only in that season), and coasted [sledded] upon the ribs of animals and buffalo robes. . . .

The "mud-and-willow" fight was rather a severe and dangerous sport. A lump of soft clay was stuck on the end of a limber and springy willow wand and thrown as boys throw apples from sticks, with considerable force. When there were fifty or a hundred players on each side, the battle became warm; but anything to arouse the bravery of Indian boys seemed to them a good and wholesome diversion.

Wrestling was largely indulged in by us all. It may seem odd, but wrestling was done by a great many boys at once—from ten to any number on a side. It was really a battle, in which each one chose his opponent. The rule was that if a boy sat down, he was let alone, but as long as he remained standing within the field, he was open to an attack. No one struck with the hand, but all manner of tripping with legs and feet and butting with the knees was allowed. Altogether it was an exhausting pastime—fully equal to the American game of football, and only the young athlete could really enjoy it.

One of our most curious sports was a war upon the nests of wild bees. We imagined ourselves about to make an attack upon the Ojibways or some tribal foe. We all painted and stole cautiously upon the nest; then, with a rush and war-whoop, sprang upon the object of our attack and endeavored to destroy it. But it seemed that the bees were always on the alert and never entirely surprised, for they always raised quite as many scalps as did their bold assailants! After the onslaught upon the nest was ended, we usually followed it by a pretended scalp dance. . . .

We had some quiet plays which we alternated with the more severe and warlike ones. Among them were throwing wands and snow-arrows. In the winter we coasted much. We had no "double-rippers" or toboggans, but six or seven of the long ribs of a buffalo, fastened together at the larger end, answered all practical purposes. Sometimes a strip of bass-wood bark, four feet long and about six inches wide, was used with considerable skill. We stood on one end and held the other, using the slippery inside of the bark for the outside, and thus coasting down long hills with remarkable speed.

Journal of Christopher Columbus

Christopher Columbus, 1492

Christopher Columbus kept a journal of his first voyage to the New World of 1492-1493 as a record for King Ferdinand and Queen Isabella of Spain, for whom he sailed. He wrote the following entry about his arrival on one of the islands of the Bahamas. It was translated by Clements R. Markham.

October 11, 1492

I, that we might form great friendship, for I knew that they were a people who could be more easily freed and converted to our holy faith by love than by force, gave to some of them red caps, and glass beads to put round their necks, and many other things of little value, which gave them great pleasure, and made them so much our friends that it was a marvel to see. They afterwards came to the ship's boats where we were, swimming and bringing us parrots, cotton threads in skeins, darts, and many other things; and we exchanged them for other things that we gave them, such as glass beads and small bells. In fine, they took all, and gave what they had with good will. It appeared to me to be a race of people very poor in everything. . . . All I saw were youths, none more than thirty years of age. They are very well made, with very handsome bodies, and very good countenances. Their hair is short and coarse, almost like the hairs of a horse's tail. They wear the hairs brought down to the eyebrows, except a few locks behind, which they wear long and never cut. They paint themselves black, and they are the color of the Canarians, neither black nor white. Some paint themselves white, others red, and others of what color they find. Some paint their faces, others the whole body, some only round the eyes, others only on the nose. They neither carry nor know anything of arms, for I showed them swords, and they took them by the blade and cut themselves through ignorance. They have no iron, their darts being wands without iron, some of them having a fish's tooth at the end, and others being pointed in various ways. They are all of fair stature and size, with good faces, and well made. I saw some with marks of wounds on their bodies, and I made signs to ask what it was, and they gave me to understand that people from other adjacent islands came with the intention of seizing them, and that they defended themselves. I believed, and still believe, that they come here from the mainland to take them prisoners. They should be good servants and intelligent, for I observed that they quickly took in what was said to them, and I believe that they would easily be made Christians, as it appeared to me that they had no religion. I, our Lord being pleased, will take hence, at the time of my departure, six natives for your Highnesses, that they may learn to speak. I saw no beast of any kind except parrots, on this island.

The Mountain Chant:
A Navajo Ceremony

Dr. Washington Matthews, 1884

Dr. Washington Matthews observed members of the Navajo nation while researching for the Smithsonian Institution. This excerpt is from a report of 1883-1884.

On two occasions I have witnessed a very pretty dance, in which an eagle plume was stuck upright in a basket, and by means of some well hidden mechanism, caused to dance in good time to the song, the beat of the drum, and the motions of the single Indian who danced at the same time; not only this, but the feather followed the motions of the Indian: if he danced toward the north, the feather leaned to the north while making its rhythmical motions; if he moved to the south,  it bent its white head in the same direction, and so on. On one occasion it was a little boy, five years old, son of the chief Manuelito, who danced with the eagle plume. He was dressed and painted much like the akáninili, or the arrow swallowers, on a diminutive scale. The sash of scarlet velvet around his hips was beautifully trimmed with feathers. They said he had been several weeks in training for the dance, and he certainly went through his varied motions with great skill. I have rarely seen a terpsichorean [dance] spectacle that struck my fancy more than that of the little Indian child and his partner, the eagle plume.

The Coyote and the Turtle

told by Guanyanum Sacknumptewa
to Hattie Greene Lockett, c. 1932

Hattie Greene Lockett learned this old Hopi folk tale when she visited in the home of a Hopi family. Guanyanum sat on the clean clay floor of her house and husked a pile of corn while she told it. Her husband and children soon gathered around to enjoy her gifted, animated story-telling.

A long time ago, there were many turtles living in the Little Colorado River near Homolovi, southeast of Winslow, where Hopi used to live. And there was a coyote living there too, and of course, he was always hungry.

Now one day the turtles decided they would climb out of the river and go hunt some food, for there was a kind of cactus around there that they like very much. But one of the turtles had a baby and she didn't like to wake it up and take it with her because it was sleeping so nicely. So they just went along and left the baby asleep.

After a while the little turtle woke up and he said, "Where is my mother? She must have gone somewhere and left me. O, I must go and find her!"

So the baby turtle saw that the others had crawled up the bank, and he followed their tracks for a little way. But he soon got tired and just stopped under a bush and began to cry.

Now the coyote was coming along and he heard the poor little turtle crying. So he came up and said, "That's a pretty song; now go on and sing for me."

But the baby turtle said, "I'm not singing, I'm crying."

"Go on and sing," said the coyote, "I want to hear you sing."

"I can't sing," said the poor baby, "I'm crying and I want my mother."

"You'd better sing for me, or I'll eat you up," said the big hungry coyote.

"O, I can't sing—I just can't stop crying," said the baby, and he cried harder and harder.

"Well," the big coyote said, "if you don't sing for me I'm going to eat you right up." The coyote was mad, and he was very hungry. "All right, then, I'll just eat you," he said.

Now the little turtle thought of something. So he said, "Well, I can't sing, so I guess you'll have to eat me. But that's all right, for it won't hurt me any; here inside of my shell I'll go right on living inside of you."

Now the coyote thought about this a little bit and didn't like the idea very well.

Then the baby turtle said, "You can do anything you want with me, just so you don't throw me into the river, for I don't want to drown."

Now the old coyote was pretty mad and he wanted to be as mean as possible. So he just picked that baby up in his mouth and carried him over to the river and threw him in.

Then the baby turtle was very happy; he stuck his little head out of his shell and stretched out his feet and started swimming off toward the middle of the river. And he said, "Goodbye, Mr. Coyote, and thank you very much for bringing me back to my house so that I didn't have to walk back." And the little turtle laughed at the old coyote, who got madder and madder because he had let the little turtle go. But he couldn't get him now, so he just went home. And the baby turtle was still laughing when his mother got home, and she laughed, too. And those turtles are still living in that water.

Mesa Verde Wonderland Is Easy to Reach

Willa Cather, 1916

To American author Willa Cather, Mesa Verde was a special place. This excerpt is from an article published in The Denver Times *on January 31, 1916, when Mesa Verde National Park was less than ten years old.*

The Denver Times　　　　　　　　　　　　　　**January 31, 1916**

Mesa Verde Wonderland Is Easy to Reach

By Willa Cather

The journey to the Mesa Verde . . . is now a very easy one, and the railway runs within thirty miles of the mesa. You leave Denver in the evening, over the Denver & Rio Grande. From the time when your train crawls out of La Veta pass at about 4 in the morning, until you reach Durango at nightfall, there is not a dull moment. All day you are among high mountains, swinging back and forth between Colorado and New Mexico, with the Sangre de Cristo and the Culebra ranges always in sight until you cross the continental divide at Cumbres and begin the wild scurry down the westward slope.

That particular branch of the Denver & Rio Grande is called the Whiplash, and most of the way you can signal to the engineer from the rear car . . . .

From the streets of Mancos and from the hills about it one can always see the green mesa—not green at that distance but a darkish purple, a rather grim mass bulking up in the West. It sits like a cheese box in the plain, the deep canyons with which it is slashed imperceptible from far away. The mesa is forty-five miles long and twenty-five wide, and its sides are so steep that it is accessible from only one point. The government wagon road is recent. Until within a few years there was only a difficult horse trail. Charles Kelly, who now takes travelers out to the mesa by wagon or motor, is the same guide who formerly provided mounts and provisions and pack horses for people who came to see ruins on the mesa. There is now a very comfortable tent camp on the mesa, just above the fine spring at Spruce Tree House, and the wife of the forest ranger provides excellent food. Anyone can be very comfortable there for several weeks.

Any approach to the Mesa Verde is impressive, but one must always think with envy of the entrada of Richard Wetherill, the first white man who discovered the ruins in its canyons forty-odd years ago. . . . One December day a boy brought word to the ranch house that a bunch of cattle had got away and gone up into the mesa. The same thing had happened before, and young Richard Wetherill said that this time he was going after his beasts. He rode off with one of his cow men and they entered the mesa by a deep canyon from the Mancos river, which flows at its base. They followed the canyon toward the heart of the mesa until they could go no farther with horses. They tied their mounts and went on foot up a side canyon, now called Cliff Canyon. After a long stretch of hard climbing, young Wetherill happened to glance up at the great cliffs above him, and there, through a veil of lightly falling snow, he saw practically as it stands today and as it had stood for 800 years before, the cliff palace—not a cliff dwelling, but a cliff village; houses, courts, terraces and towers, a place large enough to house 300 people, lying in a natural archway let back into the cliff. It stood as if it had been deserted yesterday; undisturbed and undesecrated, preserved by the dry atmosphere and by its great inaccessibility.

That is what the Mesa Verde means; its ruins are the highest achievement of stone-age man—preserved in bright, dry sunshine, like a fly in amber—sheltered by great canyon walls and hidden away in a difficult mesa into which no one had ever found a trail. When Wetherill rode in after his cattle no later civilization blurred the outlines there. Life had been extinct upon the mesa since the days of the Cliff

Dwellers. Not only their buildings, but their pottery, linen cloth, feather cloth, sandals, stone and bone tools, dried pumpkins, corn and onions, remained as they had been left. . . .

Florida Tourism Advertisement

New York Tribune, December 19, 1920

This advertisement encouraged New Yorkers to enjoy the vacation wonderland of Florida. Look for the names of Henry Flagler's famous St. Augustine hotels. Henry Flagler also purchased and developed railroad lines in Florida, which are also mentioned in this advertisement.

NEW YORK TRIBUNE   DECEMBER 19, 1920

The Charm of Color

Have you ever realized the exhilarating effect that warm, pleasing colors, even in a picture, have upon your physical well-being? For instance, visualize this illustration in your mind's eye, in all its natural coloring—the blue sky, the verdant foliage and brilliant flowers, the sunlit buildings with their purple shadows, the sparkling iridescent waters—and—presto, your troubles vanish and you are filled with a warm spirit of contentment. The interesting feature of the illustration, is, however, that this is no vision, but just a fragment of the real, summer-like environment that you find everywhere

On the Wonderful Florida East Coast

Leave those gray skies and drab walls that oppress you and linger awhile among those radiant resorts, where every day is a holiday, and where Health, Happiness and Contentment are waiting to welcome you with open arms.

Golf   Surf-Bathing   Fishing   Sailing
Tennis   Motoring   Aviation   Etc.,   Etc.

St. Augustine—Ponce de Leon, Alcazar
Ormond-on-the-Halifax—Ormond
Palm Beach—Breakers, Royal Poinciana
Miami—Royal Palm
Long Key—Long Key Fishing Camp
Key West—Casa Marina
Nassau—Colonial
Bahama Islands—Royal Victoria

Through Pullman Trains, New York to Miami. Excellent dining car service to Key West, connecting with high-class Passenger ships for Cuba.

For Booklets and Information Write:
Florida East Coast (Flagler System)
243 Fifth Avenue, New York
General Offices, St. Augustine, Fla.

The Founding of Jamestown

Captain John Smith, 1624

John Smith was one of the first leaders of the Jamestown settlement and one of the primary keys to its success. He also explored, made maps, and recorded the history of the early settlement of America. Below is an excerpt concerning the journey to and early days of Jamestown. The title of Smith's extensive work of history, with the original spelling, is: The Generall Historie of Virginia, New-England, and the Summer Isles: With the Names of the Adventurers, Planters, and Governours from Their First Beginning, Ano[1]: 1584. To This Present 1624. *The drawing at the bottom was sketched by Alfred R. Waud in 1864 and shows the ruins of the church tower at Jamestown begun in 1639. The ruins are still standing today.*

We watered at the Canaries, we traded with the savages at Dominica; three weeks we spent in refreshing ourselves amongst these west-India Isles; in Gwardalupa we found a bath so hot, as in it we boiled Pork as well as over the fire. And at a little Isle called Monica, we took from the bushes with our hands, near two hogsheads [barrels] full of Birds in three or four hours. In Mevis, Mona, and the Virgin Isles, we spent some time, where, with a loathsome beast like a crocodile, called a gwayn, tortoises, pelicans, parrots, and fishes, we daily feasted. Gone from thence in search of Virginia, the company was not a little discomforted, seeing the mariners [sailors] had 3 days passed their reckoning and found no land, so that Captain Ratliffe (Captain of the Pinnace) rather desired to bear up the helm to return for England, than make further search. But God the guider of all good actions, forcing them by an extreme storm to hull all night, did drive them by His providence to their desired Port, beyond all their expectations, for never any of them had seen that coast. The first land they made they called Cape Henry; where thirty of them recreating [resting] themselves on shore, were assaulted by five savages, who hurt two of the English very dangerously. That night was the box opened[2], and the orders read, in which Bartholomew Gosnoll, John Smith, Edward Wingfield, Christopher Newport, John Ratliffe, John Martin, and George Kendall, were named to be the Council, and to choose a President amongst them for a year, who with the Council should govern. . . . Until the 13 of May they sought a place to plant in, then the Council was sworn, Mr Wingfield was chosen President. . . .

Now falleth every man to work, the Council contrive the Fort, the rest cut down trees to make place to pitch their Tents; some provide clapboard to reload the ships, some make gardens, some nets, &c. The Savages often visited us kindly . . . .

[1] Ano is an abbreviation for anno domini which is Latin for "the year of the Lord."

[2] The box John Smith mentioned contained the orders of the Virginia Company, which supervised the founding of Jamestown from England. The settlers were ordered to leave the box sealed until they reached the site of the new colony.

Great Lakes Poems

Denise Rogers, 2003

Denise Rogers is a contemporary children's poet who lives in Michigan and loves to write poetry about her home state. The first poem is about Michigan's special geography and city names, many of which come from Native American words. The second poem celebrates a native Michigan resident—the porcupine. These poems are from Denise Rogers' book Great Lakes Rhythm and Rhyme.

Michigan Map Poem

Saginaw Bay is the crook of a mitten.
Port Hope is right up near the thumb.
Manistee sits right where you'd put your pinky.
The Lansing spot taps on a drum.
Sturgis is south, at the base of the wrist
And there's Mackinac at the tip top.
There are so many cities in Michigan's mitten.
Recite them and you'll never stop.

Mount Pleasant, Ann Arbor and Kalamazoo,
Adrian, Midland and Frost,
Alpena, Kalkaska, Boyne City and Bath.
Keep driving until you get lost.
The mitten is grand, it is large, it is super,
But down there you'll never get close to a
    yooper.
A yooper's a person who's from the U.P.
The part of the state where there's much more
    to see.

There's Laurium, Skandia, Limestone and Tula,
Marquette, Iron Mountain and Gay.
There's Drummond and White Pine
    and Greenland
And Johnsville and Witch Lake and
    Keweenaw Bay.
So go for a ride, get out there exploring
No matter how long it might take.
And if you get finished with finding the cities,
Then next you can look for the lakes . . . .

Porcupine

The thing about the porcupine -
He has no pork. He has no pine.
He does have quills, these long thin spikes
That no one but the porc'pine likes.
He'll use them when he's in a mood.
(Like when you're loud or mean or rude.)
They won't feel good. They'll make you pout.
They go in quick. They won't come out.
So if a porcupine is present,
Make sure that you are nice and pleasant.

Of Plimoth Plantation

William Bradford, c. 1620

William Bradford, Governor of Plymouth Plantation, wrote a detailed history of the journey of the Pilgrims (Separatists) of England: to the Netherlands, back to England, and to the founding of a new home in the New World. The following are excerpts from his work.

On the arrival of the Mayflower in America:

Being thus arrived in a good harbor and brought safe to land, they fell upon their knees & blessed the God of heaven, who had brought them over the vast & furious ocean, and delivered them from all the perils and miseries thereof, again to set their feet on the firm and stable earth, their proper element. . . .

On their explorations and first encounter with Native Americans:

Being thus arrived at Cape Cod the 11th of November, and necessity calling them to look out a place for habitation . . . whereupon a few of them tendered themselves to go by land and discover those nearest places. . . . It was conceived there might be some danger in the attempt, yet seeing them resolute, they were permitted to go, being sixteen of them well armed, under the conduct of Captain Standish, having such instructions given them as was thought meet. They set forth the 15th of November and when they had marched about the space of a mile by the sea side, they espied five or six persons with a dog coming towards them, who were savages, but they [the Native Americans] fled from them and ran up into the woods and the English followed them partly to see if they could speak with them, and partly to discover if there might not be more of them lying in ambush. But the Indians seeing themselves thus followed, they again forsook [left] the woods and ran away on the sands as hard as they could. . . . So, night coming on, they made their rendezvous and set out their sentinels, and rested in quiet that night, and the next morning followed their tract till they had headed a great creek, and so left the sands, and turned another way into the woods. But they still followed them by guess, hoping to find their dwellings; but they soon lost both them and themselves, falling into such thickets as were ready to tear their clothes and armor in pieces, but were most distressed for want of drink. But at length they found water & refreshed themselves, being the first New-England water they drunk of . . . .

On the discovery of the place for settlement in the midst of a storm at sea:

And though it was very dark, and rained sore, yet in the end they got under the lee of a small island, and remained there all that night in safety. But they knew not this to be an island till morning, but were divided in their minds; some would keep [stay on] the boat for fear they might be amongst the Indians; others were so weak and cold, they could not endure, but got ashore, and with much ado got fire, (all things being so wet,) and the rest were glad to come to them; for after midnight the wind shifted to the north-west, and it froze hard. But though this had been a day and night of much trouble and danger unto them, yet God gave them a morning of comfort and refreshing (as usually He doth to his children), for the next day was a fair sunshining day, and they found themselves to be on an island secure from the Indians, where they might dry their stuff, fix their pieces, and rest themselves, and gave God thanks for His mercies, in their manifold deliverances. And this being the last day of the week, they prepared there to keep the Sabbath. On Monday they sounded the harbor, and found it fit for shipping; and marched into the land, and found diverse cornfields, and little running brooks, a place (as they supposed) fit for situation [to live in]; at least it was the best they could find, and the season, and their present necessity, made them glad to accept of it. So they returned to their ship again with this news to the rest of their people, which did much comfort their hearts.

On the 15th of December: they weighed [lifted] anchor to go to the place they had discovered, and came within leagues of it, but were fain [inclined] to bear up again; but the 16th day the wind came fair and they arrived safe in this harbor. And afterwards took better view of their place, and resolved where to pitch their dwelling, and the 25th day began to erect the first house for common use to receive them and their goods.

Flushing Remonstrance

Edward Hart, 1657

One of Governor Peter Stuyvesant's harsh policies was denial of religious freedom to Quakers. The town of Flushing in the colony of New Netherlands had many Quakers. In 1657 thirty brave citizens of Flushing sent a remonstrance (protest) to Peter Stuyvesant stating that they would follow God instead of his unfair law. An excerpt from the "Flushing Remonstrance," one of the first documents of the struggle for religious freedom in America, is printed below. The Quaker meeting house in Flushing, New York, was built in 1694. The building still stands and houses an active congregation.

Right Honorable,

You have been pleased to send up unto us a certain prohibition or command that we should not receive or entertain any of those people called Quakers. . . .

The law of love, peace and liberty in the states extending to Jews, Turks, and Egyptians, as they are considered the sons of Adam, which is the glory of the outward state of Holland, so love, peace and liberty, extending to all in Christ Jesus, condemns hatred, war and bondage. And because our Saviour saith it is impossible but that offenses will come, but woe unto him by whom they cometh, our desire is not to offend one of his little ones, in whatsoever form, name or title he appears in, whether Presbyterian, Independent, Baptist or Quaker, but shall be glad to see anything of God in any of them, desiring to do unto all men as we desire all men should do unto us, which is the true law both of Church and State; for our Savior saith this is the law and the prophets. Therefore, if any of these said persons come in love unto us, we cannot in conscience lay violent hands upon them, but give them free egresse and regresse [coming and going] unto our town, and houses, as God shall persuade our consciences. And in this

we are true subjects both of Church and State, for we are bound by the law of God and man to do good unto all men and evil to no man. And this is according to the patent and charter of our town, given unto us in the name of the States General [the country of Holland], which we are not willing to infringe, and violate, but shall hold to our patent and shall remain, your humble subjects, the inhabitants of Vlishing. [Flushing]

Written this 27th day of December, in the year 1657, by me

Edward Hart, Clericus [Town Clerk]

Salvation from Sin
by Christ Alone

William Penn, 1694

This is an excerpt from a sermon William Penn preached in a Quaker Meeting House in London, England, on August 12, 1694. The portait below shows William Penn in 1666.

. . . Friends, I beseech you, in the fear of God, "look up unto Jesus, the great mediator of the new covenant, the author and finisher of your faith; that by patient continuance in well doing, you may seek for glory, honor, immortality, and eternal life." Which you shall obtain, if you persevere to the end: "For he that endureth unto the end shall be saved."

"Be not weary of well doing; for in due time you shall reap if you faint not." He that hath appeared, as a God of salvation, and a mighty preserver of His people in all ages of the world, and hath been so both to the primitive Christians, and to all our Christian friends that are gone before us to an eternal rest, if you faint not, but follow them, who through faith and patience do inherit the promises, you shall lay down your heads in peace in Him, when you come to die. And when time shall be no more, you shall be forever with the Lord.

To God be praise, honor, and glory, who hath stretched forth His mighty arm to save: Who is the arm of the Lord but Christ Jesus, the redeemer of souls? When we had undone ourselves, and lost ourselves, in wandering and departing from the Lord, the true and living God, into darkness and the shadow of death, He stretched forth his Almighty arm, to gather us, and to bring us into the paradise of God again, when we were driven out by our own sin, from the face and presence of the Lord. Christ Jesus, the great and good shepherd of his sheep, came to seek and to save them that were lost: The lost sheep that have wandered from Him, He will take them on His shoulder, and bring them to His fold: and He will make them lie down in green pastures, and lead them by the still waters, and satisfy them with the rivers of pleasure that are at God's right hand forevermore. He hath promised, "That He will feed His flock like a shepherd, and gather His lambs with His arm, and carry them in His bosom." I hope Christ Jesus, the Great Shepherd, will find some here this day, that have gone astray, and gather them with His divine arm, and keep them by His mighty power, through faith unto salvation. To Him be all praise, honor, glory, dominion, and thanksgiving: For He alone is worthy, who is God over all, blessed for ever and ever. Amen.

New England Primer
Rhyming Alphabet
c. 1687

The New England Primer *was published around 1687 by Benjamin Harris. It is thought to be the first American textbook and remained popular for many years. The Puritans encouraged children to learn how to read so that they could know for themselves what the Bible says. This rhyming alphabet reveals some of the beliefs of the Puritans. The original capitalizations are shown here.*

A In Adam's Fall
We sinned all.

B Thy Life to mend
This Book attend.

C The Cat doth play
And after slay.

D A dog will Bite
A Thief at Night.

E An Eagle's Flight
Is out of Sight.

F An idle Fool
Is whipt at School.

G As runs the Glass
Man's life doth pass.

H My Book and Heart
Shall never part.

J Sweet Jesus He
Died on a Tree.

K King William's Dead
and left the Throne
To Ann our Queen
of great Renown.

L The Lion bold
The Lamb does hold.

M Moon gives light
In time of Night.

N Nightingales sing
in time of Spring.

O The Royal Oak
It was the Tree
That favored his
Royal Majesty.

P Peter denies
His Lord and cries.

Q Queen Esther came
in Royal State,
To save the Jews
from dismal Fate.

R Rachel doth mourn
for her first-born.

S Samuel anoints
whom God appoints.

T Time cuts down all
both great and small.

U Uriah's beauteous Wife
Made David seek his Life.

W Whales in the Sea,
God's Voice obey.

X Xerxes the Great did die,
And so must you and I.

Y Youth forward slips
Death soonest nips.

Z Zaccheus he
did climb the Tree,
his Lord to see.

The Pharisee and the Publican

Isaac Watts, c. 1700

The Great Awakening caused an explosion in the popularity of hymns and hymn-singing in America. The hymns of Isaac Watts of England (1674-1748) were beloved in America. This hymn is from his collection entitled Hymns and Spiritual Songs. *In response to the great demand for religious books at the time, Benjamin Franklin printed an American edition of this book in 1741, which sold many copies.*

Behold how sinners disagree,
    The Publican and Pharisee!
One doth his righteousness proclaim,
    The other owns his guilt and shame.

This man at humble distance stands,
    And cries for grace with lifted hands;
That boldly rises near the throne,
    And talks of duties he has done.

The Lord their different language knows,
    And different answers he bestows;
The humble soul with grace he crowns,
    Whilst on the proud his anger frowns.

Dear Father, let me never be
    Joined with the boasting Pharisee;
I have no merits of my own,
    But plead the sufferings of thy Son.

The Village Blacksmith

Henry Wadsworth Longfellow, 1839

Henry Wadsworth Longfellow wrote this well-loved poem in 1839. It was inspired by a real blacksmith who stood under a chestnut tree that Longfellow passed every day. Longfellow wrote to his father that this poem was a song of praise for one of their ancestors who was a blacksmith.

Under a spreading chestnut-tree
   The village smithy stands;
The smith, a mighty man is he,
   With large and sinewy hands;
And the muscles of his brawny arms
   Are strong as iron bands.

His hair is crisp, and black, and long,
   His face is like the tan;
His brow is wet with honest sweat,
   He earns whate'er he can,
And looks the whole world in the face,
   For he owes not any man.

Week in, week out, from morn till night,
   You can hear his bellows blow;
You can hear him swing his heavy sledge,
   With measured beat and slow,
Like a sexton ringing the village bell,
   When the evening sun is low.

And children coming home from school
   Look in at the open door;
They love to see the flaming forge,
   And hear the bellows roar,
And catch the burning sparks that fly
   Like chaff from a threshing-floor.

He goes on Sunday to the church,
   And sits among his boys;
He hears the parson pray and preach,
   He hears his daughter's voice,
Singing in the village choir,
   And it makes his heart rejoice.

It sounds to him like her mother's voice,
   Singing in Paradise!
He needs must think of her once more,
   How in the grave she lies;
And with his hard, rough hand he wipes
   A tear out of his eyes.

Toiling, — rejoicing, — sorrowing,
   Onward through life he goes;
Each morning sees some task begin,
   Each evening sees it close;
Something attempted, something done,
   Has earned a night's repose.

Thanks, thanks to thee, my worthy friend,
   For the lesson thou hast taught!
Thus at the flaming forge of life
   Our fortunes must be wrought;
Thus on its sounding anvil shaped
   Each burning deed and thought.

20

The Evening of the 5th of March

John Adams, c. 1805

John Adams wrote down the story of his life for his children. This excerpt from his autobiography contains his memories of the Boston Massacre of March 5, 1770. On the morning of the next day, John Adams was asked to represent the British soldiers in the trial for this event. John Adams bravely agreed, knowing he was taking a position that would be unpopular among many Americans.

The year 1770 was memorable enough in these little annals of my pilgrimage. The evening of the fifth of March I spent at Mr. Henderson Inches's house, at the south end of Boston, in company with a club with whom I had been associated for several years. About nine o'clock we were alarmed with the ringing of bells, and, supposing it to be the signal of fire, we snatched our hats and cloaks, broke up the club, and went out to assist in quenching the fire, or aiding our friends who might be in danger. In the street we were informed that the British soldiers had fired on the inhabitants, killed some and wounded others, near the town-house. A crowd of people was flowing down the street to the scene of action. When we arrived, we saw nothing but some field-pieces placed before the south door of the town-house, and some engineers and grenadiers drawn up to protect them. Mrs. Adams was then in circumstances to make me apprehensive of the effect of the surprise upon her, who was alone, excepting her maids and a boy, in the house. Having therefore surveyed round the town-house, and seeing all quiet, I walked down Boylston Alley into Brattle Square, where a company or two of regular soldiers were drawn up in front of Dr. Cooper's old church, with their muskets all shouldered, and their bayonets all fixed. I had no other way to proceed but along the whole front in a very narrow space which they had left for foot passengers. Pursuing my way, without taking the least notice of them, or they of me, any more than if they had been marble statues, I went directly home to Cole Lane.

My wife having heard that the town was still and likely to continue so, had recovered from her first apprehensions, and we had nothing but our reflections to interrupt our repose. These reflections were to me disquieting enough.

Autobiography and Poor Richard's Almanack

Benjamin Franklin, c. 1788

Benjamin Franklin wrote down the story of his life for his son. In the following excerpt, he relates the origins of Poor Richard's Almanack, *one of Franklin's many important and famous achievements. An almanac is a book published usually once a year that contains information about weather, length of days, planting crops, and a host of other information. Almanacs were especially popular and useful to farmers during America's early days. Following the excerpt from Franklin's autobiography is a selection of his famous proverbs from the* Almanack.

In 1732 I first published my Almanack, under the name of *Richard Saunders;* it was continued by me about twenty-five years, commonly called *Poor Richard's Almanack.* I endeavored to make it both entertaining and useful; and it accordingly came to be in such demand, that I reaped considerable profit from it, vending annually near ten thousand. And observing that it was generally read, scarce any neighborhood in the province being without it, I considered it as a proper vehicle for conveying instruction among the common people, who bought scarcely any other books; I therefore filled all the little spaces that occurred between the remarkable days in the calendar with proverbial sentences, chiefly such as inculcated industry and frugality as the means of procuring wealth, and thereby securing virtue; it being more difficult for a man in want to act always honestly, as, to use here one of those proverbs, *it is hard for an empty sack to stand upright.*

These proverbs, which contained the wisdom of many ages and nations, I assembled and formed into a connected discourse prefixed to the Almanack of 1757, as the harangue of a wise old man to the people attending an auction. The bringing all these scattered counsels thus into a focus enabled them to make greater impression. The piece, being universally approved, was copied in all the newspapers of the Continent; reprinted in Britain on a broadside, to be stuck up in houses; two translations were made of it in French, and great numbers bought by the clergy and gentry, to distribute gratis among their poor parishioners and tenants. In Pennsylvania, as it discouraged useless expense in foreign superfluities, some thought it had its share of influence in producing that growing plenty of money which was observable for several years after its publication.

After crosses and losses, men grow humbler and wiser.

A good example is the best sermon.

A lie stands on one leg, truth on two.

An honest man will receive neither money nor praise, that is not his due.

Bad gains are truly losses.

Be always ashamed to catch thyself idle.

Be at war with your vices, at peace with your neighbors.

Being ignorant is not so much a shame, as being unwilling to learn.

Beware of little expenses, a small leak will sink a great ship.

Do good to thy friend to keep him, to thy enemy to gain him.

Early to bed and early to rise, makes a man healthy, wealthy, and wise.

Fools need advice most, but wise men only are the better for it.

Glass, china, and reputation are easily crack'd, and never well mended.

Haste makes waste.

He that can compose himself is wiser than he that composes books.

Lost time is never found again.

Little strokes fell great oaks.

Take this remark from Richard, poor and lame, whate'er is begun in anger, ends in shame.

Tim was so learned, that he could name a horse in nine languages. So ignorant, that he bought a cow to ride on.

What you would seem to be, be really.

Who is rich? He that is content.

Who is strong? He that can conquer his bad habits.

Who is wise? He that learns from every one.

Advertisements in the
Virginia Gazette
December 31, 1772

This variety of advertisements appeared in Williamsburg's Virginia Gazette *newspaper.*

VIRGINIA GAZETTE   DECEMBER 31, 1772

ADVERTISEMENTS

If one Doctor Mariner, and his Son James Mariner who went from Bristol about the Year 1758 to Virginia, are living, they may hear of Something to their Advantage by applying at the Post Office in Williamsburg.

To be SOLD, at the late Dwelling-House of Colonel John Fleming, deceased, in Cumberland County, on Thursday the 21st of January next, if fair, otherwise next fair Day, about fifty choice SLAVES, among whom there is a good Blacksmith, and several other valuable Tradesmen. Also Stocks of HORSES, CATTLE, and SHEEP, a large Quanitiy of CORN and FODDER, PLANTATION UTENSILS, and several other useful Articles.

JUST arrived, in the *Unity*, Captain Goosley, and to be sold at John Carter's Store, for ready Money, a Variety of fresh GARDEN SEEDS, namely, Early Golden Hotspur Peas, Early Charlton Peas, Ledman's Dwarf Peas, Short Sugar Peas, Dwarf Marrow Peas, Long Pod Beans, Windsor Beans, Canterbury Dwarf Kidney Beans, Silver Skin Onion Seed, Carrot Seed, white round Turnip seed, Salmon Radish Seed, Spinnage, solid Celery, curled Parsley, curled Cress, Early Dwarf Sugar Loaf Cabbage, large Ditto, large English Ditto, best Colliflower Seed, purple and green Broccoli, white Coss Lettice, Silesia Ditto, best Hyson Teas at eighteen, twenty, and twenty two Shillings and Six-pence a Pound, Bohea Tea at five Shillings, best Jar Raisins and Currens, white and brown Sugar Candy, and a Variety of Paper Hangings.

JONATHAN PROSSER, TAILOR, WILLIAMSBURG, Returns Thanks to his Customers, and others from whom he has received Favors, and begs Leave to acquaint them that he continues his Business in all its Branches, which, from many Years Experience in London, he is bold to say he understands as well as any Man in Europe, and has given the greatest Satisfaction to all Gentlemen of Fashion and Dignity who have been pleased to employ him in Virginia. In Order to enable him the better to fulfill his Engagements, as well as to support his Family, he gives this publick Notice, that he is determined to work for none but such as choose to pay him upon the Delivery of their Clothes.

JUST IMPORTED, in the *Unity*, Captain Goosley, from London, an Assortment of almost all Sorts of GARDEN SEEDS, with various Sorts of PEAS and BEANS, and red and white CLOVER SEED. Likewise, from Liverpool, a fine Assortment of TABLE LINEN of all Sizes, consisting of Damask, Dornock, Diaper, and Dimity; also a large Quantity of CHESHIRE CHEESE, sold reasonable by ALLAN & TURNER.

On Monday, the 25th of January next (being Middlesex Court Day) will be sold to the highest Bidder, a TRACT of very fine LAND, containing six Hundred and twenty four Acres, agreeably situated on the River Pianketank, and convenient to Church, Mill, and Warehouse.

The Declaration of Independence

Thomas Jefferson, 1776

Delegates to the Second Continental Congress of 1776 in Philadelphia selected Benjamin Franklin, Thomas Jefferson, John Adams, Robert Livingston, and Roger Sherman as a committee to compose a declaration to the British government and to the world at large. Thomas Jefferson did most of the actual writing of the declaration, an excerpt of which is below. At the end of the document, fifty-six men signed their names. As representatives of all thirteen colonies, the signers were taking a bold, courageous step toward freedom for their country.

July 4, 1776

The Unanimous Declaration of the thirteen united States of America.

When, in the course of human events, it becomes necessary for one people to dissolve the Political Bands which have connected them with another, and to assume among the Powers of the Earth, the separate and equal Station to which the Laws of Nature and of Nature's God entitle them, a decent Respect to the Opinions of Mankind requires that they should declare the causes which impel them to the Separation.

We hold these Truths to be self-evident, that all Men are created equal, that they are endowed by their Creator with certain unalienable Rights, that among these are Life, Liberty and the Pursuit of Happiness—That to secure these Rights, Governments are instituted among Men, deriving their just Powers from the Consent of the Governed, that whenever any Form of Government becomes destructive to these Ends, it is the Right of the People to alter or to abolish it, and to institute new Government, laying its Foundation on such Principles and organizing its Powers in such Form, as to them shall seem most likely to effect their Safety and Happiness. . . .

We, therefore, the Representatives of the UNITED STATES of AMERICA, in General Congress, Assembled, appealing to the Supreme Judge of the World for the Rectitude of our Intentions, do, in the Name, and by the Authority of the good People of these Colonies, solemnly Publish and Declare, that these United Colonies are, and of Right ought to be, FREE AND INDEPENDENT STATES; that they are absolved from all Allegiance to the British Crown, and that all political Connection between them and the State of Great Britain, is and ought to be totally dissolved; and that as FREE AND INDEPENDENT STATES, they have full Power to levy War, conclude Peace, contract Alliances, establish Commerce, and to do all other Acts and Things which INDEPENDENT STATES may of right do. And for the support of this Declaration, with a firm Reliance on the Protection of Divine Providence, we mutually pledge to each other our Lives, our Fortunes, and our sacred Honor.

Letter from Valley Forge

Nathanael Green, 1778

George Washington asked Nathanael Green to be Quartermaster General of the Continental Army, the officer in charge of acquiring supplies. In this position, General Green wrote this letter to Joseph Webb of Wethersfield, Connecticut, a successful shopkeeper and trader. The town of Fishkill mentioned in this letter was a small New York town that the Continental Army used as a supply center. The original capitalization and spelling (except for words that were abbreviated) have been retained.

Camp Valley Forge, 2nd of April 1778

Sir:

In order to lessen the Quantity of Baggage in the Army & enable it to move with the greater Ease, it is proposed to lay aside as much as possible, the Use of Chests and Trunks: A large Number of Portmanteaus and Valeeses [suitcases] is therefore become necessary for the Officers; and as I am informed some of these may be collected in Connecticut, I request the Favour of you to procure as many good leather Portmanteaus, of about the middling Size, as can be got ready to send forward by or before the middle of May — the Number I shall expect from you will be about 200. at least; and 20, or 30 Valeeses for Matrasses [mattress covers] to be made of pretty strong Canvas. If you can meet with any Canvas, Ticklenburgs, and Oznaburgs [heavy fabrics] suitable for Tents, Knapsacks &c, I should be glad you would  purchase it for me. As fast as you can collect any of these Articles in any considerable Quantity, be pleased to forward them to the Care of Mr. Hugh Hughes, Deputy Quartermaster at Fishkill who will send them on to Camp.

I expect in very short Time to remit you Money sufficient to pay for the Articles you may purchase, so that I think you may rely on being enabled to make punctual Payments, which I doubt not will not only facilitate the Business but enable you to do it on better Terms than it could otherwise be done. In the mean Time I beg you will inform me what Quantity of these articles are likely to be procured in Connecticut within the Time I have mentioned, and that you will give me the speediest Information when any Goods shall be sent forward.

I rely on your Zeal in the Publick Service to take upon you this Trouble, and to employ such Persons in the Business, as you shall think most likely to effect it to the best Advantage & with the greatest Dispatch [speed], allowing them such Compensation [payment] as you shall think reasonable; and for your own Troubles, besides your Expences of which be pleased to make a Charge, you will be allowed a Commission adequate to the Business.

I take it for granted you have been informed of my Appointment to the Office of Quarter-Master-General of the Army of the United States, and it is in that Character I now apply to you. I am, with Regard, Sir

Your most obedient
Humble servant
Nathanael Greene,
Quartermaster General

The Liberty Song

John Dickinson, 1768

John Dickinson wrote "The Liberty Song," one of America's first patriotic songs, to fit a famous British tune called "Heart of Oak." The song was first published in the Boston Gazette *newspaper in July of 1768. It was popular throughout the colonies and was sung at meetings and social gatherings. It contains the origin of a phrase well-known to Americans: "united we stand, divided we fall."*

Come, join hand in hand, brave Americans all,
    And rouse your bold hearts at fair Liberty's call;
No tyrannous acts shall suppress your just claim,
    Or stain with dishonor America's name.

Chorus
In Freedom we're born and in Freedom we'll live.
    Our purses are ready. Steady, friends, steady;
Not as slaves, but as Freemen our money we'll give.

Our worthy forefathers, let's give them a cheer,
    To climates unknown did courageously steer;
Thro' oceans to deserts for Freedom they came,
    And dying, bequeath'd us their freedom and fame. *Chorus*

The tree their own hands had to Liberty rear'd,
    They lived to behold growing strong and revered;
With transport they cried, Now our wishes we gain,
    For our children shall gather the fruits of our pain. *Chorus*

Then join hand in hand, brave Americans all,
    By uniting we stand, by dividing we fall;
In so righteous a cause let us hope to succeed,
    For heaven approves of each generous deed. *Chorus*

Chester

William Billings, 1770

William Billings was born in Boston in 1746. He was a tanner as well as America's first professional composer. He published The New England Psalm Singer *at age 24. It was the first book of music entirely composed by an American. Billings also organized the first church choir in America. He was a passionate Revolutionary and adapted many of his hymns into war songs. "Chester" was a favorite of patriots during the American Revolution. It has been called America's first national anthem.*

Let tyrants shake their iron rods,
    And Slavery clank her galling chains.
We fear them not, we trust in God.
    New England's God forever reigns.

Howe and Burgoyne and Clinton, too,
    With Prescott and Cornwallis joined,
Together plot our overthrow,
    In one infernal league combined.

When God inspired us for the fight,
    Their ranks were broke, their lines were forced,
Their ships were shattered in our sight,
    Or swiftly driven from our coast.

The foe comes on with haughty stride,
    Our troops advance with martial noise;
Their veterans flee before our youth,
    And generals yield to beardless boys.

What grateful offering shall we bring,
    What shall we render to the Lord?
Loud hallelujahs let us sing,
    And praise his name on every chord!

Preamble to the Constitution

1787

These are the opening words to the United States Constitution, written in Philadelphia in 1787.

We the people of the United States, in order to form a more perfect union, establish justice, insure domestic tranquility, provide for the common defense, promote the general welfare, and secure the blessings of liberty to ourselves and our posterity, do ordain and establish this Constitution for the United States of America.

Independence Hall

Letter to Abigail Adams

John Adams, 1789

During their long, loving marriage, John and Abigail Adams wrote hundreds of letters to each other. They were frequently apart due to John Adams' service to his country at home and abroad while Abigail stayed in Massachusetts to run their farm. John Adams wrote the following letter upon his arrival in New York City (then the nation's capital) as the new Vice President. Adams' spelling and capitalization are retained.

New York. April 22. 1789

My dearest Friend

This is the first Moment I have been able to Seize, in order to acquaint you of my Arrival and Situation. Governor Clinton The Mayer of New York, all the old officers of the Continental Government, and the Clergy, Magistrates and People, have seemed to emulate the two houses of Congress, in shewing every respect to me and to my office. For Particulars I must refer you to the public Papers. Yesterday for the first time I attended the Senate. Tomorrow or next day, The President is expected. Mr. Jay with his usual Friendship, has insisted on my taking Apartments in his noble house. No Provision No arrangement, has been made for the President or Vice P. and I see, clearly enough, that Minds are not conformed to the Constitution, enough, as yet, to do any Thing, which will support the Government in the Eyes of the People or of Foreigners. Our Countrymens Idea of the "L'Air imposant" [nobleness, grandness] is yet confined to volunteer Escorts, verbal Compliments &c.

You and I however, are the two People in the World the best qualified for this situation. We can conform to our Circumstances. —And if they determine that We must live on little, we will not spend much.—every Body enquires respectfully for Mrs. A. of her affectionate

J. A.

George Washington and the Cherry Tree

Mason Locke Weems, 1806

A few months after George Washington died, Mason Locke Weems published a book about Washington's life, knowing that Americans were eager to know more about their beloved hero. In a later edition, Weems included the following story of young George Washington. It has become one of the most famous stories about Washington, read by schoolchildren for generations. Weems said that the story was told to him by a woman who was a distant relative of Washington, but no one has found other evidence for this tale. Weems likely invented the story to make Washington look noble even as a boy. Nonetheless, it has instructed and entertained Americans for over two hundred years.

When George was about six years old, he was made the wealthy master of a hatchet! Of which, like most little boys, he was immoderately fond, and was constantly going about chopping every thing that came in his way. One day, in the garden, where he often amused himself hacking his mother's pea-sticks, he unluckily tried the edge of his hatchet on the body of a beautiful young English cherry-tree, which he barked so terribly, that I don't believe the tree ever got the better of it. The next morning the old gentleman, finding out what had befallen his tree, which, by the by, was a great favorite, came into the house; and with much warmth asked for the mischievous author, declaring at the same time, that he would not have taken five guineas for his tree. Nobody could tell him any thing about it. Presently George and his hatchet made their appearance.

"George," said his father, "do you know who killed that beautiful little cherry tree yonder in the garden?"

This was a tough question; and George staggered under it for a moment; but quickly recovered himself and looking at his father, with the sweet face of youth brightened with the inexpressible charm of all-conquering truth, he bravely cried out, "I can't tell a lie, Pa; you know I can't tell a lie. I did cut it with my hatchet."

"Run to my arms, you dearest boy," cried his father in transports, "Run to my arms. Glad am I, George, that you killed my tree; for you have paid me for it a thousand fold. Such an act of heroism in my son is more worth than a thousand trees, though blossomed with silver, and their fruits of purest gold."

Rules of Civility & Decent Behavior in Company & Conversation

George Washington, c. 1747

When George Washington was fourteen or fifteen years old, he copied by hand 110 rules for polite living. These maxims originated in France in the 1600s. They reflect the good manners, respectfulness, and kindness that Washington was known for in his adult life. A selection of the rules is below.

Every action done in company ought to be with some sign of respect to those that are present.

If you cough, sneeze, sigh or yawn, do it not loud but privately, and speak not in your yawning, but put your handkerchief or hand before your face and turn aside.

Shake not the head, feet, or legs; roll not the eyes; lift not one eyebrow higher than the other, wry not the mouth, and bedew no man's face with your spittle by approaching too near him when you speak.

Associate yourself with men of good quality if you esteem your own reputation; for 'tis better to be alone than in bad company.

Speak not injurious words neither in jest nor earnest; scoff at none although they give occasion.

Think before you speak, pronounce not imperfectly, nor bring out your words too hastily, but orderly and distinctly.

When another speaks, be attentive yourself and disturb not the audience. If any hesitate in his words, help him not nor prompt him without desired. Interrupt him not, nor answer him till his speech be ended.

Be not curious to know the affairs of others, neither approach those that speak in private.

Undertake not what you cannot perform but be careful to keep your promise.

Speak not evil of the absent, for it is unjust.

Being set at meat scratch not, neither spit, cough or blow your nose except there's a necessity for it.

Put not another bite into your mouth 'til the former be swallowed. Let not your morsels be too big for the jowls.

If others talk at table be attentive, but talk not with meat in your mouth.

When you speak of God or His attributes, let it be seriously and with reverence. Honor and obey your natural parents although they be poor.

Labor to keep alive in your breast that little spark of celestial fire called conscience.

O Sing a Song of Bethlehem

Louis F. Benson, 1899

Louis Benson was born in Philadelphia, Pennsylvania, in 1855 and died there in 1930. He was a Presbyterian minister and an authority on hymns. He wrote many hymns himself and compiled several hymn books.

O sing a song of Bethlehem, of shepherds watching there,
    And of the news that came to them from angels in the air.
The light that shone on Bethlehem fills all the world today;
    Of Jesus' birth and peace on earth the angels sing alway.

O sing a song of Nazareth, of sunny days of joy;
    O sing of fragrant flowers' breath, and of the sinless Boy.
For now the flowers of Nazareth in every heart may grow;
    Now spreads the fame of His dear Name on all the winds that blow.

O sing a song of Galilee, of lake and woods and hill,
    Of Him Who walked upon the sea and bade the waves be still.
For though like waves on Galilee, dark seas of trouble roll,
    When faith has heard the Master's Word, falls peace upon the soul.

O sing a song of Calvary, its glory and dismay,
    Of Him Who hung upon the tree, and took our sins away.
For He Who died on Calvary is risen from the grave,
    And Christ, our Lord, by Heaven adored, is mighty now to save.

The Adventures of Colonel Daniel Boone

John Filson, 1784

John Filson, a Kentucky pioneer, wrote Discovery, Settlement, and Present State of Kentucke, *which included a biography of one of Kentucky's most famous settlers, Daniel Boone. Filson wrote the biography as if it were written by Daniel Boone himself. He titled the biography "The Adventures of Colonel Daniel Boone, Formerly a Hunter; Containing A Narrative of the Wars of Kentucky, As Given By Himself."*

To conclude, I can now say that I have verified the saying of an old Indian . . . . Taking me by the hand . . . "Brother," said he, "we have given you a fine land, but I believe you will have much trouble in settling it." My footsteps have often been marked with blood, and therefore I can truly subscribe to its original name. Two darling sons and a brother have I lost by savage hands, which have also taken from me forty valuable horses, and abundance of cattle. Many dark and sleepless nights have I been a companion for owls, separated from the cheerful society of men, scorched by the summer's sun, and pinched by the winter's cold—an instrument ordained to settle the wilderness. But now the scene is changed: peace crowns the sylvan shade.

What thanks, what ardent and ceaseless thanks are due to that all-superintending Providence which has turned a cruel war into peace, brought order out of confusion, made the fierce savages placid, and turned away their hostile weapons from our country! May the same Almighty Goodness banish the accursed monster, war, from all lands, with her hated associates, rapine and insatiable ambition! Let peace, descending from her native heaven, bid her olives spring amid the joyful nations; and plenty, in league with commerce, scatter blessings from her copious hand!

This account of my adventures will inform the reader of the most remarkable events of this country. I now live in peace and safety, enjoying the sweets of liberty, and the bounties of Providence, with my once fellow-sufferers, in this delightful country, which I have seen purchased with a vast expense of blood and treasure: delighting in the prospect of its being, in a short time, one of the most opulent and powerful states on the continent of North America; which, with the love and gratitude of my countrymen, I esteem a sufficient reward for all my toil and dangers.

DANIEL BOONE.
Fayette County, Kentucky.

Letter to
Thomas Jefferson Smith

Thomas Jefferson, 1825

The year before Thomas Jefferson died, a father wrote to him asking Jefferson to write a letter to his baby son, whom he had named Thomas Jefferson Smith. Jefferson wrote the following letter. The poem he included is a song based on Psalm 15 written by Nicholas Brady and Nahum Tate. At the end is a list of personal mottoes Jefferson acquired or developed during his life. He sent a similar list in a letter to his granddaughter.

Thomas Jefferson to Thomas Jefferson Smith

This letter will, to you, be as one from the dead. The writer will be in the grave before you can weigh its counsels. Your affectionate and excellent father has requested that I would address to you something which might possibly have a favorable influence on the course of life you have to run, and I too, as a namesake, feel an interest in that course. Few words will be necessary, with good dispositions on your part. Adore God. Reverence and cherish your parents. Love your neighbor as yourself, and your country more than yourself. Be just. Be true. Murmur not at the ways of Providence. So shall the life into which you have entered, be the portal to one of eternal and ineffable bliss. And if to the dead it is permitted to care for the things of this world, every action of your life will be under my regard. Farewell.

Monticello February 21, 1825

The portrait of a good man by the most sublime of poets, for your imitation.

> Lord, who's the happy man that may to thy blest courts repair;
> Not stranger-like to visit them but to inhabit there?
> 'Tis he whose every thought and deed by rules of virtue moves;
> Whose generous tongue disdains to speak the thing his heart disproves.
> Who never did a slander forge, his neighbor's fame to wound;
> Nor hearken to a false report, by malice whispered round.
> Who vice in all its pomp and power, can treat with just neglect;
> And piety, though clothed in rags, religiously respect.
> Who to his plighted vows and trust has ever firmly stood;
> And though he promise to his loss, he makes his promise good.
> Whose soul in usury disdains his treasure to employ;
> Whom no rewards can ever bribe the guiltless to destroy.
> The man, who, by his steady course, has happiness insured.
> When earth's foundations shake, shall stand, by Providence secured.

A Decalogue of Canons for observation in practical life.

1. Never put off till to-morrow what you can do to-day.

2. Never trouble another for what you can do yourself.

3. Never spend your money before you have it.

4. Never buy what you do not want, because it is cheap; it will be dear to you.

5. Pride costs us more than hunger, thirst and cold.

6. We never repent of having eaten too little.

7. Nothing is troublesome that we do willingly.

8. How much pain have cost us the evils which have never happened.

9. Take things always by their smooth handle.

10. When angry, count ten, before you speak; if very angry, an hundred.

Journals of Lewis and Clark

Meriwether Lewis and William Clark, 1804-1806

Lewis and Clark kept extensive journals detailing their travels and adventures as part of the records of their Voyage of Discovery. Following are four selections from their journals about different parts of their mission.

Ready to Set Out, May 20, 1804, by Meriwether Lewis

The morning was fair, and the weather pleasant. At 10 o'clock a.m. agreeably to an appointment of the preceding day, I was joined by Captain Stoddard, Lieutenants Milford and Worrell, together with Messrs. A. Chouteau, C. Gratiot, and many other respectable inhabitants of St. Louis, who had engaged to accompany me to the village of St. Charles; accordingly at 12 o'clock after bidding an affectionate adieu to my hostess, that excellent woman the spouse of Mr. Peter Chouteau, and some of my fair friends of St. Louis, we set forward to that village in order to join my friend, companion and fellow laborer Captain William Clark who had previously arrived at that place with the party destined for the discovery of the interior of the continent of North America. The first 5 miles of our route laid through a beautiful high, level, and fertile prairie which encircles the town of St. Louis from northwest to southeast. The lands through which we then passed are somewhat broken up fertile. The plains and woodlands are here indiscriminately interspersed until you arrive within three miles of the village when the woodland commences and continues to the Missouri. The latter is extremely fertile. At half after one p.m. our progress was interrupted [by] the near approach of a violent thunder storm from the northwest and concluded to take shelter in a little cabin hard by until the rain should be over; accordingly we alighted and remained about an hour and a half and regaled ourselves with a cold collation [light meal] which we had taken the precaution to bring with us from St. Louis.

The clouds continued to follow each other in rapid succession, insomuch that there was but little prospect of its ceasing to rain this evening; as I had determined to reach St. Charles this evening and knowing that there was now no time to be lost, I set forward in the rain. Most of the gentlemen continued with me. We arrived at half after six and joined Captain Clark. Found the party in good health and spirits.

Winter on the Pacific, December 27, 1805, by William Clark

Rained last night as usual and the greater part of this day. The men complete chimneys and bunks today. In the evening a chief and 4 men come of the Clotsop nation, Chief Co-ma wool. We sent out R. Fields and Collins to

hunt and order Drewyer, Shannon and Labiach to set out early tomorrow to hunt; Jo Fields, Bratten, and Gibson to make Salt at Point Addams; Willard and Wiser, to assist them in carrying the Kitties and the rest to the ocean, and all the others to finish the pickets and gates. Warm weather. I saw a mosquito which I showed Captain Lewis. Those Indians gave us a black root they call Shan-na-tah que, a kind of licorice which they roast in embers and call Cul ho-mo, a black berry the Size of a cherry and dried which they call Shel-well. All of which they prize highly and make use of as food to live on, for which Captain Lewis gave the chief a cap of sheep skin and I his son, ear bobs, piece of ribbon, a piece of brass, and 2 small fishing hooks, of which they were much pleased. Those roots and berries, are grateful to our stomachs as we have nothing to eat but poor elk meat, nearly spoiled; and this accident of spoiled meat, is owing to warmth and the repeated rains, which cause the meat to taint before we can get it from the woods. Mosquitoes troublesome.

On the Return Journey, July 12, 1806, by Meriwether Lewis

We arose early and resumed our operations in completing our canoes which we completed by 10 a.m. About this time two of the men whom I had dispatched this morning in quest of the horses returned with seven of them only. The remaining ten of our best horses were absent and not to be found. I fear that they are stolen. I dispatch two men on horseback in search of them. The wind blew so violently that I did not think it prudent to attempt passing the river. At noon Werner returned having found three others of the horses near Fort Mountain. Sergeant Gass did not return until 3 p.m. not having found the horses. He had been about 8 miles up Medicine River. I now dispatched Joseph Fields and Drewyer in quest of them. The former returned at dark unsuccessful and the latter continued absent all night. At 5 p.m. the wind abated and we transported our baggage and meat to the opposite shore in our canoes which we found answered [performed] even beyond our expectations. We swam our horses over also and encamped at sunset. Mosquitoes extremely troublesome. I think the river is somewhat higher than when we were here last summer. The present season has been much more moist than the preceding one. The grass and weeds are much more luxuriant than they were when I left this place on the 13th of July 1805. Saw the brown thrush, pigeons, doves &c. The yellow currants beginning to ripen.

Returning to St. Charles, September 21, 1806, by William Clark

Rose early this morning. Collected our men. Several of them had accepted of the invitation of the citizens and visited their families. At half after 7 a.m. we set out. Passed 12 canoes of Kickapoos ascending on a hunting expedition. Saw several persons, also stock of different kinds on the bank which revived the party very much. At 3 p.m. we met two large boats ascending. At 4 p.m. we arrived in sight of St. Charles. The party rejoiced at the sight of this hospitable village. Played [rowed] their ores with great dexterity and we soon arrived opposite the town. This day being Sunday we observed a number of gentlemen and ladies walking on the bank. We saluted the village by three rounds from our blunderbuts [guns] and the small arms of the party, and landed near the lower part of the town. We were met by great numbers of the inhabitants. We found them excessively polite. We received invitations from several of those gentlemen, a Mr. Proulx, Taboe, Decett, Tice, Dejonah, and Quarie and several who were pressing on us to go to their houses. We could only visit Mr. Proulx and Mr. Deucett in the course of the evening. Mr. Querie undertook to Supply our party with provisions and the rest. The inhabitants of this village appear much delighted at our return and seem to vie with each other in their politeness to us all. We came only 48 miles today. The banks of the river thinly settled etc.

Myths and Legends of the Sioux

Mrs. Marie L. McLaughlin, 1916

Marie McLaughlin was born in 1842. She was one-fourth Sioux and was raised in Native American communities. Marie collected Sioux folk tales and published them in 1916 with this dedication: "In loving memory of my mother, Mary Graham Buisson, at whose knee most of the stories contained in this little volume were told to me, this book is affectionately dedicated."

The Little Mice

Once upon a time a prairie mouse busied herself all fall storing away a cache of beans. Every morning she was out early with her empty cast-off snake skin, which she filled with ground beans and dragged home with her teeth.

The little mouse had a cousin who was fond of dancing and talk, but who did not like to work. She was not careful to get her cache of beans and the season was already well gone before she thought to bestir herself. When she came to realize her need, she found she had no packing bag. So she went to her hardworking cousin and said:

"Cousin, I have no beans stored for winter and the season is nearly gone. But I have no snake skin to gather the beans in. Will you lend me one?"

"But why have you no packing bag? Where were you in the moon when the snakes cast off their skins?"

"I was here."

"What were you doing?"

"I was busy talking and dancing."

"And now you are punished," said the other. "It is always so with lazy, careless people. But I will let you have the snake skin. And now go, and by hard work and industry, try to recover your wasted time."

The Rabbit and the Elk

The little rabbit lived with his old grandmother, who needed a new dress. "I will go out and trap a deer or an elk for you," he said. "Then you shall have a new dress."

When he went out hunting he laid down his bow in the path while he looked at his snares. An elk coming by saw the bow.

"I will play a joke on the rabbit," said the elk to himself. "I will make him think I have been caught in his bow string." He then put one foot on the string and lay down as if dead.

By and by the rabbit returned. When he saw the elk he was filled with joy and ran home crying, "Grandmother, I have trapped

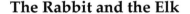

39

a fine elk. You shall have a new dress from his skin. Throw the old one in the fire!" This the old grandmother did.

The elk now sprang to his feet laughing. "Ho, friend rabbit," he called, "You thought to trap me; now I have mocked you." And he ran away into the thicket.

The rabbit who had come back to skin the elk now ran home again. "Grandmother, don't throw your dress in the fire," he cried. But it was too late. The old dress was burned.

The Pet Donkey

There was a chief's daughter once who had a great many relations so that everybody knew she belonged to a great family.

When she grew up she married and there were born to her twin sons. This caused great rejoicing in her father's camp, and all the village women came to see the babes. She was very happy.

As the babes grew older, their grandmother made for them two saddle bags and brought out a donkey.

"My two grandchildren," said the old lady, "shall ride as is becoming to children having so many relations. Here is this donkey. He is patient and surefooted. He shall carry the babes in the saddle bags, one on either side of his back."

It happened one day that the chief's daughter and her husband were making ready to go on a camping journey. The father, who was quite proud of his children, brought out his finest pony, and put the saddle bags on the pony's back.

"There," he said, "my sons shall ride on the pony, not on a donkey; let the donkey carry the pots and kettles."

So his wife loaded the donkey with the household things. She tied the tepee poles into two great bundles, one on either side of the donkey's back; across them she put the travois net and threw into it the pots and kettles and laid the skin tent across the donkey's back.

But no sooner done than the donkey began to rear and bray and kick. He broke the tent poles and kicked the pots and kettles into bits and tore the skin tent. The more he was beaten the more he kicked.

At last they told the grandmother. She laughed. "Did I not tell you the donkey was for the children?" she cried. "He knows the babies are the chief's children. Think you he will be dishonored with pots and kettles?" and she fetched the children and slung them over the donkey's back, when he became at once quiet again.

The camping party left the village and went on their journey. But the next day as they passed by a place overgrown with bushes, a band of enemies rushed out, lashing their ponies and sounding their war whoop. All was excitement. The men bent their bows and seized their lances. After a long battle the enemy fled. But when the camping party came together again—where were the donkey and the two babes? No one knew. For a long time they searched, but in vain. At last they turned to go back to the village, the father mournful, the mother wailing. When they came to the grandmother's tepee, there stood the good donkey with the two babes in the saddle bags.

Domestic Economy, or the History of Thrifty and Unthrifty

Noah Webster, 1803

This tale is from Noah's Webster's textbook The American Spelling Book; Containing the Rudiments of the English Language, for the Use of Schools in the United States. *After the explanations of correct pronunciation and lists of words to read and spell, Webster included some lessons about upright living.*

. . . I know a farmer by the name of Thrifty, who manages his affairs in this manner: He rises early in the morning, looks to the condition of his house, barn, home lot, and stock—sees that his cattle, horses, and hogs are fed, examines the tools to see whether they are all in good order for the workmen—takes care that breakfast is ready in due season, and begins work in the cool of the day. When in the field he keeps steadily at work, though not so violently as to fatigue and exhaust the body, nor does he stop to tell or hear long stories. When the labor of the day is past, he takes refreshment and goes to rest at an early hour. In this manner he earns and gains money.

When Thrifty has acquired a little property, he does not spend it or let it slip from him, without use or benefit. He pays his tax and debts when due or called for, so that he has no officers' fees to pay, nor expense of courts. He does not frequent the tavern and drink up all his earnings in liquor that does him no good. He puts his money to use, that is, he buys more land or stock, or lends his money at interest—in short, he makes his money produce some profit or income. . . . Thrifty becomes a wealthy farmer, with several hundred acres of land, and a hundred head of cattle.

Very different is the management of Unthrifty: he lies in bed till a late hour in the morning, then rises, and goes to the bottle for a dram, or to the tavern for a glass of bitters. Thus he spends six cents before breakfast, for a dram that makes him dull and heavy all day. He gets his breakfast late, when he ought to be at work. When he supposes he is ready to begin the work of the day, he finds he has not the necessary tools, or some of them are out of order. . . . Now, he is in a great hurry, he bustles about to make preparation for work, and what is done in a hurry is ill done. He loses a part of the day in getting ready, and perhaps the time of his workmen. At ten or eleven o'clock, he is ready to go to work, then comes a boy and tells him the sheep have escaped from the pasture, or the cows have got among his corn or the hogs into the garden. He frets and storms, and runs to drive them out, a half hour or more time is lost in driving the cattle from mischief. . . . After all this bustle, the fatigue of which is worse than common labor, Unthrifty is ready to begin a day's work at twelve o'clock . . . . His small crops are damaged or destroyed by unruly cattle. His barn is open and leaky, and what little he gathers is injured by the rain and snow. His house is in a like condition—the shingles and clapboards fall off and let in the water, which causes the timber, floors, and furniture to decay. And exposed to inclemences of weather, his wife and children fall sick. Their time is lost, and the mischief closes with a ruinous dram of expense for medicines and physicians. After dragging out some years of disappointment, misery, and poverty, the lawyer and the sheriff sweep away the scanty remains of his estate. This is the history of Unthrifty—his principal is spent. He has no interest.

The Star-Spangled Banner

Francis Scott Key, 1814

During the War of 1812, Francis Scott Key witnessed the British navy attack Fort McHenry from the Baltimore harbor. The morning after the battle, Key saw the United States flag still waving proudly, signifying that the British attack had failed. Key was inspired to write this triumphant poem. Congress declared "The Star-Spangled Banner" the national anthem of the United States on March 3, 1931. The flag that Key saw that morning is now in the Smithsonian's National Museum of American History.

O say can you see, by the dawn's early light,
    What so proudly we hail'd at the twilight's last gleaming,
Whose broad stripes and bright stars through the perilous fight
    O'er the ramparts we watch'd were so gallantly streaming?
And the rocket's red glare, the bombs bursting in air,
    Gave proof through the night that our flag was still there,
O say does that star-spangled banner yet wave
    O'er the land of the free and the home of the brave?

On the shore dimly seen through the mists of the deep
    Where the foe's haughty host in dread silence reposes,
What is that which the breeze, o'er the towering steep,
    As it fitfully blows, half conceals, half discloses?
Now it catches the gleam of the morning's first beam,
    In full glory reflected now shines in the stream,
'Tis the star-spangled banner–O long may it wave
    O'er the land of the free and the home of the brave!

And where is that band who so vauntingly swore,
    That the havoc of war and the battle's confusion
A home and a Country should leave us no more?
    Their blood has wash'd out their foul footstep's pollution.
No refuge could save the hireling and slave
    From the terror of flight or the gloom of the grave,
And the star-spangled banner in triumph doth wave
    O'er the land of the free and the home of the brave.

O thus be it e'er when freemen shall stand
    Between their lov'd home and the war's desolation!
Blest with vict'ry and peace may the heav'n rescued land
    Praise the Power that hath made and preserv'd us a nation!
Then conquer we must, when our cause it is just,
    And this be our motto - "In God is our trust,"
And the star-spangled banner in triumph shall wave
    O'er the land of the free and the home of the brave.

Low Bridge, Everybody Down

Thomas S. Allen, 1905

This is a folk song about the days when mules pulled barges along the Erie Canal. Like most folk songs, there are many different versions of the words. Originally, Thomas Allen wrote about the singer and his mule Sal serving "fifteen years on the Erie Canal." Now the words "fifteen miles on the Erie Canal" are more common. The title phrase refers to riders on the barge having to duck down to pass under bridges.

I've got a mule and her name is Sal,
　　Fifteen years on the Erie Canal,
She's a good old worker and a good old pal,
　　Fifteen years on the Erie Canal,
We've hauled some barges in our day,
　　Filled with lumber, coal, and hay,
And every inch of the way I know,
　　From Albany to Buffalo.
Low bridge, everybody down,
　　Low bridge, we must be getting near a town,
You can always tell your neighbor,
　　You can always tell your pal,
If he's ever navigated on the Erie Canal.

Come, Holy Spirit, Dove Divine

Adoniram Judson, 1832

The Cherokee man Sequoyah gave his nation the gift of literacy. The ability to read and write opens many good possibilities. In 1877 the American Baptist Publication Society in Philadelphia printed a hymnal in the Cherokee language. The front cover had the title Cherokee Hymnal *written in both Cherokee and English. The back cover showed the Cherokee syllabary chart. Sequoyah's work helped the Cherokee nation learn to sing hymns in their own language.*

"Come, Holy Spirit, Dove Divine" was written in 1832 by Adoniram Judson, pictured below. Judson was born in Massachusetts in 1788. He and his wife Ann were among the first Americans to go to a foreign land as missionaries. They spent their lives serving in Burma. Judson developed a grammar for the Burmese language and translated the Bible into that language.

Come, Holy Spirit, Dove divine,
   On these baptismal waters shine,
And teach our hearts, in highest strain,
   To praise the Lamb for sinners slain.

We love Thy name, we love Thy laws,
   And joyfully embrace Thy cause;
We love Thy cross, the shame, the pain,
   O Lamb of God for sinners slain.

We sink beneath the water's face,
   And thank Thee for Thy saving grace;
We die to sin and seek a grave
   With Thee, beneath the yielding wave.

And as we rise with Thee to live,
   O let the Holy Spirit give
The sealing unction from above,
   The joy of life, the fire of love.
                 Amen.

The Legend of Paul Bunyan

Bethany Poore, from traditional sources, 2010

Generations of Americans have enjoyed tall tales about Paul Bunyan, Pecos Bill, Johnny Appleseed, and other larger-than-life heroes, some real people and some imagined. Tall tales use exaggeration for fun and to represent the independent, ambitious American spirit.

Well kids, there's some debate about how tall Paul Bunyan really was. Most folks claim that he was only about as tall as a two-story house, but some say he was surely taller than that if he could stick trees in his pockets and blow the birds out of the air when he sneezed. He was born (to regular-sized people, by the way) in the old state of Maine. When Paul Bunyan's papa found him holding a saw and chewing on a bed post, he grew a mite concerned. But Paul's parents were proud of him and gave him a good raisin'. His Papa taught him, "Don't lean on buildings or on regular-sized trees, son," and his Mama said, "Paul, never pick on anyone who is smaller than you," which meant he was kind to everyone.

Paul Bunyan started in the lumber trade by knocking down trees as he was learning to crawl, so it was only natural for him to take it up as his life's work. Back in those days, America had a passel of trees that were in the way of the houses, farms, churches, and schools that people wanted to put up. Since Paul Bunyan could chop down a couple of miles of trees before breakfast, he was a handy chap to have around. Of course people made good use of all that lumber, too, for they needed plenty of wagons, furniture, barrels, and pencils. Paul scooped up handfuls of trees to send down the river to the lumber mills. Everyone appreciated his help, but being the tallest one around by about fifty feet, Paul Bunyan got a little lonely.

One day Paul took himself a solitary walk and tripped over what he thought was a mountain. The mountain sighed and stirred. "Well, excuse me," said Paul. He saw two big black eyes blinking at him and two furry ears almost as big as Massachusetts sticking out. It was nothing other than a blue ox, just a companionable size for Paul. After the two made their acquaintance, (Paul named the ox Babe) they set out together to do some big-time logging on the American frontier. They made room for farms and fields, houses and towns as the settlers kept pouring in. With Paul choppin' and Babe the Blue Ox haulin', you can bet they did some mighty efficient loggin'.

Paul and Babe haven't been heard from in quite a spell, but anyone can see where they've been. Babe's footprints are all over the state of Minnesota; they've filled up with water and made about a million lakes. While they were working in the Dakotas, Paul got in a bad habit of forgettin' about the stumps when he was fellin' them trees. Fortunately he was about as clever as he was big. Paul had his blacksmith make him a hammer so big he had to store it in the Missouri River. Paul just went over the cleared ground and hammered in every one of those stumps.

It was a let down for the pair of big friends when they reached California and knew they had logged clear across America. No one knows for sure where they've gone off to, but I can tell you for certain that when your granpappy built his cabin and didn't have to deal with a tree coming up through the middle of the living room, he said a big thank you in his heart to old Paul Bunyan.

Letter from the Alamo

William Barret Travis, 1836

William Barret Travis, commander of Texian soldiers at the Alamo, sent this letter by a courier to seek reinforcements for the besieged troops defending the Alamo. San Felipe was an important commercial and political town in Texas at the time. Bejar was the name of the town now called San Antonio. Beeves refers to cattle.

Send this to San Felipe by Express night & day

To The People of Texas and All Americans
Commandancy of the Alamo—
Bejar, Febuary 24th 1836—
To the People of Texas & all Americans in the world—
Fellow citizens & compatriots—

I am besieged, by a thousand or more of the Mexicans under Santa Anna—I have sustained a continual Bombardment & cannonade for 24 hours & have not lost a man—The enemy has demanded a surrender at discretion, otherwise, the garrison are to be put to the sword, if the fort is taken—I have answered the demand with a cannon shot, & our flag still waves proudly from the walls—I shall never surrender or retreat. Then, I call on you in the name of Liberty, of patriotism & every thing dear to the American character, to come to our aid, with all dispatch—The enemy is receiving reinforcements daily & will no doubt increase to three or four thousand in four or five days. If this call is neglected, I am determined to sustain myself as long as possible & die like a soldier who never forgets what is due to his own honor & that of his country—Victory or Death.

William Barret Travis
Lt. Col. Commandant

P.S. The Lord is on our side—When the enemy appeared in sight we had not three bushels of corn—We have since found in deserted houses 80 or 90 bushels & got into the walls 20 or 30 head of Beeves—

Travis

Letter to Papa
Maria Jay Banyer, 1821

John Jay's daughter Maria wrote this letter from New York City to her father in Rye, New York, after he was offered the position of president of the American Bible Society.

New York 19th December 1821

My dear Papa,

I was happy to hear from Sister that your health had not suffered from the long continuance of unfavorable weather we have had. I was very sorry to hear of poor Mrs. Nichols's protracted illness, and would on no account have deprived her of Ruth's services had I know her situation and fear that she must be missed at home, too, now that Jenny is sick. Mary continues much better, she went to church yesterday. We had all great cause to keep the day with thankful hearts, few families are so blessed. John's leg is nearly well, but he has now a sore throat, from which I hope he will soon be relieved. Brother has for some time wished to give a dinner to Mr. Hale, an English gentleman who married Miss Amherst whom you and Peter know, and who enjoined it on him to see you both. Mary said if I would assist he could ask him for next Friday (tomorrow week). I could not refuse, tho' I am sorry to be prevented leaving town on that day as it was my wish to get home the Saturday before Christmas and it would be hazardous to permit Mary to incur much fatigue or exposure and brother had engagements which prevented his fixing on an earlier day. He has too some hopes of going with me, the children too are begging that they may spend the holidays with you. Will it be perfectly convenient to you to send the carriage to Rye on Saturday—if not Sister can write me next week and we will take a Hack all the way.

Your friends all seem very much gratified that you are to succeed Mr. Boudinot as President of the American Bible Society and many of them have expressed strong hopes that in consequence of it they should have the pleasure of seeing you here. That I know and lament your health will not permit it, but I too heartily rejoice in the only appointment we could wish you to accept. General Clarkson has quite recovered his health.

I saw Mr. Bunorus today and made some inquiries respecting your houses. He said the frequent rains had retarded the workmen very much, but that the first coat of plaster was finished in one and nearly so in the other and that the stairs would be put up in a few days.

Will you be so good as to thank Sister for her frequent and satisfactory letters. It will not be in my power to write to her by this post and it is time to bid you good night. Please to remember me very affectionately to Brother, Augusta, Nancy, and the Children. The Family here all desired their love to you and them. I am dear Papa,

Most gratefully and affectionately,
Your dutiful daughter,
M. Banyer

A Soldier Remembers the Trail of Tears

John G. Burnett, 1890

In 1890, when John Burnett was eighty years old, he wrote about his experiences during the Trail of Tears for his children.

Children: This is my birthday, December 11, 1890, I am eighty years old today. I was born at Kings Iron Works in Sullivan County, Tennessee, December the 11th, 1810. I grew into manhood fishing in Beaver Creek and roaming through the forest hunting the deer and the wild boar and the timber wolf. Often spending weeks at a time in the solitary wilderness with no companions but my rifle, hunting knife, and a small hatchet that I carried in my belt in all of my wilderness wanderings.

On these long hunting trips I met and became acquainted with many of the Cherokee Indians, hunting with them by day and sleeping around their camp fires by night. I learned to speak their language, and they taught me the arts of trailing and building traps and snares. . . .

The removal of Cherokee Indians from their life long homes in the year of 1838 found me a young man in the prime of life and a Private soldier in the American Army. Being acquainted with many of the Indians and able to fluently speak their language, I was sent as interpreter into the Smoky Mountain Country in May, 1838, and witnessed the execution of the most brutal order in the History of American Warfare. I saw the helpless Cherokees arrested and dragged from their homes, and driven at the bayonet point into the stockades. And in the chill of a drizzling rain on an October morning, I saw them loaded like cattle or sheep into six hundred and forty-five wagons and started toward the west.

One can never forget the sadness and solemnity of that morning. Chief John Ross led in prayer and when the bugle sounded and the wagons started rolling many of the children rose to their feet and waved their little hands good-by to their mountain homes, knowing they were leaving them forever. Many of these helpless people did not have blankets and many of them had been driven from home barefooted. . . .

The long painful journey to the west ended March 26th, 1839, with four-thousand silent graves reaching from the foothills of the Smoky Mountains to what is known as Indian territory in the West. And covetousness on the part of the white race was the cause of all that the Cherokees had to suffer. . . .

Twenty-five years after the removal it was my privilege to meet a large company of the Cherokees in uniform of the Confederate Army under command of Colonel Thomas. They were encamped at Zollicoffer and I went to see them. Most of them were just boys at the time of the removal but they instantly recognized me as "the soldier that was good to us." Being able to talk to them in their native language I had an enjoyable day with them. From them I learned that Chief John Ross was still ruler in the nation in 1863. And I wonder if he is still living? He was a noble-hearted fellow and suffered a lot for his race. . . .

Let the historian of a future day tell the sad story with its sighs, its tears and dying groans. Let the great Judge of all the earth weigh our actions and reward us according to our work.

Children — Thus ends my promised birthday story. This December the 11th 1890.

To the People of the United States

John Tyler, 1841

President William Henry Harrison died on April 4, 1841, after one month in office. His Vice President, John Tyler, succeeded to the presidency and took the oath of office on April 6. A few days later, the new President issued this proclamation to the people of the United States.

TO THE PEOPLE OF THE UNITED STATES

A RECOMMENDATION

WASHINGTON, *April 13, 1841*

When a Christian people feel themselves to be overtaken by a great public calamity, it becomes them to humble themselves under the dispensation of Divine Providence, to recognize His righteous government over the children of men, to acknowledge His goodness in time past, as well as their own unworthiness, and to supplicate His merciful protection for the future.

The death of William Henry Harrison, late President of the United States, so soon after his elevation to that high office, is a bereavement peculiarly calculated to be regarded as a heavy affliction and to impress all minds with a sense of the uncertainty of human things and of the dependence of nations, as well as individuals, upon our Heavenly Parent.

I have thought, therefore, that I should be acting in conformity with the general expectation and feelings of the community in recommending, as I now do, to the people of the United States of every religious denomination that, according to their several modes and forms of worship, they observe a day of fasting and prayer by such religious services as may be suitable on the occasion; and I recommend Friday, the 14th day of May next, for that purpose, to the end that on that day we may all with one accord join in humble and reverential approach to Him in whose hands we are, invoking Him to inspire us with a proper spirit and temper of heart and mind under these frowns of His providence and still to bestow His gracious benedictions upon our Government and our country.

John Tyler

Life on the Mississippi

Mark Twain, 1883

Mark Twain, one of America's most famous and widely-read authors, grew up in Hannibal, Missouri, a small town on the Mississippi River. The river plays a prominent part in several of Twain's books. This excerpt from his autobiographical Life on the Mississippi *is titled "A Boy's Ambition."*

When I was a boy, there was but one permanent ambition among my comrades in our village on the west bank of the Mississippi River. That was, to be a steamboatman. We had transient ambitions of other sorts, but they were only transient. When a circus came and went, it left us all burning to become clowns; the first negro minstrel show that ever came to our section left us all suffering to try that kind of life; now and then we had a hope that, if we lived and were good, God would permit us to be pirates. These ambitions faded out, each in its turn; but the ambition to be a steamboatman always remained.

Once a day a cheap, gaudy packet [ship] arrived upward from St. Louis, and another downward from Keokuk. Before these events, the day was glorious with expectancy; after them, the day was a dead and empty thing. Not only the boys, but the whole village, felt this. After all these years I can picture that old time to myself now, just as it was then: the white town drowsing in the sunshine of a summer's morning; the streets empty, or pretty nearly so; one or two clerks sitting in front of the Water Street stores, with their splint-bottomed chairs tilted back against the wall, chins on breasts, hats slouched over their faces, asleep—with shingle-shavings enough around to show what broke them down; a sow and a litter of pigs loafing along the sidewalk, doing a good business in watermelon rinds and seeds; two or three lonely little freight piles scattered about the "levee;" a pile of "skids" on the slope of the stone-paved wharf . . . two or three wood flats at the head of the wharf, but nobody to listen to the peaceful lapping of the wavelets against them; the great Mississippi, the majestic, the magnificent Mississippi, rolling its mile-wide tide along, shining in the sun; the dense forest away on the other side; the "point" above the town, and the "point" below, bounding the river-glimpse and turning it into a sort of sea, and withal a very still and brilliant and lonely one. Presently a film of dark smoke appears above one of those remote points; instantly a negro drayman [load hauler], famous for his quick eye and prodigious voice, lifts up the cry, "S-t-e-a-m-boat a-comin'!" and the scene changes! The town drunkard stirs, the clerks wake up, a furious clatter of drays [wagons] follows, every house and store pours out a human contribution, and all in a twinkling the dead town is alive and moving. Drays, carts, men, boys, all go hurrying from many quarters to a common centre, the wharf. Assembled there, the people fasten their eyes upon the coming boat as upon a wonder they are seeing for the first time. And the boat *is* rather a handsome sight, too. She is long and sharp and trim and pretty; she has two tall, fancy-topped chimneys, with a gilded device of some kind swung between them; a fanciful pilot-house, all glass and "gingerbread," perched on top of the "texas" [uppermost] deck behind them; the paddle-boxes are gorgeous with a picture or with gilded rays above the boat's name: the boiler deck, the hurricane deck, and the texas deck are fenced and ornamented with clean white railings; there is a flag gallantly flying from the jack-staff; the furnace doors are open and the fires glaring bravely; the upper decks are black with passengers; the captain stands by the big bell, calm, imposing, the envy of all; great volumes of the blackest smoke are rolling and tumbling out of the chimneys—a husbanded [purposely created] grandeur created with a bit of pitch pine just before arriving at a town; the crew are grouped on the forecastle; the broad stage is run far out over the port bow, and an envied deck-hand stands picturesquely on the end of it with a coil of rope in his hand; the pent steam is screaming through the gauge-cocks; the captain lifts his hand, a bell rings, the wheels stop; then they turn back, churning the water to foam, and the steamer is at rest. Then such a scramble as there is to get aboard, and to get ashore, and to take in freight and to discharge freight, all at one and the same time. . . . Ten minutes later the steamer is under way again, with no flag on the jackstaff and no black smoke issuing from the chimneys. After ten more minutes the town is dead again. . . .

Steamboat Songs

These folk songs are from the days when steamboats were the kings of the Mississippi and many other American rivers.

I'm Goin' Down the River Before Long

I'm goin' down the river before long,
   oh Baby,
Goin' down the river before long,
I'm goin' down the river before long.

I'm goin' where the chilly winds don't blow,
   oh Baby,
Goin' where the chilly winds don't blow,
I'm goin' where the chilly winds don't blow.

Ain't comin' back till 'bout in the fall,
   oh Baby,
Ain't comin' back till 'bout in the fall,
Ain't comin' back till 'bout in the fall.

I'm goin' down the river to carry some sacks,
   oh Baby,
Goin' down the river to carry some sacks,
I'm goin' down the river to carry some sacks.

I'll have the money when I get back,
   oh Baby,
I'll have the money when I get back,
I'll have the money when I get back.

I Was Born on the River

I was born on the river
   And the river is my home,
As long as I can carry a chain,
   I won't let the river alone.

Oh captain, captain,
   Has the money come?
The reason why I asked you,
   I want to borrow some.

Well the captain is a-standin'
   Up on the hurricane roof,
He's a-hollerin' down on the deckhead
   Tellin' the boys what to do.

Oh let us hurry, boys,
   If you want to get home,
Let's load the boat out,
   Let the cards and dice alone.

I'm Workin' My Way Back Home

Chorus
I'm workin' my way back home,
I'm workin' my way back home,
I'm workin' my way back home, Baby,
I'm workin' my way back home.

Timber don't get too heavy for me,
　　And sacks too heavy to stack,
All that I crave for many a long day,
　　Is your lovin' when I get back. *(Chorus)*

Oh fireman, keep her rollin' for me,
　　Let's make it to Memphis, Tennessee,
For my back is gittin' tired,
　　And my shoulder is gittin' sore. *(Chorus)*

Down in the Mississippi to the Gulf of Mexico,
　　Down below Natchez,
But if the boat keep steppin'
　　I'll be seein' you soon. *(Chorus)*

Now Paducah's layin' round the bend,
　　Now Paducah's layin' round the bend,
Captain, don't whistle, just ring your bell,
　　For my woman will be standin' right there.
　　　　　　　　　　　　　(Chorus)

The Macombrey Queen

Hear the boat a-whistlin'
　　Comin' round the bend,
Hear the boat a-whistlin'
　　Comin' round the bend,
With its tank pipes painted,
　　Bringin' my true love back agin.

So I got to get ready,
　　We're goin' to New Orleans,
So I got to get ready,
　　We're goin' to New Orleans,
On the purtiest steamboat,
　　It's the Macombrey Queen.

Ferd Herold Blues

Big boat's up the river and
　　she won't come down,
Big boat's up the river and
　　she won't come down,
I believe to my soul that
　　the boat's run aground.

When I come to town, Baby,
　　what you want me to bring you back,
When I come to town, Baby,
　　what you want me to bring you back,
I want a new pair of shoes and a
　　Merry Widow hat.

Blow your whistle, Captain,
　　tell me the time of day,
Blow your whistle, Captain,
　　tell me the time of day,
I believe it's time I'm eatin',
　　for the mules done had their oats and hay.

Every time I hear that big boat blow,
　　Every time I hear that big boat blow,
My mind rambles and
　　my feet are bound to go.

Ferd Herold been up the river twenty days,
　　and she won't come down,
Ferd Herold been up the river twenty days,
　　and she won't come down,
Low water's up the river and
　　the boat has run aground.

What Hath God Wrought!

Samuel F. B. Morse, 1844

On May 24, 1844, Samuel F. B. Morse sent the first long-distance message with the electric telegraph, from Washington, D.C., to his associate Alfred Vail in Baltimore, Maryland. Morse let a young friend named Annie Ellsworth have the privilege of choosing the words for this historic message. She chose a phrase from Numbers 23:23: "What hath God wrought!" Morse wrote the following letter to his brother Sidney on May 31, 1844. The convention he mentions was the political convention of the Democratic Party at which James K. Polk was the surprise presidential nominee.

. . . You will see by the papers how great success has attended the first efforts of the Telegraph. That sentence of Annie Ellsworth's was divinely indited, for it is in my thoughts day and night. "What hath God wrought!" It is His work, and He alone could have carried me thus far through all my trials and enabled me to triumph over the obstacles, physical and moral, which opposed me.

"Not unto us, not unto us, but to thy name, O Lord, be all the praise."

I begin to fear now the effects of public favor, lest it should kindle that pride of heart and self-sufficiency which dwells in my own as well as in others' breasts, and which, alas! is so ready to be inflamed by the slightest spark of praise. I do indeed feel gratified, and it is right I should rejoice, but I rejoice with fear, and I desire that a sense of dependence upon and increased obligation to the Giver of every good and perfect gift may keep me humble and circumspect.

The conventions at Baltimore happened most opportunely for the display of the powers of the Telegraph, especially as it was the means of correspondence, in one instance, between the Democratic Convention and the first candidate elect for the Vice-Presidency. The enthusiasm of the crowd before the window of the Telegraph Room in the Capitol was excited to the highest pitch at the announcement of the nomination of the Presidential candidate, and the whole of it afterwards seemed turned upon the Telegraph. They gave the Telegraph three cheers, and I was called to make my appearance at the window when three cheers were given to me by some hundreds present, composed mainly of members of Congress.

Such is the feeling in Congress that many tell me they are ready to grant anything. Even the most inveterate [firmly established] opposers have changed to admirers, and one of them, Hon.

Cave Johnson, who ridiculed my system last session by associating it with the tricks of animal magnetism, came to me and said: "Sir, I give in. It is an astonishing invention."

When I see all this and such enthusiasm everywhere manifested, and contrast the present with the past season of darkness and almost despair, have I not occasion to exclaim "What hath God wrought"? Surely none but He who has all hearts in his hands, and turns them as the rivers of waters are turned could so have brought light out of darkness. "Sorrow may continue for a night, but joy cometh in the morning." Pray for me then, my dear brother, that I may have a heart to praise the great Deliverer, and in future, when discouraged or despairing, be enabled to remember His past mercy, and in full faith rest all my cares on Him who careth for us. . . .

Hail to the Chief

Music by James Sanderson, 1812
Lyrics by Albert Gamse, c. early 1900s

"Hail to the Chief" is the official song played when the President of the United States arrives at a formal occasion. It was first used to honor a President in 1815, when it was played both to honor the late George Washington and to celebrate the end of the War of 1812. The first President to be honored with "Hail to the Chief" while in office was Andrew Jackson in 1829. The tune had a part in the inauguration ceremony of Martin Van Buren. Julia Tyler, wife of John Tyler, first requested that it be played to announce the arrival of the President. Sarah Childress Polk made that practice a ritual during her husband James K. Polk's presidency. He is pictured below. President Harry Truman, who was a musician and a student of music, studied the background of "Hail to the Chief." In 1945, while Truman was in office, the Department of Defense made "Hail to the Chief" the official musical tribute to the President. It is commonly played by a military band. It is most familiar as an instrumental tune written by James Sanderson, but Albert Gamse wrote the following lyrics.

Hail to the Chief we have chosen for the nation,
 Hail to the Chief! We salute him, one and all.
Hail to the Chief, as we pledge cooperation
 In proud fulfillment of a great, noble call.

Yours is the aim to make this grand country grander,
 This you will do, that's our strong, firm belief.
Hail to the one we selected as commander,
 Hail to the President! Hail to the Chief!

First Woman on the Oregon Trail

Narcissa Whitman, 1836

This is an excerpt from a journal-style letter that Narcissa Whitman wrote in 1836 while she traveled with her new husband and their mission party to Oregon.

April 1st. - Nothing of much importance occurred to-day. My eyes are satiated with the same beautiful scenery all along the coasts of this mighty river, so peculiar to this western country. One year ago today since my husband first arrived in St. Louis on his exploring route to the mountains. We are one week earlier passing up the river this spring than he was last year. While the boat stopped to take in wood we went on shore, found some rushes, picked a branch of cedar, went to a spring for clear water (the river water is very rily [muddy] at all times), and rambled considerably in pursuit of new objects. One of these circumstances I must mention, which was quite diverting to us. On the rocks near the river we found a great quantity of the prickly pear. Husband knew from experience the effects of handling them, and cautioned me against them, but I thought I could just take one and put it in my india-rubber apron pocket, and carry it to the boat. I did so, but after rambling a little I thought to take it out, and behold, my pocket was filled with its needles, just like a caterpillar's bristles. I became considerably annoyed with them; they covered my hands, and I have scarcely got rid of them yet. My husband would have laughed at me a little, were it not for his own misfortune. He thought to discover what kind of mucilage [plant juice] it was by tasting it - cut one in two, bit it, and covered his lips completely. We then had to sympathize with each other, and were glad to render mutual assistance in a case of extermination. . . .

Thursday, 7th. - Very pleasant, but cold. This morning the thermometer stood at 24 at nine o'clock. I have not seen any snow since we left the Allegheny mountains, before the 15th of March. I should like to know about the snow in New York. Is it all gone? How did it go, and the consequences? Mary, we have had a sick one with us all the way since we joined Dr. Satterlee. Mrs. Satterlee has had a very bad cough and cold, which has kept her feeble. She is now recovering, and is as well as can be expected. The rest of us have been very well, except feeling the effects of drinking the river water. I am in exception, however. My health was never better than since I have been on the river. . . . Mrs. Spalding does not look nor feel quite healthy enough for our enterprise. Riding affects her differently from what it does me. Everyone who sees me compliments me as being the best able to endure the journey over the mountains. Sister S[paulding] is very resolute— no shrinking with her. She possesses much fortitude. I like her very much. She wears well upon acquaintance. She is a very suitable person for Mr. Spalding— has the right temperament to match him. I think we shall get along very well together; we have so far. I have such a good place to shelter—under my husband's wings. He is so excellent. I love to confide in his judgment, and act under him, for it gives me a chance to improve. Jane, if you want to be happy get as good a husband as I have got, and be a missionary. Mary, I wish you were with us. You would be happy, as I am. The way looks pleasant, notwithstanding we are so near encountering the difficulties of an unheard-of journey for females. . . .

An Act to Establish the Smithsonian Institution

1846

When the United States government received Englishman James Smithson's mysterious gift in his will, Congress had to determine how to use the money to fulfill his wishes. Congress passed this bill in 1846 and it was signed into law by President James K. Polk.

29th Congress, 1st Session

Begun and held at the City of Washington and the District of Columbia on Monday, the first day of December, eighteen hundred and forty-five.

AN ACT TO ESTABLISH THE "SMITHSONIAN INSTITUTION" FOR THE INCREASE AND DIFFUSION OF KNOWLEDGE AMONG MEN.

James Smithson, esquire, of London, in the Kingdom of Great Britain, having by his last will and testament given the whole of his property to the United States of America, to found at Washington, under the name of the "Smithsonian Institution," an establishment for the increase and diffusion of knowledge among men; and the United States having, by an act of Congress, received said property and accepted said trust; Therefore, for the faithful execution of said trust, according to the will of the liberal and enlightened donor . . . .

SEC. 4. *And be it further enacted*, That, after the board of regents shall have met and become organized, it shall be their duty forthwith to proceed to select a suitable site for such building as may be necessary for the institution, which ground may be taken and appropriated out of that part of the public ground in the city of Washington lying between the Patent Office and Seventh Street . . . .

SEC. 5. *And be it further enacted*, That, so soon as the board of regents shall have selected the said site, they shall cause to be erected a suitable building, of plain and durable materials and structure, without unnecessary ornament, and of sufficient size, and with suitable rooms or halls, for the reception and arrangement, upon a liberal scale, of objects of natural history, including a geological and mineralogical cabinet; also a chemical laboratory, a library, a gallery of art, and the necessary lecture rooms . . . .

SEC. 6. *And be it further enacted*, That, in proportion as suitable arrangements can be made for their reception, all objects of art and of foreign and curious research, and all objects of natural history, plants, and geological and mineralogical specimens, belonging, or hereafter to belong, to the United States, which may be in the city of Washington, in whosesoever custody the same may be, shall be delivered to such persons as may be authorized by the board of regents to receive them . . . .

SEC. 10. *And be it further enacted*, That the author or proprietor of any book, map, chart, musical composition, print, cut, or engraving, for which a copy-right shall be secured under the existing acts of Congress, or those which shall hereafter be enacted respecting copy-rights, shall, within three months from the publication . . . deliver, or cause to be delivered, one copy of the same to the Librarian of the Smithsonian institution, and one copy to the Librarian of Congress Library, for the use of the said Libraries.

This article appeared in the St. Paul, Minnesota, Globe *newspaper the day after Annie Edson Taylor went over Niagara Falls in a barrel as a publicity stunt.*

THE GLOBE   OCTOBER 25, 1901

OVER NIAGARA

MRS. ANNIE EDSON TAYLOR MAKES THE TRIP IN A CLOSED BARREL

HAS NO SERIOUS INJURIES

Anvil in the Bottom of the Barrel Kept It in an Upright Position.

NOT A BONE WAS BROKEN

Niagara Falls, N.Y., Oct. 24—Mrs. Annie Edson Taylor, fifty years old, went over Niagara Falls on the Canadian side, this afternoon and survived, a feat never before accomplished. . . . She made the trip in a barrel. Not only did she survive, but she escaped without a broken bone, her only apparent injuries being a scalp wound one and one-half inches long, a slight concussion of the brain, some shock to her nervous system and bruises about the body. She was conscious when taken out of the barrel. The doctors in attendance upon her tonight said that though she was somewhat hysterical, her condition is not at all serious and that she probably will be out of bed within a few days.

Mrs. Taylor's trip covered a mile ride through the Canadian rapids before she reached the brink of the precipice. Her barrel, staunch as a barrel could be made, was twirled and buffeted through those delirious waters, but escaped serious contact with rocks. As it passed through the smoother, swifter waters that rushed over into the abyss it rode in an almost perpendicular position with its upper half out of the water. As it passed over the brink

it rode at an angle of about 45 degrees on the outer surface of the deluge and descended gracefully to the white foaming waters, 158 feet below.

True to her calculations, an anvil fastened to the bottom of the barrel kept it foot downward and so it landed. . . . The ride through the rapids occupied eighteen minutes. It was 4:23 o'clock when the barrel took its leap. It could not be seen as it struck the water below, because of the spray, but in less than half a minute after it passed over the brink it was seen on the surface of the scum-covered water below the falls. It was carried swiftly down to the green water beyond the scum; then halfway to the *Maid of the Mist* landing it was caught in what is known as the *Maid of the Mist* eddy, and held there until it floated so close to the shore that it was reached by means of a pole and hook and drawn in upon the rocks at 4:40 o'clock, seventeen minutes after it shot the cataract. The woman was lifted from the barrel and half an hour later she lay on a cot at her boarding place, in Niagara Falls on the American side. She said she would never do it again, but that she was not sorry she had done it, "if it would help her financially."

She said she had prayed all during the trip, except during "a few moments" of unconsciousness just after her descent.

The barrel in which Mrs. Taylor made the journey is 4½ feet high and about 3 feet in diameter. A leather harness and cushions inside protected her body. Air was secured through a rubber tube connected with a small opening near the top of the barrel. Mrs. Taylor is a school teacher and recently came here from Bay City, Michigan.

From Audubon's Journal

John James Audubon, 1843

In March of 1843, John James Audubon and his son Victor left on a journey to research for a project called Quadrupeds of North America. *Even with the objective of observing animals, it is obvious from these journal entries that Audubon always had an eye out for birds!*

April 26. A rainy day, and the heat we had experienced yesterday was now all gone. We saw a Wild Goose running on the shore, and it was killed by Bell [a traveling companion]; but our captain did not stop to pick it up, and I was sorry to see the poor bird dead, uselessly. We now had found out that our berths were too thickly inhabited for us to sleep in; so I rolled myself in my blanket, lay down on deck, and slept very sound.

27th. A fine clear day, cool this morning . . . saw a few Gray Squirrels, and an abundance of our common Partridges in flocks of fifteen to twenty, very gentle indeed. . . . At a woodyard above us we saw a White Pelican that had been captured there, and which, had it been clean, I should have bought. I saw that its legs and feet were red, and not yellow, as they are during autumn and winter. Marmots are quite abundant, and here they perforate their holes in the loose, sandy soil of the river banks, as well as the same soil wherever it is somewhat elevated . . . at sunrise, we were in sight of the seat of government, Jefferson. The State House stands prominent, with a view from it up and down the stream of about ten miles; but, with the exception of the State House and the Penitentiary, Jefferson is a poor place, the land round being sterile and broken. This is said to be 160 or 170 miles above St. Louis. We saw many Gray Squirrels this morning. Yesterday we passed under long lines of elevated shore, surmounted by stupendous rocks of limestone, with many curious holes in them, where we saw Vultures and Eagles enter towards dusk. Harris saw a Peregrine Falcon; the whole of these rocky shores are ornamented with a species of white cedar quite satisfactorily known to us. We took wood at several places; at one I was told that Wild Turkeys were abundant and Squirrels also, but as the squatter observed, "Game is very scarce, especially Bears." Wolves begin to be troublesome to the settlers who have sheep; they are obliged to drive the latter home, and herd

them each night. . . . We saw a pair of Peregrine Falcons, one of them with a bird in its talons; also a few White-fronted Geese, some Blue-winged Teal, and some Cormorants, but none with the head, neck, and breast pure white, as the one I saw two days ago. . . .

29th. We were off at five this rainy morning, and at 9 A.M. reached Booneville, distant from St. Louis about 204 miles. We bought at this place an axe, a saw, three files, and some wafers; also some chickens, at one dollar a dozen. We found here some of the Santa Fe traders with whom we had crossed the Alleghenies. They were awaiting the arrival of their goods, and then would immediately start. I saw a Rabbit sitting under the shelf of a rock, and also a Gray Squirrel. . . .

Ho! for California

Jesse Hutchinson, 1849

This song of the California Gold Rush of 1849 reveals the bright (and unrealistic) hopes of men setting out to strike it rich. The last verse is a reminder of the heated controversy over slavery at the time. "Ho! for California" is a song of the Hutchinson Family Singers, a musical group that became popular in America in the 1840s and performed more than twelve thousand concerts.

We've formed our band and are well manned,
    To journey afar to the promised land,
Where the golden ore is rich in store,
    On the banks of the Sacramento shore.

Chorus
Then, ho! Brothers ho! To California go.
    There's plenty of gold in the world
        we're told,
On the banks of the Sacramento.
    Heigh O, and a way we go,
Digging up gold in Francisco.

O! don't you cry, nor heave a sigh,
    For we'll all come back again, bye and bye,
Don't breathe a fear, nor shed a tear,
    But patiently wait for about two year.
                 (Chorus)

As the gold is thar, most any whar,
    And they dig it out with an iron bar,
And where 'tis thick, with a spade or pick,
    They can take out lumps as heavy as brick.
                 (Chorus)

As we explore that distant shore,
    We'll fill our pockets with the shining ore;
And how 'twill sound, as the word goes round,
    Of our picking up gold by the dozen pound.
                 (Chorus)

We expect our share of the coarsest fare,
    And sometimes to sleep in the open air,
Upon the cold ground we shall all sleep sound
    Except when the wolves are howling round.
                 (Chorus)

And off we roam over the dark sea foam,
    We'll never forget our friends at home
For memories kind will bring to mind
    The thoughts of those we leave behind.
                 (Chorus)

O! the land we'll save, for the bold and brave—
    Have determined there never shall
        breathe a slave;
Let foes recoil, for the sons of toil
    Shall make California GOD'S FREE SOIL.

Final Chorus
Then ho! Brothers ho! To California go,
    No slave shall toil on God's Free Soil,
On the banks of the Sacramento,
    Heigh O, and away we go,
Chanting our songs of Freedom, O.

Letter from a Forty-Niner

Enos Christman, 1850

Enos Christman was a forty-niner who sailed in July of 1849 for California, making the dangerous trip around South America, to seek his fortune in the gold mines. He left a fiancée named Ellen Apple back home in Pennsylvania. The two exchanged several letters during Enos's sojourn in California. This letter is from Enos to Ellen on his arrival in California.

Happy Valley, near San Francisco
St. Valentine's Day, Feb 14, 1850

Betrothed Ellen:—This day a year ago, I little dreamed that in a twelvemonth I should have encountered the terrors of Cape Horn, and after many days of severe suffering, reached the shores of this golden land, and been penning you an epistle like this. But strange as this would have sounded then, it is now nevertheless true.

When we landed on the beach at Happy Valley, we pitched our tent and commenced life in true California fashion. Every evening the merry notes of the violin are heard, and judging from appearances the place is not inaptly named.

After our arrival, I received many letters and papers at the post office, and not seeing any in your handwriting, I impatiently tore the envelopes off Mr. Prizer's and therein found the precious documents so eagerly looked for. The words therein were a soothing balm to all misgivings, and assure me of your abiding and unchanging love and affection, and should I return home without a dollar, I flatter myself that in you I would still possess a jewel more precious than all the glittering ore in this dazzling country, but I expect to return with a better hand than when I left or perish in the pursuit.

You speak with great earnestness of your anxiety for my future comfort and speedy return. I can assure you that thus far I have suffered many hardships to which I have been unaccustomed, but with the exception of a slight cold, consequent upon sleeping on the ground, I feel as well in health as ever I did in my life. . . .

You and Cad must have had a merry time when you walked up to Miss Hoffinton's as Quakers. Give my compliments to Cad and tell her she had better not wait for the California boys; they may not get back very soon.

And some of your acquaintances think you have an investment in the California Stock. Well, if they consider me an investment it is even so.

You still rob yourself of much enjoyment, I fear, on my account, by not allowing yourself to walk with or attend parties with other acquaintances. If any expedition is on foot that promises enjoyment, I pray you accept the invitation on my account, for nothing can give me more pleasure than to know you are well and happy. I pray you also to abate your anxiety about me, for a continual weight upon the mind must eventually affect the system and undermine health.

Before I started and bid farewell to as good friends as ever lived, I counted the cost. I had strong and honorable motives for encountering the terrors of Cape Horn and the dangers of a long sea voyage and here, just on my arrival in the land of promise, would be a poor place indeed to regret the undertaking. No danger must be met half way, every difficulty should be met with manly fortitude, and my intention is to meet them in such a manner that I need never be ashamed. I now boldly turn my face toward the celebrated Sierra Nevada. What we may there have to encounter, I cannot anticipate; perhaps we shall have to engage with the native Indian in some sanguinary and bloody conflict, or be hugged to death by the fierce and savage grizzly bear. But whatever may be my fate—should the worst come and I be fated to leave my bones to whiten on the bleak plains of this golden land, I can never forget the image that has been present to my mind's eye for so long a time. . . .

In a few days we hope to leave for the diggings and what our opportunities may there be to receive or send letters, I know not, and should you not hear from me for a long time do not despair or think that I intentionally delay writing to you. We may have to penetrate the country many hundred miles, and if so of course our mail conveniences will be few, but what there are shall be embraced by me to write to you. I wish you to write monthly to San Francisco, and I will get your letters some time. Theodore and his party are at the Middle diggings, I believe, Thornbury at the same we are going to, but I fear we shall meet none of them. Remember me to your sister, and your parents. Although a stranger to Miss Hatch, please give my compliments to her also.

That happiness may be found in your footsteps is the prayer of your devoted

Enos Christman

Let the Lower Lights Be Burning

Philip P. Bliss, 1871

Philip P. Bliss was born in Pennsylvania in 1838 and died in a train accident in 1876. He is the author of many of America's best-loved hymns, including "Hallelujah! What a Savior," "Wonderful Words of Life," and "More Holiness Give Me." This hymn, written in 1871, uses the imagery of a lighthouse to represent God's mercy, and the lights along the shore to represent Christians doing their part to point the way for those who are lost.

Brightly beams our Father's mercy from His lighthouse evermore,
　But to us He gives the keeping of the lights along the shore.
Let the lower lights be burning! Send a gleam across the wave!
　For to us He gives the keeping of the lights along the shore.

Chorus
Let the lower lights be burning,
　Send a gleam across the wave!
Some poor fainting, struggling seaman
　You may rescue, you may save.

Dark the night of sin has settled, loud the angry billows roar;
　Eager eyes are watching, longing, for the lights, along the shore.
Let the lower lights be burning! Send a gleam across the wave!
　Eager eyes are watching, longing, for the lights, along the shore. *(Chorus)*

Trim your feeble lamp, my brother, some poor sailor tempest tossed,
　Trying now to make the harbor, in the darkness may be lost.
Let the lower lights be burning! Send a gleam across the wave!
　Trying now to make the harbor, some poor sailor may be lost. *(Chorus)*

Poems of Longfellow

Henry Wadsworth Longfellow

Henry Wadsworth Longfellow (1807-1882) is one of the greatest American poets of all time. His many poems were popular during his lifetime and have remained popular ever since. Many of the lines from his poems, such as "Into each life some rain must fall," have become American proverbs. Longfellow was well educated, widely traveled, and highly respected. He was a man of faith who expressed praise to God and understanding of people in his poetry.

Daybreak
1858

A wind came up out of the sea,
And said, "O mists, make room for me."

It hailed the ships, and cried, "Sail on,
Ye mariners, the night is gone."

And hurried landward far away,
Crying, "Awake! it is the day."

It said unto the forest, "Shout!
Hang all your leafy banners out!"

It touched the wood-bird's folded wing,
And said, "O bird, awake and sing."

And o'er the farms, "O chanticleer,
Your clarion blow; the day is near."

It whispered to the fields of corn,
"Bow down, and hail the coming morn."

It shouted through the belfry-tower,
"Awake, O bell! proclaim the hour."

It crossed the churchyard with a sigh,
And said, "Not yet! in quiet lie."

Hymn for My Brother's Ordination
1850

Christ to the young man said:
　"Yet one thing more;
　If thou would perfect be,
Sell all thou hast and give it to the poor,
　And come and follow me!"

Within this temple Christ again, unseen,
　Those sacred words hath said,
And his invisible hands to-day have been
　Laid on a young man's head.

And evermore beside him on his way
　The unseen Christ shall move,
That he may lean upon his arm and say,
　"Dost thou, dear Lord, approve?"

Beside him at the marriage feast shall be,
　To make the scene more fair;
Beside him in the dark Gethsemane
　Of pain and midnight prayer.

O holy trust! O endless sense of rest!
　Like the beloved John
To lay his head on the Saviour's breast,
　And thus to journey on!

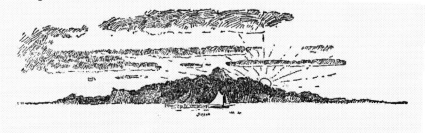

65

I Heard the Bells on Christmas Day
1864

*Longefellow wrote this song after his
son was injured during the Civil War.*

I heard the bells on Christmas day
 Their old familiar carols play,
And wild and sweet the words repeat
 Of peace on earth, good will to men.

And thought how, as the day had come,
 The belfries of all Christendom
Had rolled along the unbroken song
 Of peace on earth, good will to men.

Till ringing, singing on its way
 The world revolved from night to day,
A voice, a chime, a chant sublime
 Of peace on earth, good will to men.

Then from each black, accursed mouth
 The cannon thundered in the South,
And with the sound the carols drowned
 Of peace on earth, good will to men.

It was as if an earthquake rent
 The hearth-stones of a continent,
And made forlorn, the households born
 Of peace on earth, good will to men.

And in despair I bowed my head
 "There is no peace on earth," I said,
"For hate is strong and mocks the song
 Of peace on earth, good will to men."

Then pealed the bells more loud and deep:
 "God is not dead, nor doth He sleep;
The wrong shall fail, the right prevail
 With peace on earth, good will to men."

The Rainy Day
1842

The day is cold, and dark, and dreary;
 It rains, and the wind is never weary;
The vine still clings to the mouldering wall,
 But at every gust the dead leaves fall,
And the day is dark and dreary.

My life is cold, and dark, and dreary;
 It rains, and the wind is never weary;
My thoughts still cling to the mouldering Past,
 But the hopes of youth fall thick in the blast,
And the days are dark and dreary.

Be still, sad heart! and cease repining;
 Behind the clouds is the sun still shining;
Thy fate is the common fate of all,
 Into each life some rain must fall,
Some days must be dark and dreary.

Letters from Abraham Lincoln

1860s

One of the most famous letters in American history was written by an eleven-year-old girl:

Westfield, Chautauqua Co. NY
Oct. 15, 1860

Honorable Abraham Lincoln
Dear Sir

My father has just come from the fair and brought home your picture and Mr. Hamlin's. I am a little girl only 11 years old, but want you should be President of the United States very much so I hope you won't think me very bold to write to such a great man as you are. Have you any little girls about as large as I am if so give them my love and tell her to write to me if you cannot answer this letter. I have got 4 brothers and part of them will vote for you any way and if you let your whiskers grow I will try and get the rest of them to vote for you you would look a great deal better for your face is so thin. All the ladies like whiskers and they would tease their husbands to vote for you and then you would be President. My father is going to vote for you and if I was a man I would vote for you too but I will try to get every one to vote for you that I can I think that rail fence around your picture makes it look very pretty I have got a little baby sister she is nine weeks old and is just as cunning as can be. When you direct your letter direct to Grace Bedell Westfield Chautauqua County New York I must not write any more answer this letter right off.

Good bye   Grace Bedell

Lincoln replied:

Miss Grace Bedell
My dear little Miss

Your very agreeable letter of the 15th is received—I regret the necessity of saying I have no daughters—I have three sons—one seventeen, one nine, and one seven years of age—They, with their mother, constitute my whole family - As to the whiskers, having never worn any, do you not think people would call it a piece of silly affection if I were to begin it now? Your very sincere well wisher

A. Lincoln

Despite his reservations, Lincoln soon afterwards followed Grace Bedell's suggestion and grew a beard.

Abraham Lincoln wrote the following letter to General Ulysses S. Grant on July 13, 1863.

My dear General, I do not remember that you and I ever met personally. I write this now as a grateful acknowledgment for the almost inestimable service you have done the country. I wish to say a word further. When you first reached the vicinity of Vicksburg, I thought you should do what you finally did—march the troops across the neck, run the batteries with the transports, and thus go below; and I never had any faith, except a general hope that you knew better than I, that the Yazoo Pass expedition and the like could succeed. When you got below and took Port Gibson, Grand Gulf, and vicinity, I thought you should go down the river and join General Banks, and when you turned northward, east of the Big Black, I feared it was a mistake. I now wish to make the personal acknowledgment that you were right and I was wrong.

Yours very truly, A. Lincoln

The Gettysburg Address

Abraham Lincoln, 1863

When the Soldiers' National Cemetery was dedicated at Gettysburg on November 19, 1863, Abraham Lincoln made his speech after the famous orator Edward Everett, who spoke to the crowd for two hours. On the next day, Everett wrote to Lincoln: "I should be glad, if I could flatter myself that I came as near to the central idea of the occasion, in two hours, as you did in two minutes." Everett's speech is forgotten, while Lincoln's has become one of the most famous of all time.

Fourscore and seven years ago our fathers brought forth on this continent a new nation, conceived in liberty and dedicated to the proposition that all men are created equal. Now we are engaged in a great civil war, testing whether that nation or any nation so conceived and so dedicated can long endure. We are met on a great battlefield of that war. We have come to dedicate a portion of that field as a final resting-place for those who here gave their lives that that nation might live. It is altogether fitting and proper that we should do this. But in a larger sense, we cannot dedicate, we cannot consecrate, we cannot hallow this ground. The brave men, living and dead, who struggled here have consecrated it far above our poor power to add or detract. The world will little note nor long remember what we say here, but it can never forget what they did here. It is for us the living rather to be dedicated here to the unfinished work which they who fought here have thus far so nobly advanced. It is rather for us to be here dedicated to the great task remaining before us—that from these honored dead we take increased devotion to that cause for which they gave the last full measure of devotion—that we here highly resolve that these dead shall not have died in vain, that this nation under God shall have a new birth of freedom, and that government of the people, by the people, for the people shall not perish from the earth.

Recollections of General Robert E. Lee

Robert E. Lee Jr., 1904

Robert E. Lee's son, also named Robert E. Lee and a veteran of the Confederate Army, published a book entitled Recollections and Letters of Robert E. Lee *in 1904. This excerpt relates an incident soon after the Civil War ended, when Lee received a visit from a solider who had served under him in the United States Army before the Civil War. Lee refers to a black man as a darkey, which was common at the time; but it is an offensive term today.*

As well as I can recall my father at this time, he appeared to be very well physically, though he looked older, grayer, more quiet and reserved. He seemed very tired, and was always glad to talk of any other subject than that of the war or anything pertaining thereto. We all tried to cheer and help him. And the people of Richmond and of the entire South were as kind and considerate as it was possible to be. Indeed, I think their great kindness tired him. He appreciated it all, was courteous, grateful, and polite, but he had been under such a terrible strain for several years that he needed the time and quiet to get back his strength of heart and mind. All sorts and conditions of people came to see him: officers and soldiers from both armies, statesmen, politicians, ministers of the Gospel, mothers and wives to ask about husbands and sons of whom they had heard nothing. To keep him from being overtaxed by this incessant stream of visitors, we formed a sort of guard of the young men in the house, some of whom took it by turns to keep the door and, if possible, turn strangers away. My father was gentle, kind, and polite to all, and never willingly, so far as I know, refused to see any one.

Dan Lee, late of the Confederate States Navy, my first cousin, and myself, one day had charge of the front door, when at it appeared a Federal soldier, accompanied by a darkey carrying a large willow basket filled to the brim with provisions of every kind. The man was Irish all over, and showed by his uniform and carriage that he was a "regular," and not a volunteer. On our asking him what he wanted, he replied that he wanted to see General Lee, that he had heard down the street the General and his family were suffering for lack of something to eat, that he had been with "the Colonel" when he commanded the Second Cavalry, and, as long as he had a cent, his old colonel should not suffer. My father, who had stepped into another room as he heard the bell ring, hearing something of the conversation, came out into the hall. The old Irishman, as soon as he saw him, drew himself up and saluted, and repeated to the General, with tears streaming down his cheeks, what he had just said to us. My father was very much touched, thanked him heartily for his kindness and generosity, but told him that he did not need the things he had brought and could not take them. This seemed to disappoint the old soldier greatly, and he pleaded so hard to be allowed to present the supplies to his old colonel, whom he believed to be in want of them, that at last my father said that he would accept the basket and send it to the hospital, for the sick and wounded, who were really in great need. Though he was not satisfied, he submitted to this compromise, and then to our surprise and dismay, in bidding the General good-bye, threw his arms around him and was attempting to kiss him, when "Dan" and I interfered. As he was leaving, he said, "Good-bye, Colonel! God bless ye! If I could have got over in time I would have been with ye!"

Childhood Reminiscences

Susie King Taylor, 1902

Susie King Taylor, born into slavery in Georgia but raised by her free grandmother, served as a nurse with a regiment of African American soldiers fighting with the Union army during the Civil War. Her husband, Edward King, was a member of that regiment. In 1902 she published her memoirs, Reminiscences of My Life in Camp with the 33rd United States Colored Troops, Late 1st S.C. Volunteers. *She began her memoirs with a history of her family and memories of her childhood and the beginning of the Civil War. She uses the terms "colored" and "negro" for African Americans. These were standard in her time, though not acceptable today. The photographs illustrating Taylor's reminiscences show slave and free children at the time of the Civil War.*

My great-great-grandmother was 120 years old when she died. She had seven children, and five of her boys were in the Revolutionary War. She was from Virginia, and was half Indian. She was so old she had to be held in the sun to help restore or prolong her vitality.

My great-grandmother, one of her daughters, named Susanna, was married to Peter Simons, and was one hundred years old when she died, from a stroke of paralysis

in Savannah. She was the mother of twenty-four children, twenty-three being girls. She was one of the noted midwives of her day. In 1820 my grandmother was born, and named after her grandmother, Dolly, and in 1833 she married Fortune Lambert Reed. Two children blessed their union, James and Hagar Ann. James died at the age of twelve years.

My mother was born in 1834. She married Raymond Baker in 1847. Nine children were born to them, three dying in infancy. I was the first born. I was born on the Grest Farm (which was on an island known as Isle of Wight), Liberty County, about thirty-five miles from Savannah, Georgia, on August 6, 1848, my mother being waitress for the Grest family. I have often been told by mother of the care Mrs. Grest took of me. She was very fond of me, and I remember when my brother and I were small children, and Mr. Grest would go away on business, Mrs. Grest would place us at the foot of her bed to sleep and keep her company. Sometimes he would return home earlier than he had expected to; then she would put us on the floor.

When I was about seven years old, Mr. Grest allowed my grandmother to take my brother and me to live with her in Savannah. There were no railroad connections in those days between this place and Savannah; all travel was by stagecoaches. I remember, as if it were yesterday, the coach which ran in from Savannah, with its driver, whose beard nearly reached his knees. His name was Shakespeare, and often I would go to the stable where he kept his horses, on Barnard Street in front of the old Arsenal, just to look at his wonderful beard.

My grandmother went every three months to see my mother. She would hire a wagon to carry bacon, tobacco, flour, molasses, and sugar. These she would trade with people in the neighboring places, for eggs, chickens, or cash, if they had it. These, in turn, she carried back to the city market, where she had a customer who sold them for her. The profit from these, together with laundry work and care of some bachelors' rooms, made a good living for her.

The hardest blow to her was the failure of the Freedmen's Savings Bank in Savannah, for in that bank she had placed her savings, about three thousand dollars, the result of her hard labor and self-denial before the war, and which, by dint of shrewdness and care, she kept together all through the war. She felt it more keenly, coming as it did in her old age, when her life was too far spent to begin anew; but she took a practical view of the matter, for she said, "I will leave it all in God's hand. If the Yankees did take all our money, they freed my race; God will take care of us."

. . . I was born under the slave law in Georgia, in 1848, and was brought up by my grandmother in Savannah. There were three of us with her, my younger sister and brother. My brother and I being the two eldest, we were sent to a friend of my grandmother, Mrs. Woodhouse, a widow, to learn to read and write. She was a free woman and lived on Bay Lane, between Habersham and Price streets, about half a mile from my house. We went every day about nine o'clock, with our books wrapped in paper to prevent the police or white persons from seeing them. We went in, one at a time, through the gate, into the yard to the L kitchen, which was the schoolroom. She had twenty-five or thirty children whom she taught, assisted by her daughter, Mary Jane. The neighbors would see us going in sometimes, but they supposed we were there learning trades, as it was the custom to give children a trade of some kind. After school we left the same way we entered, one by one, when we would go to a square, about a block from the school, and wait for each other. We would gather laurel leaves and pop them on our hands, on our way home. I remained at her school for two years or more, when I was sent to a Mrs. Mary Beasley, where I continued until May, 1860, when she told my grandmother she had taught me all she knew, and grandmother had better get some one else who could teach me more, so I stopped my studies for a while.

I had a white playmate about this time, named Katie O'Connor, who lived on the next corner of the street from my house, and who attended a convent. One day she told me, if I would promise not to tell her father, she would give me some lessons. On my promise not to do so, and getting her mother's consent, she gave me lessons about four months, every evening. At the end of this time she was put into the convent permanently, and I have never seen her since.

A month after this, James Blouis, our landlord's son, was attending the High School, and was very fond of grandmother, so she asked him to give me a few lessons, which he did until the middle of 1861, when the Savannah Volunteer Guards, to which he and his brother belonged, were ordered to the front under General Barton. In the first battle of Manassas, his brother Eugene was killed, and James deserted over to the Union side, and at the close of the war went to Washington, D. C., where he has since resided. . . .

About this time I had been reading so much about the "Yankees" I was very anxious to see them. . . . I wanted to see these wonderful "Yankees" so much, as I heard my parents say the Yankee was going to set all the slaves free. Oh, how those people prayed for freedom! I remember, one night, my grandmother went out into the suburbs of the city to a church meeting, and they were fervently singing this old hymn,—

Yes, we all shall be free,
Yes, we all shall be free,
Yes, we all shall be free,
When the Lord shall appear . . . .

—when the police came in and arrested all who were there, saying they were planning freedom, and sang "the Lord," in place of "Yankee," to blind any one who might be listening. Grandmother never forgot that night, although she did not stay in the guard-house, as she sent to her guardian, who came at once for her; but this was the last meeting she ever attended out of the city proper.

On April 1, 1862, about the time the Union soldiers were firing on Fort Pulaski, I was sent out into the country to my mother. I remember what a roar and din the guns made. They jarred the earth for miles. The fort was at last taken by them. Two days after the taking of Fort Pulaski, my uncle took his family of seven and myself to St. Catherine Island. We landed under the protection of the Union fleet, and remained there two weeks, when about thirty of us were taken aboard the gunboat P—, to be transferred to St. Simon's Island; and at last, to my unbounded joy, I saw the "Yankee."

After we were all settled aboard and started on our journey, Captain Whitmore, commanding the boat, asked me where I was from. I told him Savannah, Georgia. He asked if I could read; I said, "Yes!" "Can you write?" he next asked. "Yes, I can do that also," I replied, and as if he had some doubts of my answers he handed me a book and a pencil and told me to write my name and where I was from. I did this; when he wanted to know if I could sew. On hearing I could, he asked me to

hem some napkins for him. He was surprised at my accomplishments (for they were such in those days), for he said he did not know there were any negroes in the South able to read or write. He said, "You seem to be so different from the other colored people who came from the same place you did." "No!" I replied, "the only difference is, they were reared in the country and I in the city, as was a man from Darien, Georgia, named Edward King." That seemed to satisfy him, and we had no further conversation that day on the subject.

Camp Songs of the Civil War

A host of new songs—brave, sad, and humorous—were inspired by the Civil War. Songs expressed feelings of victory and grief and helped cheer the soldiers in camp.

The New York Volunteer
Anonymous

'Twas in the days of seventy-six,
    When Freemen young and old,
All fought for Independence then,
    Each hero brave and bold!
'Twas then the noble Stars and Stripes
    In triumph did appear,
And defended by brave patriots,
    The Yankee Volunteers.

Chorus
'Tis my delight to march and fight
    Like a New York Volunteer.

Now, there's our City Regiments,
    Just see what they have done:
The first to offer to the State
    To go to Washington,
To protect the Federal Capital
    And the flag they love so dear!
And they've done their duty nobly,
    Like New York Volunteers! *(Chorus)*

The Rebels out in Maryland,
    They madly raved and swore,
They'd let none of our Union troops
    Pass through Baltimore;
But the Massachusetts Regiment,
    No traitors did they fear;
But fought their way to Washington,
    Like Yankee Volunteers. *(Chorus)*

Johnny Is My Darling
Father Reed, 1863

Chorus
Johnny is my darling, my darling, my darling,
Johnny is my darling, the Union Volunteer.

'Twas on a sunny morning,
    The brightest of the year,
When Johnny came to my town,
    A Union Volunteer. *(Chorus)*

As he came marching up the street,
    The bands played loud and clear;
And everyone came out to greet
    The Union Volunteer. *(Chorus)*

With proudly waving starry flags
    And hearts that knew no fear;
He came to fight for Freedom's rights,
    A Union Volunteer. *(Chorus)*

But though he's gone to glory win,
    And I left lonely here,
He'll soon return to me again
    As Cupid's Volunteer. *(Chorus)*

The Southern Soldier Boy
Captain G. W. Alexander, 1863

Bob Roebuck is my sweetheart's name,
    He's off to the wars and gone;
He's fighting for his Nannie dear,
    His sword is buckled on;
He's fighting for his own true love,
    His foes he does defy,
He is the darling of my heart,
    My Southern Soldier Boy.

When Johnny Comes Marching Home
Patrick S. Gilmore, 1863

When Johnny comes marching home again,
  Hurrah! Hurrah!
We'll give him a hearty welcome then,
  Hurrah! Hurrah!
The men will cheer, and the boys will shout,
  The ladies, they will all turn out,
And we'll all feel gay when
  Johnny comes marching home.

The old church bell will peal with joy,
  Hurrah! Hurrah!
To welcome home our darling boy,
  Hurrah! Hurrah!
The village lads and lassies say,
  With roses they will strew the way,
And we'll all feel gay when
  Johnny comes marching home.

Get ready for the Jubilee,
  Hurrah! Hurrah!
We'll give the hero three times three,
  Hurrah! Hurrah!
The laurel wreath is ready now
  To place upon his loyal brow,
And we'll all feel gay when
  Johnny comes marching home.

Let love and friendship on that day,
  Hurrah! Hurrah!
Their choicest treasures then display,
  Hurrah! Hurrah!
And let each one perform some part,
  To fill with joy the warrior's heart,
And we'll all feel gay when
  Johnny comes marching home.

Goober Peas
A. Pindar / P. Nutt

Sitting by the roadside on a summer's day,
  Chatting with my mess-mates, passing time
    away,
Lying in the shadow underneath the trees,
  Goodness, how delicious, eating goober
    peas[1]!

Chorus
Peas, peas, peas, peas,
  Eating goober peas!
Goodness, how delicious,
  Eating goober peas!

When a horse-man passes, the soldiers have a
    rule,
  To cry out at their loudest, "Mister, here's
    your mule!"
But another pleasure, enchantinger than these,
  Is wearing out your grinders, eating
    goober peas! *(Chorus)*

Just before the battle, the General hears a row,
  He says "The Yanks are coming, I hear their
    rifles now."
He turns around in wonder, and what do you
    think he sees?
The Georgia Militia eating goober peas!
  (Chorus)

I think my song has lasted almost long enough,
  The subject's interesting, but the rhymes are
    mighty rough,
I wish this war was over, when free from rags
    and fleas,
  We'd kiss our wives and sweethearts,
    and gobble goober peas! *(Chorus)*

[1] Goober peas are peanuts

The Discovery of Yellowstone Park

Nathaniel Pitt Langford, 1905

Nathaniel Pitt Langford was part of the Washburn Expedition of 1870 that explored the area that is now Yellowstone National Park. He kept an extensive journal of the wonders he observed. Langford went on to join the effort to ensure that Yellowstone was preserved as a national park.

Wednesday, August 31. This has been a "red-letter" day with me, and one which I shall not soon forget, for my mind is clogged and my memory confused by what I have today seen. General Washburn and Mr. Hedges are sitting near me, writing, and we have an understanding that we will compare our notes when finished. We are all overwhelmed with astonishment and wonder at what we have seen, and we feel that we have been near the very presence of the Almighty. General Washburn has just quoted from the psalm: "When I behold the work of Thy hands, what is man that Thou art mindful of him!" My own mind is so confused that I hardly know where to commence in making a clear record of what is at this moment floating past my mental vision. I cannot confine myself to a bare description of the falls of the Yellowstone alone, for these two great cataracts are but one feature in a scene composed of so many of the elements of grandeur and sublimity, that I almost despair of giving to those who on our return home will listen to a recital of our adventures, the faintest conception of it. . . .

The place where I obtained the best and most terrible view of the canyon was a narrow projecting point situated two or three miles below the lower fall. Standing there or rather lying there for greater safety, I thought how utterly impossible it would be to describe to another the sensations inspired by such a presence. As I took in this scene, I realized my own littleness, my helplessness, my dread exposure to destruction, my inability to cope with or even comprehend the mighty architecture of nature. More than all this I felt as never before my entire dependence upon that Almighty Power who had wrought these wonders. A sense of danger, lest the rock should crumble away, almost overpowered me. My knees trembled, and I experienced the terror which causes men to turn pale and their countenances to blanch with fear, and I recoiled from the vision I had seen, glad to feel the solid earth beneath me and to realize the assurance of returning safety.

. . . Mr. Hedges and I sat on the table-rock to which I have referred, opposite the upper fall, as long as our limited time would permit; and as we reluctantly left it and climbed to the top, I expressed my regret at leaving so fascinating a spot, quoting the familiar line: "A thing of beauty is a joy forever."

. . . Yes! This stupendous display of nature's handiwork will be to me "a joy forever." It lingers in my memory like the faintly defined outlines of a dream. I can scarcely realize that in the unbroken solitude of this majestic range of rocks, away from civilization and almost inaccessible to human approach, the Almighty has placed so many of the most wonderful and magnificent objects of His creation, and that I am to be one of the few first to bring them to the notice of the world. Truly has it been said, that we live to learn how little may be known, and of what we see, how much surpasses comprehension. . . .

Dedication Prayer

Dr. John Todd, 1869

Congregational minister John Todd of Pittsfield, Massachusetts, offered this dedication prayer at the Golden Spike Ceremony celebrating the completion of the transcontinental railroad on May 10, 1869.

Our Father and God, and our fathers' God, God of Creation and God of Providence, Thou hast created the heavens and the earth, the valleys and the hills; Thou art also the God of mercies and blessings. We rejoice that Thou hast created the human mind with its power of invention, its capacity of expansion, and its guardian of success. We have assembled here this day, upon the height of the continent, from varied sections of our country, to do homage to Thy wonderful name, in that Thou hast brought this mighty enterprise, combining the commerce of the east with the gold of the west to so glorious a completion. And now we ask Thee that this great work, so auspiciously begun and so magnificently completed, may remain a monument to our faith and good works. We here consecrate this great highway for the good of Thy people. O God, we implore Thy blessings upon it and upon those that may direct its operations. O Father, God of our fathers, we desire to acknowledge Thy handiwork in this great work, and ask Thy blessing upon us here assembled, upon the rulers of our government and upon Thy people everywhere; that peace may flow unto them as a gentle stream, and that this mighty enterprise may be unto us as the Atlantic of Thy strength, and the Pacific of Thy love. Through Jesus, the Redeemed, Amen.

Hymns of Fanny J. Crosby

Fanny J. Crosby of Putnam County, New York, wrote over 8,000 hymns in her lifetime, many of which are among the most famous and beloved hymns in the church. Crosby was blind from the time she was very young. However, she saw her blindness not as a burden, but as a blessing from the Lord. Fanny Crosby lived from 1820 to 1915.

Near the Cross
Before 1869

Jesus, keep me near the cross:
    There a precious fountain,
Free to all, a healing stream,
    Flows from Calvary's mountain.

Chorus
In the cross, in the cross,
    Be my glory ever;
Till my raptured soul shall find
    Rest beyond the river.

Near the cross, a trembling soul,
    Love and mercy found me;
There the Bright and Morning Star
    Sheds its beams around me. *(Chorus)*

Near the cross! O Lamb of God,
    Bring its scenes before me;
Help me walk from day to day
    With its shadows o'er me. *(Chorus)*

Near the cross I'll watch and wait
    Hoping, trusting ever,
Till I reach the golden strand,
    Just beyond the river. *(Chorus)*

All the Way My Savior Leads Me
Before 1875

All the way my Savior leads me;
    What have I to ask beside?
Can I doubt His tender mercy,
    Who through life has been my Guide?
Heav'nly peace, divinest comfort,
    Here by faith in Him to dwell!
For I know, whate'er befall me,
    Jesus doeth all things well;
For I know, whate'er befall me,
    Jesus doeth all things well.

All the way my Savior leads me,
    Cheers each winding path I tread;
Gives me grace for every trial,
    Feeds me with the living Bread.
Though my weary steps may falter,
    And my soul athirst may be,
Gushing from the Rock before me,
    Lo! A spring of joy I see;
Gushing from the Rock before me,
    Lo! A spring of joy I see.

All the way my Savior leads me
    O the fullness of His love!
Perfect rest to me is promised
    In my Father's house above.
When my spirit, clothed immortal,
    Wings its flight to realms of day
This my song through endless ages—
    Jesus led me all the way;
This my song through endless ages—
    Jesus led me all the way.

I Am Thine, O Lord
Before 1875

I am Thine, O Lord, I have heard Thy voice,
    And it told Thy love to me;
But I long to rise in the arms of faith
    And be closer drawn to Thee.

Chorus
Draw me nearer, nearer blessed Lord,
    To the cross where Thou hast died.
Draw me nearer, nearer, nearer blessed Lord,
    To Thy precious, bleeding side.

Consecrate me now to Thy service, Lord,
    By the power of grace divine;
Let my soul look up with a steadfast hope,
    And my will be lost in Thine. *(Chorus)*

O the pure delight of a single hour
    That before Thy throne I spend,
When I kneel in prayer, and with Thee, my God
    I commune as friend with friend! *(Chorus)*

There are depths of love that I cannot know
    Till I cross the narrow sea;
There are heights of joy that I may not reach
    Till I rest in peace with Thee. *(Chorus)*

Blessed Assurance
1873

Blessed assurance, Jesus is mine!
    O what a foretaste of glory divine!
Heir of salvation, purchase of God,
    Born of His Spirit, washed in His blood.

Chorus
This is my story, this is my song,
    Praising my Savior, all the day long;
This is my story, this is my song,
    Praising my Savior, all the day long.

Perfect submission, perfect delight,
    Visions of rapture now burst on my sight;
Angels descending bring from above
    Echoes of mercy, whispers of love. *(Chorus)*

Perfect submission, all is at rest;
    I in my Savior am happy and blest;
Watching and waiting, looking above,
    Filled with His goodness, lost in His love.
                        (Chorus)

Cowboy Songs

Cowboy culture began with the real-life, skilled, hardworking men who drove cattle across the open range. However, interest in cowboy culture spread far beyond the laborers themselves. For generations, Americans have gobbled up all things cowboy: from boots to TV and movie heroes to rodeos to cowboy ballads. The music born of the cowboy life has taken its place among popular American folk music.

Oh, Give Me a Home Where the Buffalo Roam
Brewster Higley, 1876

Oh, give me a home where the buffalo roam
    Where the deer and the antelope play;
Where seldom is heard a discouraging word,
    And the sky is not cloudy all day.

Chorus
Home! Home on the range!
    Where the deer and the antelope play,
Where seldom is heard a discouraging word,
    And the sky is not clouded all day.

Oh! give me a land where the bright diamond
    sand
    Throws its light from the glittering streams,
Where glideth along the graceful white swan,
    Like the maid in her heavenly dreams.
                    (Chorus)

Oh! give me a gale of the Solomon vale,
    Where the life streams with buoyancy flow;
On the banks of the Beaver, where seldom if
      ever,
    Any poisonous herbage doth grow. *(Chorus)*

How often at night, when the heavens were
      bright,
    With the light of the twinkling stars
Have I stood here amazed, and asked as I
      gazed,
    If their glory exceed that of ours. *(Chorus)*

I love the wild flowers in this bright land of
      ours,
    I love the wild curlew's shrill scream;
The bluffs and white rocks, and antelope flocks
    That graze on the mountains so green.
                    (Chorus)

Red River Valley

Late 1800s

From this valley they say you are going,
  I shall miss your sweet face and bright smile.
For they say you are taking the sunshine
  That has brightened my pathway awhile.

I've been thinking a long time my darling,
  Of those sweet words you never would say,
But the last of my fond hopes have vanished
  For they say you are going away.

Then come sit here awhile ere you leave us
  Do not hasten to bid us adieu,
And remember the Red River Valley
  And the cowboy who loves you so true.

I have promised you, darling, that never
  Would words from my lips cause you pain;
My life will be yours forever
  If only you will love me again.

There never could be such a longing
  In the heart of a poor cowboy's breast,
As dwells in this heart you are breaking
  While I wait in my home in the West.

Do you think of this valley you are leaving,
  Oh, how lonely and dreary it will be?
Do you think of the kind hearts you're breaking,
  And the pain you are causing to me?

I'd Like To Be in Texas

Jack C. Williams and Carl Copeland , c. 1916

In the lobby of a big hotel,
  in New York town one day,
Sat a bunch of fellers tellin' yarns
  to pass the time away.
They told of places they had been and
  different things they'd seen.
Some preferred Chicago town
  and others New Orleans.
In a corner, in an old arm chair,
  sat a man whose hair was gray.
He listened to them eagerly,
  to what they had to say.
They asked him where he'd like to be
  and his clear old voice did ring,
"I'd like to be in Texas
  for the roundup in the spring."

They sat and listened carefully
  to what he had to say
For they knew the old man sitting there
  had been a top hand in his day.
They asked him for a story
  of his life out on the plains,
Slowly he removed his hat
  and quietly began.
"I've seen 'em stampede over hills
  till you'd think they'd never stop,
I've seen 'em run for miles and miles
  until their leader dropped,
I was Foreman on a cow ranch,
  the callin' of a king.
I'd like to be in Texas
  for the roundup in the spring." *(Chorus)*

Chorus
I can see the cattle grazing
  o'er the hills at early morn;
I can see the campfire smoking
  at the breaking of the dawn.
I can hear the broncos neighing,
  I can hear the cowboys sing.
I'd like to be in Texas
  for the roundup in the spring.

80

How Arthur Was Inaugurated

September 20, 1881

President James A. Garfield died on September 19, 1881, several weeks after he was shot by an assassin at a Washington train station. Garfield's Vice President, Chester A. Arthur, then became the President of the United States. He took the oath of office at his home in New York City early the next morning after the President died. This article appeared in Washington, D.C.'s The Evening Critic newspaper later that day.

THE EVENING CRITIC SEPTEMBER 20, 1881

HOW ARTHUR WAS INAUGURATED

New York, Sept. 20— General Arthur was sworn in at 2:15 o'clock this morning at his house. Two judges of the New York Supreme Court had been sent for, J. R. Brady and Charles Donohue. Judge Brady arrived with Mr. Rollins and Mr. Roat at 1:50, but the ceremony was out of courtesy deferred until Judge Donohue's arrival, at a

little after two o'clock, with ex-Commissioner French. On Judge Donohue's arrival General Arthur rose from his seat in the library and advanced to the front parlor. It is a large room, with large French windows. Oil paintings, by old masters, hang from the ceiling. Dispatches, books, and writing materials were scattered all over the large table that stands in the centre. General Arthur stood behind this table, facing the window. He had regained his composure; his eye was clear, and his manner dignified. The gas in the library was burning dimly, and his fine, tall form stood out grandly from the dark background. Old allegorical pictures loomed out from the darkness. Pictures of conquests and of triumphs, of defeats and of despairs, and above all was a white marble bust of Henry Clay.

Judge Brady stood on the other side of the table, facing General Arthur. Grouped around the two men were Judge Donohue, Elihu Root, Commissioner French, and Daniel G. Rollins, and General Arthur's son. Judge Brady slowly advanced a step and raised his right hand. General Arthur did likewise.

A moment of impressive silence followed. General Arthur's features were almost fixed. Then Judge Brady administered the oath, General Arthur speaking in a clear, ringing voice: "I do solemnly swear that I will faithfully execute the office of President of the United States, and will, to the best of my ability, preserve, protect, and defend the Constitution of the United States." After this he remained standing a moment longer, his hand still raised. No one spoke, nor did the President afterward give expression to any emotion. Up to 3 o'clock he had not decided when to leave the city for Washington.

Colonel Anderson and Books

Andrew Carnegie, 1920

In Andrew Carnegie's autobiography, he wrote about his friend Colonel Anderson who offered his books for working boys to borrow. His generosity inspired Andrew Carnegie to donate millions of dollars later in his life to help other young people as Colonel Anderson had helped him. This excerpt from the autobiography is from the chapter entitled "Colonel Anderson and Books."

With all their pleasures the messenger boys were hard worked. Every other evening they were required to be on duty until the office closed, and on these nights it was seldom that I reached home before eleven o'clock. On the alternating nights we were relieved at six. This did not leave much time for self-improvement, nor did the wants of the family leave any money to spend on books. There came, however, like a blessing from above, a means by which the treasures of literature were unfolded to me.

Colonel James Anderson—I bless his name as I write—announced that he would open his library of four hundred volumes to boys, so that any young man could take out, each Saturday afternoon, a book which could be exchanged for another on the succeeding Saturday. . . .

My dear friend, Tom Miller, one of the inner circle, lived near Colonel Anderson and introduced me to him, and in this way the windows were opened in the walls of my dungeon through which the light of knowledge streamed in. Every day's toil and even the long hours of night service were lightened by the book which I carried about with me and read in the intervals that could be snatched from duty. And the future was made bright by the thought that when Saturday came a new volume could be obtained. In this way I became familiar with Macaulay's essays and his history, and with Bancroft's "History of the United States," which I studied with more care than any other book I had then read. Lamb's essays were my special delight, but I had at this time no knowledge of the great master of all, Shakespeare, beyond the selected pieces in the school books. My taste for him I acquired a little later at the old Pittsburgh Theater.

John Phipps, James R. Wilson, Thomas N. Miller, William Cowley—members of our circle—shared with me the invaluable privilege of the use of Colonel Anderson's library. Books which it would have been impossible for me to obtain elsewhere were, by his wise generosity, placed within my reach; and to him I owe a taste for literature which I would not exchange for all the millions that were ever amassed by man. Life would be quite intolerable without it. Nothing contributed so much to keep my companions and myself clear of low fellowship and bad habits as the beneficence of the good Colonel. Later, when fortune smiled upon me, one of my first duties was the erection of a monument to my benefactor. It stands in front of the Hall and Library in Diamond Square, which I presented to Allegheny, and bears this inscription:

> To Colonel James Anderson, Founder of Free Libraries in Western Pennsylvania. He opened his Library to working boys and upon Saturday afternoons acted as librarian, thus dedicating not only his books but himself to the noble work. This monument is erected in grateful remembrance by Andrew Carnegie, one of the "working boys" to whom were thus opened the precious treasures of knowledge and imagination through which youth may ascend.

This is but a slight tribute and gives only a faint idea of the depth of gratitude which I feel for what he did for me and my companions. It was from my own early experience that I decided there was no use to which money could be applied so productive of good to boys and girls who have good within them and ability and ambition to develop it, as the founding of a public library in a community which is willing to support it as a municipal institution. I am sure that the future of those libraries I have been privileged to found will prove the correctness of this opinion. For if one boy in each library district, by having access to one of these libraries, is half as much benefited as I was by having access to Colonel Anderson's four hundred well-worn volumes, I shall consider they have not been established in vain.

"As the twig is bent the tree's inclined." The treasures of the world which books contain were opened to me at the right moment. The fundamental advantage of a library is that it gives nothing for nothing. Youths must acquire knowledge themselves. There is no escape from this. It gave me great satisfaction to discover, many years later, that my father was one of the five weavers in Dunfermline who gathered together the few books they had and formed the first circulating library in that town.

The history of that library is interesting. It grew, and was removed no less than seven times from place to place, the first move being made by the founders, who carried the books in their aprons and two coal scuttles from the hand-loom shop to the second resting-place. That my father was one of the founders of the first library in his native town, and that I have been fortunate enough to be the founder of the last one, is certainly to me one of the most interesting incidents of my life. I have said often, in public speeches, that I had never heard of a lineage for which I would exchange that of a library-founding weaver. I followed my father in library founding unknowingly—I am tempted almost to say providentially—and it has been a source of intense satisfaction to me. Such a father as mine was a guide to be followed—one of the sweetest, purest, and kindest natures I have ever known.

Summer on the Homestead

Elinore Rupert Stewart, 1909

In 1909 a young widow named Elinore Rupert and her toddler daughter, Jerrine, moved from Denver, Colorado, to seek a better life on a homestead claim in Wyoming. Elinore worked as a housekeeper for a Mr. Stewart (whom she later married) as well as claiming and improving her own piece of land under the Homestead Act. She wrote letters about her homesteading experiences to her friend and former employer in Denver.

September 11, 1909

Dear Mrs. Coney,

This has been for me the busiest, happiest summer I can remember. I have worked very hard, but it has been work that I really enjoy. Help of any kind is very hard to get here, and Mr. Stewart had been too confident of getting men, so that haying caught him with too few men to put up the hay. He had no man to run the mower and he couldn't run both the mower and the stacker, so you can fancy what a place he was in.

I don't know that I ever told you, but my parents died within a year of each other and left six of us to shift for ourselves. Our people offered to take one here and there among them until we should all have a place, but we refused to be raised on the halves and so arranged to stay at Grandmother's and keep together. Well, we had no money to hire men to do our work, so had to learn to do it ourselves. Consequently I learned to do many things which girls more fortunately situated don't even know have to be done. Among the things I learned to do was the way to run a mowing-machine. It cost me many bitter tears because I got sunburned, and my hands were hard, rough, and stained with machine oil, and I used to wonder how any Prince Charming could overlook all that in any girl he came to. . . .

. . . I almost forgot that I knew how [to mow] until Mr. Stewart got into such a panic. If he put a man to mow, it kept them all idle at the stacker, and he just couldn't get enough men. I was afraid to tell him I could mow for fear he would forbid me to do so. But one morning, when he was chasing a last hope of help, I went down to the barn, took out the horses, and went to mowing. I had enough cut before he got back to show him I knew how, and as he came back manless he was delighted as well as surprised. I was glad because I really like to mow, and besides that, I am adding feathers to my cap in a surprising way. When you see me again you will think I am wearing a feather duster, but it is only that I have been said to have almost as much sense as a "mon," [Mr. Stewart's way of saying "man" in his Scottish accent] and that is an honor I never aspired to, even in my wildest dreams.

I have done most of my cooking at night, have milked seven cows every day, and have done all the hay-cutting, so you see I have been working. But I have found time to put up thirty pints of jelly and the same amount of jam for myself. I used wild fruits, gooseberries, currants, raspberries, and cherries. I have almost two gallons of the cherry butter, and I think it is delicious. I wish I could get some of it to you, I am sure you would like it.

We began haying July 5 and finished September 8. After working so hard and so steadily I decided on a day off, so yesterday I saddled the pony, took a few things I needed, and Jerrine and I fared forth. Baby can ride behind quite well. We got away by sunup and a glorious day we had.

We followed a stream higher up into the mountains and the air was so keen and clear at first we had on our coats. There was a tang of sage and of pine in the air, and our horse was midside deep in rabbit-brush, a shrub just covered with flowers that look and smell like goldenrod. The blue distance promised many alluring adventures, so we went along singing and simply gulping in summer. Occasionally a bunch of sage chickens would fly up out of the sagebrush, or a jack rabbit would leap out. Once we saw a bunch of antelope gallop over a hill, but we were out just to be out, and game didn't tempt us. I started, though, to have just as good a time as possible, so I had a fish-hook in my knapsack.

Presently, about noon, we came to a little dell where the grass was as soft and as green as a lawn. The creek kept right up against the hills on one side and there were groves of quaking asp and cottonwoods that made shade, and service-bushes and birches that shut off the ugly hills on the other side. We dismounted and prepared to noon. We caught a few grasshoppers and I cut a birch pole for a rod. The trout are so beautiful now, their sides are so silvery, with dashes of old rose and orange, their speckles are so black, while their backs look as if they had been sprinkled with gold-dust. They bite so well that it doesn't require any especial skill or tackle to catch plenty for a meal in a few minutes.

In a little while I went back to where I had left my pony browsing, with eight beauties. We made a fire first, then I dressed my trout while it was burning down to a nice bed of coals. I had brought a frying-pan and a bottle of lard, salt, and buttered bread. We gathered a few service-berries, our trout were soon browned, and with water, clear, and as cold as ice, we had a feast. The quaking aspens are beginning to turn yellow, but no leaves have fallen. Their shadows dimpled and twinkled over the grass like happy children. The sound of the dashing, roaring water kept inviting me to cast for trout, but I didn't want to carry them so far, so we rested until the sun was getting low and then started for home, with the song of the locusts in our ears warning us that the melancholy days are almost here. We would come up over the top of a hill into the glory of a beautiful sunset with its gorgeous colors, then down into the little valley already purpling with mysterious twilight. So on, until, just at dark, we rode into our corral and a mighty tired, sleepy little girl was powerfully glad to get home. . . .

Sincerely yours,
Elinore Rupert

Thanksgiving Time

Laura Ingalls Wilder, 1916

Before gaining national fame for her beloved Little House *books, Laura Ingalls Wilder was a writer for the* Missouri Ruralist *newspaper. She wrote articles regularly from 1911 to 1924. In her column, she shared her wisdom on managing a farm and home, community involvment, friendship, and family. This article was published on November 20, 1916.*

MISSOURI RURALIST   NOVEMBER 20, 1916

THANKSGIVING TIME

As Thanksgiving day draws near again, I am reminded of an occurrence of my childhood. To tell the truth, it is a yearly habit of mine to think of it about this time and to smile at it once more.

We were living on the frontier in South Dakota then. There's no more frontier within the boundaries of the United States, more's the pity, but then we were ahead of the railroad in a new unsettled country. Our nearest and only neighbor was 12 miles away and the store was 40 miles distant.

Father had laid in a supply of provisions for the winter and among them were salt meats, but for fresh meat we depended on father's gun and the antelope which fed, in herds, across the prairie. So we were quite excited, one day near Thanksgiving, when father hurried into the house for his gun and then away again to try for a shot at a belated flock of wild geese hurrying south.

We would have roast goose for Thanksgiving dinner! "Roast goose and dressing seasoned with sage," said sister Mary. "No not sage! I don't like sage and we won't have it in the dressing," I exclaimed. Then we quarreled, sister Mary and I, she insisting that there should be sage in the dressing and I declaring there should not be sage in the dressing, until father returned,—without the

goose! I remember saying in a meek voice to sister Mary, "I wish I had let you have the sage," and to this day when I think of it I feel again just how thankful I would have been for roast goose and dressing with sage seasoning—with or without any seasoning—I could even have gotten along without the dressing. Just plain goose roasted would have been plenty good enough.

This little happening has helped me to be properly thankful even though at times the seasoning of my blessings has not been just as I would have chosen.

"I suppose I should be thankful for what we have, but I can't feel very thankful when I have to pay $2.60 for a little flour and the price still going up," writes a friend, and in the same letter she says, "we are in our usual health." The family are so used to good health that it is not even taken into consideration as a cause of thanksgiving. We are so inclined to take for granted the blessings we possess and to look for something peculiar, some special good luck for which to be thankful.

I read a Thanksgiving story, the other day, in which a woman sent her little boy out to walk around the block and look for something for which to be thankful.

One would think that the fact of his being able to walk around the block and that he had a mother to send him would have been sufficient cause for thankfulness. We are nearly all afflicted with mental farsightedness and so easily overlook the thing which is so obvious and near. There are our hands and feet, who ever thinks of giving thanks for them, until indeed they, or the use of them, are lost. We usually accept them as a matter of course, without a thought, but a year of being crippled has taught me the value of my feet and two perfectly good feet are now among my dearest possessions. Why! There is greater occasion for thankfulness just in the unimpaired possession of one of the five senses than there would be if some one left us a fortune. Indeed how could the value of one be reckoned? When we have all five in good working condition we surely need not make a search for anything else in order to feel that we should give thanks to Whom thanks are due.

I once remarked upon how happy and cheerful a new acquaintance seemed always to be and the young man to whom I spoke replied, "Oh he's just glad that he is alive." Upon inquiry, I learned that several years before this man had been seriously ill, that there had been no hope of his living, but to everyone's surprise he had made a complete recovery and since then he had always been remarkably happy and cheerful.

So if for nothing else, let's "just be glad that we are alive" and be doubly thankful if like the Scotch poet, we have a good appetite and the means to gratify it.

Some hae meat that canna eat
And some want meat that lack it,
But I hae meat and I can eat,
And sae the Lord be thanket.

Sears and Roebuck Catalog, 1897

Sears, Roebuck and Company called itself the "Cheapest Supply House on Earth" and "The Most Progressive Concern of Its Kind in the World." By 1897 they claimed to have shipped to every town in the United States. The company was certainly very popular and made a permanent mark on American commerce and everyday life. Below is a selection of item descriptions from among the thousands of items that were available in their 786-page catalog from 1897.

FANCY MIXED CANDY

A pail of fancy mixed candy, 30 lbs., in good wooden pail, for $1.95. Buy a pail of fine candy and divide it among your neighbors. They will all want candy. Three or four order together and get a pail (30 lbs) of candy for $1.95, and you get the candy at 6 ½ cents per pound and the pail for free.

LADIES' BICYCLE BELT AND BUCKLE,

made of real seal. Belt 1¾ inches wide, full length, adjustable, with black buckle and solid silver ornaments. The purse is made of seal skin with solid silver name plate, embossed and engraved. A very useful article for a lady who rides a bicycle. Price complete $2.25

THE IMPERIAL HAIR REGENERATOR

No matter how gray your hair is, or how bleached or how spoiled by dyes, makes it beautiful, natural, healthy. Restores gray hair to color of youth. Gives the hair new life. Price per bottle $1.25

LEARNER'S OUTFIT,

complete, for telegraphy, consisting of full size sounder and key, mounted on polished cherry base; has full sized battery, with wire, chemicals and complete book of instructions, with everything necessary for operating for private practice, complete weight about 10½ lbs. Price $3.00

A Graphophone Exhibition

You can hear in your own home all of the latest songs, instrumental music, speeches, etc., from the best artists in the metropolitan cities. The Graphophone or Talking Machine is a most wonderful invention, but until recently the prices were so high that their use has not become very general. All this is now changed and they are becoming so popular that thousands of private families are purchasing them for home entertainment. They also afford a most excellent means for money making by traveling from place to place and giving public exhibitions. By using the horn they can be distinctly heard in every part of a large hall. An outfit with records complete for an evening's entertainment can be purchased for a small amount of money. $35.00

Fat Folks, Take Dr. Rose's Obesity Powders

.. and watch the result. Too much fat is a disease and a source of great annoyance to those afflicted. . . . Send at once for a box of Dr. Rose's Obesity Cure. It will reduce corpulency in a safe and agreeable manner, perfectly harmless. No bad results follow its use, as is the case with many of the much advertised cures. Explicit directions and valuable information for fat folks enclosed in each box. Per box, 88 cents; per dozen, $8

Base Balls

The Genuine Spalding League Ball. . . . Warranted to last a full game without ripping or losing its elasticity or shape. Positively the finest Base Ball made. Each ball in a separate box. Our special price $1.25

Indian Cough Syrup

An old Indian remedy for coughs, colds, sore throat, bronchitis, croup, and all diseases of the throat and lungs, prepared by White Cloud of the Indian Medicine Company. Each bottle usually sold for 50 cents. Price, per bottle, 20 cents. Per dozen, $2.25

Wedding in the White House
June 3, 1886

When President Grover Cleveland married Frances Folsom during his first term in office, the event naturally attracted national attention. Across the country in Sacramento, California, the local newspaper, the Sacramento Daily Record-Union, *reported the wedding in exhausting detail for eager readers. Note the mention of John Philip Sousa as leader of the Marine Band that provided the wedding music in the article excerpts below.*

SACRAMENTO DAILY RECORD-UNION   JUNE 3, 1886

WEDDING IN THE WHITE HOUSE

Orange Blossoms.
President Cleveland Is No Longer A Bachelor.
Married to Miss Folsom—Details of the Affair— Scenes at the White House
[Special By Telegraph to the Record-Union]

OUTSIDE THE WHITE HOUSE. Washington, June 2nd—Other weddings there have been at the White House—eight in all—but never before today has the highest dignity in the land bowed his head within its historic walls to receive the blessing of the church on his union in the holy bonds of matrimony. From the very dawn of the wedding day the city seemed alive to the approaching event. . . . The successive arrivals of the guests were watched with interest. . . . Suddenly the strains of the wedding march floated through the open

windows, and there was a general exclamation from the outside crowd, "The service has begun!" Then there came a tantalizing hush within the walls, which was soon ended by the strains of the bridal chorus from "Lohengrin" and it was thereby known that the ceremony was over. One by one the lights sprung up at the windows . . . .

For a few minutes the guests chatted gaily, but conversaton was quickly suspended at 7:15, when a selected orchestra from the Marine Band, stationed in the corridor, struck up the familiar strains of the wedding march from Mendelssohn's "Midsummer Night's Dream," and all eyes were turned to the doorway to catch the first glimpse of the coming bride and groom . . . . A hush fell upon the assembly as Dr. Sunderland stepped forward to his position fronting the wedding couple, with Rev. William Cleveland (the President's brother) at his left hand. In a distinct voice, and with deliberate utterance, the Doctor began the simple and beautiful service. . . . At the conclusion of the ceremony, Mrs. Folsom, showing traces of deep emotion, was the first to tender her congratulations to the newly-married pair. She was followed by Miss Cleveland, Rev. Mr. Cleveland and other relatives and friends in turn. While the congratulations were in progress, the band, under the leadership of Professor Sousa, performed the bridal chorus and march from "Lohengrin," and to this music the President and his wife led the way into the stately East Room. . . . From the East Room the company proceeded, after a season of promenading and conversation, to the family dining-room of the mansion, where the wedding supper was served. There was no formal order observed in the supper-room, but the collation [light meal] was served, and the guests sat at small tables or slowly promenaded the room as they discussed the menu and chatted over the event of the evening. Elegantly-designed souvenirs of satin boxes, containing dainty pieces of bridal cake, and each one bearing a hand-painted monogram "C.F." were received with great admiration. . . . The wedding presents were many, but they were not exhibited, nor will any list be furnished. This is in deference to the

wishes of the President. The groom's gift to his bride was a handsome diamond necklace, composed of a single string of brilliants. The presents from the Cabinet officers and wives were mostly articles of jewelry, though there were several beautiful presents of silverware . .

THE QUEEN'S CONGRATULATIONS London, June 2—The Queen[1] has sent the following cable message to President Cleveland: Pray accept my sincere congratulations on your marriage, and my best wishes for your happiness.

[1] Queen Victoria of England

Galen Clark of Yosemite

John Muir, 1912

Conservationist John Muir published a book entitled The Yosemite *in 1912, in which he described the park's wonders and gave advice to visitors. Muir devoted one chapter to a description of his friend Galen Clark, who had died in 1910 at almost 96 years of age. Clark lived most of his life in Yosemite, exploring and showing hospitalty to visitors. He served as the park's official guardian for 24 years. Clark retired from this post in his 80s, but he continued to serve Yosemite's visitors in his retirement. John Muir and Galen Clark shared a commitment to preserving this American treasure. The photograph below shows Galen Clark at the base of a tree in a California mariposa grove.*

Galen Clark was the best mountaineer I ever met, and one of the kindest and most amiable of all my mountain friends. I first met him at his Wawona ranch forty-three years ago on my first visit to Yosemite. I had entered the Valley with one companion by way of Coulterville, and returned by what was then known as the Mariposa Trail. Both trails were buried in deep snow where the elevation was from 5,000 to 7,000 feet above sea level in the sugar pine and silver fir regions. We had no great difficulty, however, in finding our way by the trends of the main features of the topography. Botanizing [studying plants] by the way, we made slow, plodding progress, and were again about out of provisions when we reached Clark's hospitable cabin at Wawona. He kindly furnished us with flour and a little sugar and tea, and my companion, who complained of the benumbing poverty of a strictly vegetarian diet, gladly accepted Mr. Clark's offer of a piece of a bear that had just been killed. After a short talk about bears and the forests and the way to the Big Trees, we pushed on up through the Wawona firs and sugar pines, and camped in the now-famous Mariposa grove.

Later, after making my home in the Yosemite Valley, I became well acquainted with Mr. Clark, while he was guardian. He was elected again and again to this important office by different Boards of Commissioners on account of his efficiency and his real love of the Valley.

Although nearly all my mountaineering has been done without companions, I had the pleasure of having Galen Clark with me on three excursions. . . . It was on this first trip from Hetch Hetchy to the upper cataracts that I had convincing proofs of Mr. Clark's daring and skill as mountaineer, particularly in fording torrents, and in forcing his way through thick chaparral [thickets of shrubs]. I found it somewhat difficult to keep up with him in dense, tangled brush, though in jumping on boulder taluses and slippery cobble-beds I had no difficulty in leaving him behind.

After I had discovered the glaciers on Mount Lyell and Mount McClure, Mr. Clark kindly made a second excursion with me to assist in establishing a line of stakes across the McClure glacier to measure its rate of flow. On this trip we also climbed Mount Lyell together, when the snow which covered the glacier was melted into upleaning, icy blades which were extremely difficult to cross, not being strong enough to support our weight, nor wide enough apart to enable us to stride across each blade as it was met. Here again I, being lighter, had no difficulty in keeping ahead of him. While resting after wearisome staggering and falling he stared at the marvelous ranks of leaning blades, and said, "I think I have traveled all sorts of trails and canyons, through all kinds of brush and snow, but this gets me."

. . . In cooking his mess of oatmeal porridge and making tea, his pot was always the first to boil, and I used to wonder why, with all his skill in scrambling through brush in the easiest way, and preparing his meals, he was so utterly careless about his beds. He would lie down anywhere on any ground, rough or smooth, without taking pains even to remove cobbles or sharp-angled rocks protruding through the grass or gravel, saying that his own bones were as hard as any stones and could do him no harm.

His kindness to all Yosemite visitors and mountaineers was marvelously constant and uniform. He was not a good business man, and in building an extensive hotel and barns at Wawona, before the travel to Yosemite had been greatly developed, he borrowed money, mortgaged his property and lost it all.

Though not the first to see the Mariposa Big Tree grove, he was the first to explore it, after he had heard from a prospector, who had passed through the grove and who gave him the indefinite information, that there were some wonderful big trees up there on the top of the Wawona hill and that he believed they must be of the same kind that had become so famous and well-known in the Calaveras grove farther north. On this information, Galen Clark told me, he went up and thoroughly explored the grove, counting the trees and measuring the largest, and becoming familiar with it. He stated also that he had explored the forest to the southward and had discovered the much larger Fresno grove of about two square miles, six or seven miles distant from the Mariposa grove. Unfortunately most of the Fresno grove has been cut and flumed down to the railroad near Madera. . . .

He was very fond of scenery and once told me after I became acquainted with him that he liked "nothing in the world better than climbing to the top of a high ridge or mountain and looking off." He preferred the mountain ridges and domes in the Yosemite regions on account of the wealth and beauty of the forests. Often times he would take his rifle, a few pounds of bacon, a few pounds of flour, and a single blanket and go off hunting, for no other reason than to explore and get acquainted with the most beautiful points of view within a journey of a week or two from his Wawona home. On these trips he was always alone and could indulge in tranquil enjoyment of Nature to his heart's content. He said that on those trips, when he was a sufficient distance from home in a neighborhood where he wished to linger, he always shot a deer, sometimes a grouse, and occasionally a bear. After diminishing the weight of a deer or bear by eating part of it, he carried as much as possible of the best of the meat to Wawona, and from his hospitable well-supplied cabin no weary wanderer ever went away hungry or unrested. . . .

He was one of the most sincere tree-lovers I ever knew. About twenty years before his death he made choice of a plot in the Yosemite cemetery on the north side of the Valley, not far from the Yosemite Fall, and selecting a dozen or so of seedling sequoias in the Mariposa grove he brought them to the Valley and planted them around the spot he had chosen for his last rest. The ground there is gravelly and dry; by careful watering he finally nursed most of the seedlings into good, thrifty trees, and doubtless they will long shade the grave of their blessed lover and friend.

One of My Closest Friends

Henry Ford, 1922

In Henry Ford's autobiography, My Life and Work, *published in 1922, he described how he first met Thomas Edison. He wrote about their friendship and told why he believed Edison was a successful inventor.*

No man exceeds Thomas A. Edison in broad vision and understanding. I met him first many years ago when I was with the Detroit Edison Company—probably about 1887 or thereabouts. The electrical men held a convention at Atlantic City, and Edison, as the leader in electrical science, made an address. I was then working on my gasoline engine, and most people, including all of my associates in the electrical company, had taken pains to tell me that time spent on a gasoline engine was time wasted—that the power of the future was to be electricity. These criticisms had not made any impression on me. I was working ahead with all my might. But being in the same room with Edison suggested to me that it would be a good idea to find out if the master of electricity thought it was going to be the only power in the future. So, after Mr. Edison had finished his address, I managed to catch him alone for a moment. I told him what I was working on.

At once he was interested. He is interested in every search for new knowledge. And then I asked him if he thought that there was a future for the internal combustion engine. He answered something in this fashion:

"Yes, there is a big future for any light-weight engine that can develop a high horsepower and be self-contained. No one kind of motive power is ever going to do all the work of the country. We do not know what electricity can do, but I take for granted that it cannot do everything. Keep on with your engine. If you can get what you are after, I can see a great future."

That is characteristic of Edison. He was the central figure in the electrical industry, which was then young and enthusiastic. The rank and file of the electrical men could see nothing ahead but

electricity, but their leader could see with crystal clearness that no one power could do all the work of the country. I suppose that is why he was the leader.

Such was my first meeting with Edison. I did not see him again until many years after—until our motor had been developed and was in production. He remembered perfectly our first meeting. Since then we have seen each other often. He is one of my closest friends, and we together have swapped many an idea.

His knowledge is almost universal. He is interested in every conceivable subject and he recognizes no limitations. He believes that all things are possible. At the same time he keeps his feet on the ground. He goes forward step by step. He regards "impossible" as a description for that which we have not at the moment the knowledge to achieve. He knows that as we amass knowledge we build the power to overcome the impossible. That is the rational way of doing the "impossible." The irrational way is to make the attempt without the toil of accumulating knowledge. Edison is really the world's greatest scientist. In addition, he has the constructive and managerial sense. He has not only had visions, but he has made them realities. He has had management of men and affairs to a degree unusual in an inventor, who is almost always considered visionary. Although not primarily a business man, he has made himself one by sheer necessity. Edison could have done anything to which he had turned his mind. He sees through things—and there is a great lack of *seeing through*, today.

Burned Out of House and Home

Justin, 1871

Justin, a young survivor of the Great Chicago Fire, wrote this letter to his friend Philip Prescott on October 19, 1871. Justin wrote from Lake Forest, Illinois, a small town north of Chicago. On the back of his letter, Justin drew a picture of his family escaping the fire. The drawing below is an artist's rendition of a bird's-eye view of Chicago in the midst of the fire.

Dear Chum,

    We are burnt out of house and home and so we had to come up here. I suppose you would like to hear about the fire and how we escaped from it. Half past one Monday morning we were awakened by a loud knocking at the front door. We were awake in an instant and dressing ourselves. We looked about and saw a perfect shower of sparks flying over our house. I got some water and went out in the yard while my brother went up on the roof. We worked for one or two hours. At the end of that time we had to give up. We tried to get a wagon but could not so we put two trunks on a wheelbarrow and each of us shouldered a bundle and we marched for the old skating park, I leading my goat. We got along very well until the Peshtigo Lumber yard caught on fire. Then it was all we could do to breathe. Mother caught on fire once but we put it out. At last we heard that there was a little shanty that hadn't burnt down so we marched there, but had to leave our trunks and everything else, but Charlie and father went back and got one but could not get the other as the sand was blowing in their faces and cut like glass. At last a wagon drove up and we all piled in and escaped so good-bye.

Yours, Justin

The Glories of the Fair

James A. Miller, 1893

James A. Miller of Athens, Ohio, wrote the following two-part letter to the editor of his local newspaper, the Athens Messenger, *about his visit to the World's Columbian Exposition in Chicago in September 1893.*

ATHENS MESSENGER   SEPTEMBER 1893

JAMES A. MILLER WRITES FROM THE WORLD COLUMBIAN EXPOSITION!

Part 1, September 17, 1893

Editor, *Athens Messenger*: According to promise I drop you a few lines. So many Athenians have seen the Fair, each looking through his own eyes, that I approach the task of writing out an impression with a sense of hesitation, realizing that I am inviting criticism from those who looked at things through spectacles different from mine. However, I shall give you a few notes taken from a list of wonderful things I saw at the Fair.

The Electricity Building was intensely interesting. We noticed a large crowd in the upper gallery and made our way around to find the center of attention, which was an electric oven, where they were roasting meat and baking biscuits. There was not the least sign of a stove or a spark of fire, and yet the cooking was going on all the same. A little wire that leads into the oven does the whole business. Another feature in this entertaining building was the sweet strains of music coming by telephone seven miles away in the heart of the city. It was amusing to see people trying to locate the source.

The Children's Building is a beautiful structure, decorated in blue and gold. Here we met crowds of people. It was only after patient waiting that I succeeded in wedging my way up to the big windows where men and women of all sizes and complexions stood peering

through the glass. What did I see? Only a row of dainty white cribs and swinging cradles and babies that were being cared for by trained nurses in white caps. The little children seemed to be behaving very well indeed.

We took a leisurely walk through the Transportation building and saw the family carriages of President Polk and Daniel Webster, together with the little boat in which Grace Darling made her marvelous rescues.

We spent a delightful hour in Horticulture Hall amidst the lovely flowers and products of every clime. The palms and ferns are simply immense, attracting crowds of visitors interested in plant culture.

Passing down the middle aisle of the Liberal Arts Building we saw the glittering obelisk composed of Columbian half-dollars.

At the German exhibit we saw more rare jewels, the personal property of Emperor William and the Empress. I noticed a beautiful fan of German point lace, with shell sticks set with diamonds.

The most wonderful dress, perhaps, is the one made of spun glass, expressly for Eulalia. The fine work on this dress is simply beyond my description.

We took a walk through the streets of Cairo and witnessed an Egyptian wedding, which began with a wild dance and ended with a sword fight. We also saw a woman take a comfortable ride on a camel, and I have no doubt she saw more of Cairo than she could have seen afoot.

The remainder of the day was spent in the Art Gallery, and after a good look at the "discovery of America," we joined the thousands of people who had formed along the lake front to enjoy the refreshing breeze and listen to the strains of sweet music.

Our view of the White City from the lake by night was the most magnificent spectacle of all and can never be forgotten.

I came to see and not to write, and it would be as uninteresting to your readers, as I am finding myself in this vast conglomeration of nations and things. Having lost myself no less than five times in that many hours.

James A. Miller

Part 2, September 18, 1893

Taking up where I left off in my last, I found the French exhibit most interesting. The display of silks was considered handsome. And the French dresses! Was there ever such a sight for the ladies to gaze upon. The one that took the cake, and bakery thrown in, was an ivory toned satin, embroidered all over with pearls. They were not for Athens country ladies. Some of these elegant affairs were valued at seventy-five thousand dollars. The laces were not so much in my sight. But you may imagine there was a good deal of staring at one piece, marked ten thousand dollars a yard.

At the Tiffany exhibit we saw large diamonds and also saw them cut and polish these precious stones.

On my way, I passed the King of Denmark's room. The furniture is solid gold, and the draperies brocade velvet, flounced with gold and silver. I was much pleased with some of the foreign exhibits. It is probably a lack of taste on my part, but I do not take much stock in gorgeous and fierce looking colors.

I enjoyed glimpses of foreign life very well, except the Exquimaux village, which I considered more filthy than the alleys of Athens. They have their villages surrounded with fences and are living just as they live in their own country.

Watching the Venetian workmen molding beautiful forms in glass was a novel sight. They do not seem to have any patterns but work entirely by eye.

I had time for no more than a leisurely walk amid the clattering machines of Machinery Hall; but I did not forget the immense boilers and engines that set all the machines in motion.

Perhaps it will be interesting for you to know that the most beautiful state building on the exposition grounds is that of Ohio, in my opinion. True, it is not so large as some others, nor so brilliant as California's; but to one who tires of the flashy and is fond of the tranquil, is to step into Ohio and rest the eyes.

I have only given a few dashes of the glories you may experience by going to the Fair.

J. A. M.

Old Glory

David Fletcher Hunton, 1898

David Fletcher Hunton (c. 1829-1915) was a lawyer from Grand Haven, Michigan, who wrote hundreds of poems during his lifetime, some of which were published in the Grand Haven Daily Tribune *and other newspapers. He wrote several poems about the Spanish-American War. "Old Glory" was published on May 24, 1898. It is based on the song "America."*

"Old Glory," 'tis of thee,
   Emblem of Liberty,
Of thee we sing;
   Flag of our fathers brave,
Flag which they died to save,
   Long may your colors wave,
A sacred thing.

Our country's flag to thee,
   We pledge our loyalty,
Our life, our home;
   We love thy crimson hue,
Thy stars and field of blue,
   To thee we will be true,
'Till death shall come.

Oh, may our arms be found,
   With wreathes of victory crowned,
In every place;
   May haughty Spaniards feel,
The might of fire and steel,
   'Till from their pride they reel,
Into disgrace.

May Jack Tars sing this song,
   'Till right subdues the Wrong,
And Cuba's free;
   Lads, keep your Flag unfurled.
'Till you have shown the world,
   The Dons have all been hurled,
Across the sea.

May our brave soldiers make,
   For Liberty's sweet sake,
Grand history;
   Our father's God, we pray,
Be with the Blue and Gray,
   Until the world shall say,
"CUBA IS FREE."

Gains at Ellis Island

August 28, 1904

This article appeared in New York City's New York Tribune *newspaper.*

NEW YORK TRIBUNE   **AUGUST 28, 1904**

GAINS AT ELLIS ISLAND

Place for Immigrant Children to Play to Their Hearts' Content

There is, perhaps, no branch of the government service where greater improvements have been effected in the administration of President Roosevelt than in the immigration service, although so quiet have been the methods pursued and so unostentatious the direction of the service that comparatively few persons are aware of the improvements accomplished.

To speak of Ellis Island is almost to include the whole immigration service, so far as the landing of immigrants is concerned, for at that point close to 75 percent of the newcomers to the United States are inspected and pass muster. Last year, out of a total of 875,046 immigrants admitted to this country, 631,885 landed at Ellis Island. Without going into tiresome details regarding the improvements in the administration of this important function of the government, it may be said that never before were the laws so conscientiously and thoroughly enforced and yet never before was the comfort of the immigrants so carefully considered or their welfare so effectively provided for. . . .

To Commissioner General Sargent belongs the credit of one of the latest and most attractive features introduced on the island—the children's playground. Thousands of children are domiciled [housed] at Ellis Island for weeks, sometimes for months at a time. Arriving after a week or more of confinement in the fetid [bad-smelling] atmosphere of the steerage [low-cost ship accommodations], they are usually pale and listless, and when, as often occurs, their parents are necessarily detained for some time in the station hospital, their lot is not a happy one, or, rather, it formerly was not. Moved by pity for these little ones, Commissioner Sargent sought a remedy for their condition. The grounds did not furnish an appropriate place for a playground, but diligent examination revealed an ideal place on the large, flat roof of the main building. There, by the erection of awnings and the raising of the parapet [wall around the edge of the roof], the children could play to their hearts' content. There they could enjoy the sea breezes of the New York harbor, precisely the sort of tonic needed after their passage. There they could run and romp and laugh and shout without disturbing anyone or doing injury to themselves or their surroundings. Commissioner Sargent's suggestion was joyfully received by Commissioner Williams, and the result is an amply equipped play place, where the future young Americans recover from the effects of their voyage and learn their first lessons in liberty.

Experiences of a Bandmaster

John Philip Sousa, 1900

"The March King," John Philip Sousa (1854-1932), had a long and fascinating musical career that led him into acquaintance with many famous Americans and gave him opportunities to lead music at historic moments and places in American history. Sousa shared some of his favorite musical memories in an article in Youth's Companion *magazine. Selections from this article are below.*

I think I may say that more than one President, relieved from the onerous duties of a great reception, has found rest by sitting quietly in the corner of a convenient room and listening to the music.

Once, on the occasion of a state dinner, President Arthur came to the door of the main lobby of the White House, where the Marine Band was always stationed, and beckoning me to his side asked me to play the "Cachuca." When I explained that we did not have the music with us but would be glad to include it in the next programme, the President looked surprised and remarked:

"Why, Sousa, I thought you could play anything. I'm sure you can; now give us the 'Cachuca.'"

This placed me in a predicament, as I did not wish the President to believe that the band was not at all times able to respond to his wishes. Fortunately, one of the bandmen remembered the melody and played it over softly to me on his cornet in a corner. I hastily wrote out several parts for the leading instruments, and told the rest of the band to vamp in the key of E flat. Then we played the "Cachuca" to the entire satisfaction of Mr. Arthur, who came again to the door and said: "There, I knew you could play it."

During the World's Fair at Chicago my present band was giving nightly concerts in the Court of Honor surrounding the lagoon. On one beautiful night in June fully ten thousand people were gathered round the bandstand while we were playing a medley of popular songs.

Director Tomlins, of the World's Fair Choral Associations, was on the stand, and exclaiming, "Keep that up, Sousa!" he turned to the crowd and motioned the people to join him in singing. With the background of the stately buildings of the White City, this mighty chorus, led by the band, sang the songs of the people: "Home, Sweet Home," "Swanee River," "Annie Laurie," "My Old Kentucky Home," etc., and never did the familiar melodies sound so grandly beautiful.

The influence of music to quiet disorder and to allay fear is quite as potent as its power to excite and to stir enthusiasm. A case in point happened at the St. Louis Exposition, where my band was giving a series of concerts. There was an enormous audience in the music hall when, in the middle of the programme, every electric light suddenly went out, leaving the house in complete darkness.

A succession of sharp cries from women, the hasty shuffling of feet, and the nervous tension manifest in every one, gave proof that a panic was probably imminent. I called softly to the band,

"Yankee Doodle!" and the men quickly responded by playing the good old tune from memory in the darkness, quickly following it with "Dixie" on my orders. The audience began to quiet down, and some scattering applause gave assurance that the excitement was abating.

"The Star-Spangled Banner" still further restored confidence, and when we played "Oh Dear, What Can the Matter Be?" and "Wait Till The Clouds Roll By," every one was laughing and making the best of the gloom. In a short time the gas was turned on, and the concert proceeded with adequate lighting.

In the desire to do especial honor to a certain foreign representative during the World's Fair, I had a particular piece of music in which he was interested arranged for my band, and agreed to play it at a specified concert. The music was given to a member of the band with instructions to copy the parts and deliver them at the band-stand.

The foreign gentleman was present at the concert with a large party of friends, whom he had invited to hear this particular piece of music. When the librarian asked the musician for the parts, he could not find them, and a search high and low for the missing music was without avail. Much to my chagrin, it was necessary to omit the number and send explanations and regrets to the dignitary whom it was designed to honor.

At the end of the concert, when the men were packing to go home, the player found the missing band parts stuck in the bell of his instrument, where he had placed them for safe-keeping.

Once when we were playing during warm weather in a theatre situated near a railroad, the windows were left open for ventilation. The band was rendering a Wagner selection, and at the climax was playing with increasing force. The last note to be played was a unison B flat, and as I gave the sign to the musicians to play as strong as possible the volume of sound that followed fairly astonished me. I had never heard fifty men play with such force before and could not account for it, but the explanation soon became manifest. As the band ceased playing, the same note continued in the blast of a passing locomotive that had opportunely chimed in with us in unison.

One more story of the White House. At the time of the unveiling of the statue of Admiral Farragut in Washington, it was suddenly proposed to have a reception at the Executive Mansion in honor of the many distinguished visitors. The informal invitations were issued while I was participating in the parade that was part of the ceremonies.

At seven o'clock in the evening, when I was at home, tired out after the long march, word came to me to report at the Marine Barracks. I went there and was ordered to take the band to the White House at eight o'clock p.m.

The bandmen did not live in barracks, and it was practically impossible to get them together at that time of night, as they were scattered all over the city.

"Well, those are my instructions and those are your orders," said the commanding officer.

So we sent the band-messengers out to the men's lodgings, and they found just one musician at home, and he was the bass-drummer.

At eight o'clock, arrayed in all the gorgeousness of my scarlet and gold uniform, I sat in front of the band platform in the White House lobby, and the bass-drummer stationed himself back in the semi-obscurity of his corner. There was a dazzling array of music-stands and empty chairs, but no musicians! The President evidently saw the humorous side of it, and when I explained the situation he said it could not be helped. All the evening we sat there and listened to humorous remarks from the guests. We had "reported for duty," though, and the drummer and I stayed till the reception was over.

In a little Michigan town my band was booked for an afternoon concert, and on our arrival the local manager assured us that we should have a good house, although there was no advance sale. He explained this by saying that the townspeople did not like to buy their tickets until the last minute.

The theatre was on the second floor of the town hall, the ground floor being given over to the fire department, the especial pride of the community. Twenty minutes before the concert a large crowd had gathered round the box-office to buy tickets when the fire-alarm sounded, and the entire population promptly deserted the muse of music and escorted the engine and hose-cart to the scene of action, leaving the band absolutely without an audience.

When North Carolina celebrated its centenary, the Marine Band was ordered to Fayetteville to participate in the ceremonies. The little Southern town was much interested in the advent of the "President's Band," and the prevailing opinion was that "Dixie" would be tabooed music with us. Before the exercises a local committee waited upon me and intimated that "Dixie" was a popular melody in that vicinity.

"Of course," said the spokesman, "we don't want you to play anything you don't want to, but please remember, sir, that we are very fond of 'Dixie' here."

Bowing gravely, I thanked the committee for their interest in my programme, but left them completely in the dark as to whether I intended to play the loved song of the South or not. "Dixie," by the President's Band.

The ceremonies opened with a patriotic address by Governor Fowle, lauding the glories of the American flag and naturally the only appropriate music to such a sentiment was "The Star-Spangled Banner," which the crowd patriotically cheered.

The tone of the succeeding oration was equally fervid, but the speaker enlarged upon the glories of the Commonwealth whose one hundredth anniversary was being celebrated. The orator sat down, there was a momentary pause, and then as I raised my baton the strains of "Dixie" fell upon the delighted ears of the thousands round the platform.

The unexpected had happened, and such a shout as went up from that throng I have never heard equaled. Hats were tossed in the air, gray-bearded men embraced, and for a few minutes a jubilant pandemonium reigned supreme. During the rest of our stay in Fayetteville the repertoire of the Marine Band was on this order: "Yankee Doodle," —"Dixie;" "Star-Spangled Banner," —"Dixie;" "Red, White and Blue," —"Dixie."

Letters to His Children

Theodore Roosevelt

Theodore Roosevelt was a devoted father to his six children. He read to them, played with them, and when he or they were away from home, he wrote letters to them. Shortly before his death, Roosevelt helped prepare for publication a volume of these letters which had been carefully preserved by his children. Letters to His Children *was published in 1919.*

This letter was written while Roosevelt was in camp with his regiment of Rough Riders in Tampa, Florida, before they left for Cuba to fight in the Spanish-American War. He had received a visit from his wife, Edith.

Camp at Tampa, May 6th, 1898

Blessed Bunnies,

It has been a real holiday to have darling mother here. Yesterday I brought her out to the camp, and she saw it all—the men drilling, the tents in long company streets, the horses being taken to water, my little horse Texas, the colonel and the majors, and finally the mountain lion and the jolly little dog Cuba, who had several fights while she looked on. The mountain lion is not much more than a kitten as yet, but it is very cross and treacherous.

I was very much interested in Kermit's and Ethel's letters today.

We were all, horses and men, four days and four nights on the cars coming here from San Antonio, and were very tired and very dirty when we arrived. I was up almost all of each night, for it happened always to be at night when we took the horses out of the cars to feed and water them.

Mother stays at a big hotel about a mile from camp. There are nearly thirty thousand troops here now, besides the sailors from the war-ships in the bay. At night the corridors and piazzas are thronged with officers of the army and navy; the older ones fought in the great Civil War, a third of a century ago, and now they are all going to Cuba to war against the Spaniards. Most of them are in blue, but our rough-riders are in brown. Our camp is on a great flat, on sandy soil without a tree, though round about are pines and palmettos. It is very hot, indeed, but there are no mosquitoes. Marshall is very well, and he takes care of my things and of the two horses. A general was out to inspect us when we were drilling to-day.

This letter was written in the midst of the Spanish-American War near Santiago, Cuba.

Off Santiago, 1898

Darling Ethel,

We are near shore now and everything is in a bustle, for we may have to disembark to-night, and I do not know when I shall have another chance to write to my three blessed children, whose little notes please me so. This is only a line to tell you all how much father loves you. The Pawnee Indian drew you the picture of the little dog, which runs everywhere round the ship, and now and then howls a little when the band plays.

Roosevelt wrote this letter to his son, who was at a boarding school, from Sagamore Hill, the Roosevelt family home in Oyster Bay on Long Island, New York.

Oyster Bay, May 7th, 1901

Blessed Ted,

It was the greatest fun seeing you, and I really had a satisfactory time with you, and came away feeling that you were doing well. I am entirely satisfied with your standing, both in your studies and in athletics. I want you to do well in your sports, and I want even more to have you do well with your books; but I do not expect you to stand first in either, if so to stand could cause you overwork and hurt your health. I always believe in going hard at everything, whether it is Latin or mathematics, boxing or football, but at the same time I want to keep the sense of proportion. It is never worth while to absolutely exhaust one's self or to take big chances unless for an adequate object. I want you to keep in training the faculties which would make you, if the need arose, able to put your last ounce of pluck and strength into a contest. But I do not want you to squander these qualities. To have you play football as well as you do, and make a good name in boxing and wrestling, and be cox of your second crew, and stand second or third in your class in the studies, is all right. I should be rather sorry to see you drop too near the middle of your class, because, as you  cannot enter college until you are nineteen, and will therefore be a year later in entering life, I want you to be prepared in the best possible way, so as to make up for the delay. But I know that all you can do you will do to keep substantially the position in the class that you have so far kept, and I have entire trust in you, for you have always deserved it.

The weather has been lovely here. The cherry trees are in full bloom, the peach trees just opening, while the apples will not be out for ten days. The May flowers and bloodroot have gone, the anemonies and bellwort have come and the violets are coming. All the birds are here, pretty much, and the warblers troop through the woods.

To my delight, yesterday Kermit, when I tried him on Diamond, did excellently. He has evidently turned the corner in his riding, and was just as much at home as possible, although he was on my saddle with his feet thrust in the leathers above the stirrup. Poor mother has had a hard time with Yagenka, for she rubbed her back, and as she sadly needs exercise and I could not have  a saddle put upon her, I took her out bareback yesterday. Her gaits are so easy that it is really more comfortable to ride her without a saddle than to ride Texas with one, and I gave her three miles sharp cantering and trotting.

Dewey Jr. is a very cunning white guinea pig. I wish you could see Kermit taking out Dewey Sr. and Bob Evans to spend the day on the grass. Archie is the sweetest little fellow imaginable. He is always thinking of you. He has now struck up a great friendship with Nicholas, rather to Mame's [the nurse's] regret, as Mame would like to keep him purely for Quentin. The last-named small boisterous person was in fearful disgrace this morning, having flung a block at his mother's head. It was done in sheer playfulness, but of course could not be passed over lightly, and after the enormity of the crime had been brought fully home to him, he fled with howls of anguish to me and lay in an abandon of yellow-headed grief in my arms. Ethel is earning money for the purchase of the Art Magazine by industriously hoeing up the weeds in the walk. Alice is going to ride Yagenka bareback this afternoon, while I try to teach Ethel on Diamond, after Kermit has had his ride.

Yesterday at dinner we were talking of how badly poor Mrs. Blank looked, and Kermit suddenly observed in an aside to Ethel, entirely unconscious that we were listening: "Oh, Effel, I'll tell you what Mrs. Blank looks like: Like Davis' hen dat died—you know, de one dat couldn't hop up on de perch." Naturally, this is purely a private anecdote.

Roosevelt wrote this letter to his son Kermit from the White House while he was President.

White House, Jan. 6, 1903

Dear Kermit,

We felt very melancholy after you and Ted left and the house seemed empty and lonely. But it was the greatest possible comfort to feel that you both really have enjoyed school and are both doing well there.

Tom Quartz is certainly the cunningest kitten I have ever seen. He is always playing pranks on Jack and I get very nervous lest Jack should grow too irritated. The other evening they were both in the library—Jack sleeping before the fire—Tom Quartz scampering about, an exceedingly playful little wild creature—which is about what he is. He would race across the floor, then jump upon the curtain or play with the tassel. Suddenly he spied Jack and galloped up to him. Jack, looking exceedingly sullen and shame-faced, jumped out of the way and got upon the sofa, where Tom Quartz instantly jumped upon him again. Jack suddenly shifted to the other sofa, where Tom Quartz again went after him. Then Jack started for the door, while Tom made a rapid turn under the sofa and around the table, and just as Jack reached the door leaped on his hind-quarters. Jack bounded forward and away and the two went tandem out of the room—Jack not reappearing at all; and after about five minutes Tom Quartz stalked solemnly back.

Another evening the next Speaker of the House, Mr. Cannon, an exceedingly solemn, elderly gentleman with chin whiskers, who certainly does not look to be of playful nature, came to call upon me. He is a great friend of mine, and we sat talking over what our policies for the session should be until about eleven o'clock; and when he went away I accompanied him to the head of the stairs. He had gone about half-way down when Tom Quartz strolled by, his tail erect and very fluffy. He spied Mr. Cannon going down the stairs, jumped to the conclusion that he was a playmate escaping, and raced after him, suddenly grasping him by the leg the way he does Archie and Quentin when they play hide and seek with him; then loosening his hold he tore down-stairs ahead of Mr. Cannon, who eyed him with iron calm and not one particle of surprise.

Ethel has reluctantly gone back to boarding-school. It is just after lunch and Dulany is cutting my hair while I dictate this to Mr. Loeb. I left Mother lying on the sofa and reading aloud to Quentin, who as usual has hung himself over the back of the sofa in what I should personally regard as an exceedingly uncomfortable attitude to listen to literature. Archie we shall not see until this evening, when he will suddenly challenge me either to a race or a bear play, and if neither invitation is accepted will then propose that I tell a pig story or else read aloud from the Norse folk tales.

Miss Delia Torrey
Consents to Come

June 16, 1911

William Howard Taft and his wife had their twenty-fifth wedding anniversary during his term as President. They celebrated in grand style at the White House with thousands of guests. This article appeared in The Washington Times *newspaper of Washington, D.C. The big news was that Taft's elderly aunt had just decided to come to Washington for the celebration. The original article included a photograph of her in a long black dress, white hair tightly pinned up, frowning over her spectacles, sitting in a chair reading a Bible. The photograph below shows William Howard Taft in the center with his Aunt Delia Torrey on the right.*

THE WASHINGTON TIMES   JUNE 16, 1911

MISS DELIA TORREY CONSENTS TO COME

TAFT'S AUNT TO BE HERE FOR HIS SILVER WEDDING
Miss Delia Torrey consents to Come for Anniversary Festival.
SHE THOUGHT TRIP WOULD TIRE HER OUT
But Robert Soon Talked Her Into Notion, and Will Arrive With Her.

Word was received at the White House today that "Aunt Delia" Torrey will leave her home in Millbury, Massachusetts, tonight for Washington to attend the silver wedding anniversary of her "Nephew Will" and Mrs. Taft at the White House on Monday night.

"Aunt Delia," who is Miss Delia C. Torrey, is the President's favorite aunt, and noted as the maker of apple pies which appeal particularly to the Presidential appetite. Miss Torrey, when first invited, and told her presence was necessary to make the family reunion complete, feared she would be unable to attend, declaring she would not travel all the way to Washington.

But she changed her mind and her grandnephew, Robert Taft, arrived in Millbury today to accompany her to Washington. She will leave her Massachusetts home at 6:35 tonight over the New Haven line to Providence, where she will change to the Federal Express for the Capital.

Mrs. Anderson, a sister, reached Washington yesterday. Horace Taft, the New England brother of the President, will arrive in Washington tomorrow, and Henry W. Taft is expected either tomorrow night or Sunday.

By Sunday night all of the children will have reached this city. Miss Helen is now visiting in Cincinnati, while Robert and Charlie are away at school.

The White House, the scene of many splended festivities and the center of the nation's social life for a century, has never looked so well as it will Monday night when the President and Mrs. Taft entertain nearly 5,000 of their friends at their silver wedding celebration.

It was announced at the White House today that President and Mrs. Taft have invited all the surviving members of the families of former presidents to the silver wedding celebration. . . .

Two score of electricians are now dressing the exterior and nearly as many gardeners and florists will begin work in the interior decorations Saturday. The White House garden will glow with light. The lawns have been cut, the trees trimmed, and the hedges leveled.

From one end to the other, the Mansion will be strung with streams of electric globes. Every angle, cornice and gable will be outlined in fire. Never before has the White House been so illuminated.

The electrical display will not stop there. Down on the west lawn an electric flag will wave. This will be a huge piece of work, and the red, white, and blue colors will flash out in the night as though in imitation of a flag unfurled to the breezes. . . .

The invitation list will include friends of the President, not only in Washington, but in every part of the country . . . . From Cincinnati, a special train will bring more than a hundred personal friends of the Tafts . . . .

If the weather is favorable, the party will overflow on the lawns. The mansion will not hold more than a small fraction of the people, and after they have paid their compliments to the President and Mrs. Taft, they will pass out into the garden, where many features of the fete [party] will take place. . . .

Monday's reception promises to be the most interesting social event the Capital has witnessed during the present Administration, if not for many administrations. Probably never before have so many people been asked to enjoy the hospitality of the Executive Mansion at one time. At the New Year receptions more people have passed through and greeted the President, but they did not linger. They simply passed along.

The Subject of Flying

Wilbur and Orville Wright, 1922

The Wright brothers, through their Dayton-Wright Airplane Company, published a booklet entitled The Early History of the Airplane. *The booklet begins with a description of how they became interested in flight when they were boys.*

Though the subject of aerial navigation is generally considered new, it has occupied the minds of men more or less from the earliest ages. Our personal interest in it dates from our childhood days. Late in the autumn of 1878 our father came into the house one evening with some object partly concealed in his hands, and before we could see what it was, he tossed it into the air. Instead of falling to the floor, as we expected, it flew across the room, till it struck the ceiling, where it fluttered awhile, and finally sank to the floor. It was a little toy, known to scientists as a "helicoptere," but which we, with sublime disregard for science, at once dubbed a "bat." It was a light frame of cork and bamboo, covered with paper, which formed two screws, driven in opposite directions by rubber bands under torsion. A toy so delicate lasted only a short time in the hands of small boys, but its memory was abiding.

Several years later we began building these helicopteres for ourselves, making each one larger than that preceding. But, to our astonishment, we found that the larger the "bat" the less it flew. We did not know that a machine having only twice the linear dimensions of another would require eight times the power. We finally became discouraged, and returned to kite-flying, a sport to which we had devoted so much attention that we were regarded as experts. But as we became older we had to give up this fascinating sport as unbecoming to boys of our ages.

It was not till the news of the sad death of Lilienthal[1] reached America in the summer of 1896 that we again gave more than passing attention to the subject of flying. We then studied with great interest Chanute's "Progress in Flying Machines," Langley's "Experiments in Aerodynamics," the "Aeronautical Annuals" of 1895, 1896, and 1897, and several pamphlets published by the Smithsonian Institution, especially articles by Lilienthal and extracts from Mouillard's "Empire of the Air." The larger works gave us a good understanding of the nature of the flying problem,

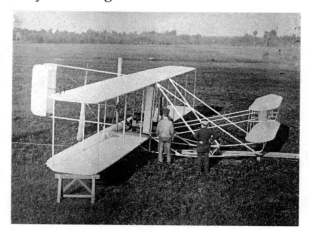

and the difficulties in past attempts to solve it, while Mouillard and Lilienthal, the great missionaries of the flying cause, infected us with their own unquenchable enthusiasm, and transformed idle curiosity into the active zeal of workers.

---

[1] Otto Lilienthal was a German aviation pioneer who died from injuries sustained in a gliding accident.

Alaska Days with John Muir

Samuel Hall Young, 1915

Samuel Hall Young arrived in Alaska in 1878 to work as a missionary to native people. Later, when a boat brought some short-term helpers for his mission work, Young met the workers' fellow-passenger, conservationist and botanist John Muir. Young and Muir became friends. They traveled in Alaska together, each pursuing his own projects and helping the other. Young published this account of his memories with Muir in 1915. The map below shows their journeys, and the photo on the next page shows Muir Glacier.

The first week in October saw the culmination of plans long and eagerly discussed . . . .

My mission in the proposed voyage of discovery was to locate and visit the tribes and villages of Thlingets to the north and west of Wrangell, to take their census, confer with their chiefs and report upon their condition, with a view to establishing schools and churches among them. The most of these tribes had never had a visit from a missionary, and I felt the eager zeal of an Eliot or a Martin at the prospect of telling them for the first time the Good News. Muir's mission was to find and study the forests, mountains and glaciers. I also was eager to see these and learn about them, and Muir was glad to study the natives with me—so our plans fitted into each other well.

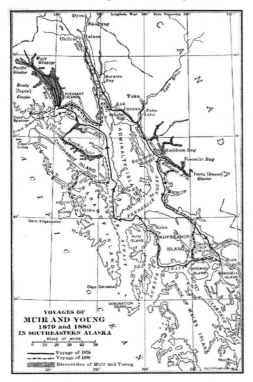

VOYAGES OF
MUIR AND YOUNG
1879 and 1880
IN SOUTHEASTERN ALASKA

"We are going to write some history, my boy," Muir would say to me. "Think of the honor! We have been chosen to put some interesting people and some of Nature's grandest scenes on the page of human record and on the map. Hurry! We are daily losing the most important news of all the world."

In many respects we were most congenial companions. We both loved the same poets and could repeat, verse about, many poems of Tennyson, Keats, Shelley and Burns. He took with him a volume of Thoreau, and I one of Emerson, and we enjoyed them together. I had my printed Bible with me, and he had his in his head—the result of a Scotch father's discipline. Our studies supplemented each other and our tastes were similar. We had both lived clean lives and our conversation together was sweet and high, while we both had a sense of humor and a large fund of stories.

Our ship for this voyage of discovery . . . was . . . a kladushu etlan (six fathom) red-cedar canoe. It belonged to our captain, old Chief Tow-a-att, a chief who had lately embraced Christianity with his whole heart—one of the simplest, most faithful, dignified and brave souls I ever knew. He fully expected to meet a martyr's death among his heathen enemies of the northern islands; yet he did not shrink from the voyage on that account. . . .

We stowed our baggage, which was not burdensome, in one end of the canoe, taking a simple store of provisions—flour, beans, bacon, sugar, salt and a little dried fruit. We were to depend upon our guns, fishhooks, spears and clamsticks for other diet. As a preliminary to our palaver with the natives we followed the old Hudson Bay custom, then firmly established in the North. We took materials for a potlatch,—leaf-tobacco, rice and sugar. Our Indian crew laid in their own stock of provisions, chiefly dried salmon and seal-grease, while our table was to be separate, set out with the white man's viands [foods]. . . .

One sunny October day we set our prow to the unknown northwest. Our hearts beat high with anticipation. Every passage between the islands was a corridor leading into a new and more enchanting room of Nature's great gallery. The lapping waves whispered enticing secrets, while the seabirds screaming overhead and the eagles shrilling from the sky promised wonderful adventures

. . . Our captain, taciturn and self-reliant, commanded Muir's admiration from the first. His paddle was sure in the stern, his knowledge of the wind and tide unfailing. Whenever we landed the crew would begin to dispute concerning the best place to make camp. But old Tow-a-att, with the mast in his hand, would march straight as an arrow to the likeliest spot of all, stick down his mast as a tent-pole and begin to set up the tent, the others invariably acquiescing in his decision as the best possible choice.

At our first meal Muir's sense of humor cost us one-third of a roll of butter. We invited our captain to take dinner with us. I got out the bread and other viands, and set the two-pound roll of butter beside the bread and placed both by Tow-a-att. He glanced at the roll of butter and at the three who were to eat, measured with his eye one-third of the roll, cut it off with his hunting knife and began to cut it into squares and eat it with great gusto. I was about to interfere and show him the use we made of butter, but Muir stopped me with a wink. The old chief calmly devoured his third of the roll, and rubbing his stomach with great satisfaction pronounced it "hyas klosh (very good) glease."

Of necessity we had chosen the rainiest season of the year in that dampest climate of North America, where there are two hundred and twenty-five rainy days out of the three hundred and sixty-five. During our voyage it did not rain every day, but the periods of sunshine were so rare as to make us hail them with joyous acclamation.

We steered our course due westward for forty miles, then through a sinuous, island-studded passage called Rocky Strait, stopping one day to lay in a supply of venison before sailing on to the village of the Kake Indians. My habit throughout the voyage, when coming to a native town, was to find where the head chief lived, feed him with rice and regale him with tobacco, and then induce him to call all his chiefs and head men together for a council. When they were all assembled I would give small presents of tobacco to each, and then open the floodgate of talk, proclaiming my mission and telling them in simplest terms the Great New Story. Muir would generally follow me, unfolding in turn some of the wonders of God's handiwork and the beauty of clean, pure living; and then in turn, beginning with the head chief, each Indian would make his speech. We were received with joy everywhere, and if there was suspicion at first old Tow-a-att's tearful pleadings and Kadishan's oratory speedily brought about peace and unity.

These palavers often lasted a whole day and far into the night, and usually ended with our being feasted in turn by the chief in whose house we had held the council. I took the census of each village, getting the heads of the families to count their relatives with the aid of beans,—the large brown beans representing men, the large white ones, women, and the small Boston beans, children. In this manner the first census of southeastern Alaska was taken.

Poetry of the Great War

Edgar A. Guest, 1918

Edgar A. Guest was born in Birmingham, England, in 1881. His family settled in Detroit, Michigan, in 1891. While still in his teens, Guest began his long career at the Detroit Free Press *newspaper. His poems first appeared in this newspaper, but they were soon read and loved throughout the United States. The following poems are from his volume titled* Over Here, *published in 1918, which Guest dedicated to "The Mothers Over Here."*

The Boy Enlists

His mother's eyes are saddened, and her cheeks are stained with tears,
    And I'm facing now the struggle that I've dreaded through the years;
For the boy that was our baby has been changed into a man.
    He's enlisted in the army as a true American.

He held her for a moment in his arms before he spoke,
    And I watched him as he kissed her, and it seemed to me I'd choke,
For I knew just what was coming, and I knew just what he'd done!
    Another little mother had a soldier for a son.

When we'd pulled ourselves together, and the first quick tears had dried,
    We could see his eyes were blazing with the fire of manly pride;
We could see his head was higher than it ever was before,
    For we had a man to cherish, and our baby was no more.

Oh, I don't know how to say it! With the sorrow comes the joy
    That there isn't any coward in the make-up of our boy.
And with pride our hearts are swelling, though with grief they're also hit,
    For the boy that was our baby has stepped forth to do his bit.

The Christmas Box

Oh, we have shipped his Christmas box with ribbons red 'tis tied,
    And he shall find the things he likes from them he loves inside,
But he must miss the kisses true and all the laughter gay
    And he must miss the smiles of home upon his Christmas Day.

He'll spend his Christmas 'neath the Flag; he'll miss each merry face,
    Old Glory smiling down on him must take his mother's place,
Yet in the Christmas box we've sent, in fancy he will find
    The laughter and the tears of joy that he has left behind.

These Boys Will Look Up To You
Tell Them What It Means To Be An American Soldier

His mother's tenderness is there, his father's kindly way,
    And all that went last year to make his merry Christmas Day;
He'll see once more his sister's smile, he'll hear the baby shout,
    And as he opens every gift we'll gather round about.

He cannot come to share with us the joys of Christmas Day;
    The Flag has called to him, and he is serving far away.
Undaunted, unafraid and fine he stands to duty grim,
    And so this Christmas we have tried to ship ourselves to him.

The Soldier on Crutches

He came down the stairs on the laughter-filled grill
    Where patriots were eating and drinking their fill,
The tap of his crutch on the marble of white
    Caught my ear as I sat all alone there that night.
I turned—and a soldier my eyes fell upon,
    He had fought for his country, and one leg was gone!

As he entered a silence fell over the place;
    Every eye in the room was turned up to his face.
His head was up high and his eyes seemed aflame
    With a wonderful light, and he laughed as he came.
He was young—not yet thirty—yet never he made
    One sign of regret for the price he had paid.

One moment before this young soldier came in
    I had caught bits of speech in the clatter and din
From the fine men about me in life's dress parade
    Who were boasting the cash sacrifices they'd made;
And I'd thought of my own paltry service with pride,
    When I turned and that hero of battle I spied.

I shall never forget the hot flushes of shame
    That rushed to my cheeks as that young fellow came.
He was cheerful and smiling and clear-eyed and fine
    And out of his face golden light seemed to shine.
And I thought as he passed me on crutches: "How small
    Are the gifts that I make if I don't give my all."

Some day in the future in many a place
    More soldiers just like him we'll all have to face.
We must sit with them, talk with them, laugh with them, too,
    With the signs of their service forever in view.
And this was my thought as I looked at him then
    —Oh, God! make me worthy to stand with such men.

Save and Serve

C. Houston and Alberta M. Goudiss, 1918

During World War I, millions of people looked to the bounty of America for food. Many of these people were the citizens of foreign countries that were America's military allies. Their homelands were devastated by the war. All Americans were called upon to help in this part of the war effort. Foods That Will Win The War and How to Cook Them *was a 1918 publication that gave dozens of recipes for dishes that saved on wheat, meat, fats, and sugar. Excerpts from this booklet are below.*

FOOD

1. Buy it with thought.
2. Cook it with care.
3. Serve just enough.
4. Save what will keep.
5. Eat what would spoil.
6. Home-grown is best.

Don't Waste It.

TO SAVE BREAD. Serve bread or rolls made from corn, rye or from coarse flours. Use breakfast foods and hot cakes composed of corn, oatmeal, buckwheat, rice or hominy. Serve no toast as garniture or under meat. Serve war breads. Use every part of the bread, either fresh or stale, for puddings and toast; or dried and sifted for baked croquettes; or use to extend flour in the making of muffins and drop cakes.

TO SAVE MEAT. Use more chicken, hare, rabbits, duck, goose, lobster, oysters, clams and egg and cheese dishes of all kinds. Use less beef, mutton, and pork and serve smaller portions at table of these meats. Have fewer of these items on the menu. Provide more entrees and made-over dishes in which a smaller quantity of meat is extended by the use of potatoes, rice, hominy, etc. Use beans, as they contain nearly the same nutritive value as meat. Serve bacon only as a dish and not as a garniture, and this way not more than once a week. Use cheese, dried vegetables and nuts. Use fish and meat chowders. Use meat extension dishes. Serve vegetable dinners.

TO SAVE SUGAR. Use less candy and sweet drinks. Use honey, maple sugar, corn syrup, molasses and dark syrups with hot cakes and waffles and in all cooking, in order to save butter and sugar. Use all classes of fruit preserves, jam, marmalades and jellies. Do not frost or ice cakes. Serve dried fruits with cereals, and no sugar is needed.

TO SAVE FATS. Serve as few fried dishes as possible, so as to save both butter and lard, and in any event use vegetable oils for frying—that is, olive oil, corn oil, cottonseed oil, vegetable oil compounds, etc. Trim all coarse fats from meats before cooking and use the waste fats for shortening and for soap. We are short of soap fats as our supplies of tropical oils used for soap-making are reduced. Do not waste soap. Save fat from soup stock and from boiled meats. Use butter substitutes where possible.

TO SAVE MILK. Use it all. Buy whole milk and let cream rise. Use this cream, and you secure your milk without cost. Economize on milk and cream except for children. Serve buttermilk. Serve cottage cheese regularly in varying forms. It is especially nutritious. Use skimmed milk in cooking. A great quantity of it goes to waste in this country. Use cheese generally. The children must have milk whole, therefore reduce the use of cream.

USE VEGETABLES. Use more vegetables and potatoes. Make fruits and vegetables into salads and attractive dishes. Feature vegetable dinners and salads of all kinds. Encourage the use of cheese with salads. Make all types of salads from vegetables. We have a great surplus of vegetables, and they can be used by substituting them for staples so that the staples most needed will be saved.

Make all kinds of vegetable soups, especially the cream soups, in which the waste from staple vegetables, such as outer leaves and wilted parts, can be utilized. These are wholesome and nutritious and save meat.

Sergeant York and His People

Sam K. Cowan, 1922

Soon after Alvin C. York returned from his heroic service in World War I, author Sam K. Cowan lived for a while among the members of York's community, developing a great respect for them. Following is an excerpt from Cowan's biography of York, published in 1922.

At his home in the "Valley of the Three Forks o' the Wolf," after the war was over, I asked Alvin York how he came to be "Sergeant York."

"Well," he said, as he looked earnestly at me, "you know we were in the Argonne Forest twenty-eight days, and had some mighty hard fighting in there. A lot of our boys were killed off. Every company has to have so many sergeants. They needed a sergeant; and they jes' took me."

In the summer of 1917 when Alvin York was called to war, he was working on the farm for $25 a month and his midday meal, walking to and from his work. He was helping to support his widowed mother with her family of eleven. When he returned to this country to be mustered out of service he had traveled among the soldiers of France [as] the guest of the American Expeditionary Force, so the men in the lines could see the man who single-handed had captured a battalion of machine guns, and he bore the emblems of the highest military honors conferred for valor by the governments composing the Allies.

At New York he was taken from the troop-ship when it reached harbor and the spontaneous welcome given him there and at Washington was not surpassed by the prearranged demonstrations for the Nation's distinguished foreign visitors.

The streets of those cities were lined with people to await his coming and police patrols made way for him. The flaming red of his hair, his young, sunburned, weather-ridged face with its smile and its strength, the worn service cap and uniform, all marked him to the crowds as the man they sought. . . .

Many business propositions were made to him. Some were substantial and others strange, the whimsical offerings of enthused admirers.

Among them were cool fortunes he could never earn at labor . . . .

He turned all down, and went back to the little worried mother who was waiting for him in a hut in the mountains, to the gazelle-like mountain girl whose blue eyes had haunted the shades of night and the shadows of trees, to the old seventy-five acre farm that clings to one of the sloping sides of a sun-kissed valley in Tennessee. He refused to capitalize his fame, his achievements that were crowded into a few months in the army of his country.

There was one influence that was ever guiding him. The future had to square to the principles of thought and action he had laid down for himself and that he had followed since he knelt, four years before, at a rough-boarded altar in a little church in the "Valley of the Three Forks o' the Wolf," whose belfry had been calling, appealing to him since childhood. . . .

The people of Tennessee filled depots, streets and tabernacles to welcome him. Gifts awaited him, which ranged from a four-hundred acre farm raised by public subscriptions by the Rotary Clubs and newspapers, to blooded stock for it, and almost every form of household furnishings that could add to man's comfort. It took a ware-room at Nashville and the courtesies of the barns of the State Fair Association to hold the gifts.

He was made a Colonel by the Governor of Tennessee, and appointed a member of his staff. He was elected to honorary membership in many organizations. As far away as Spokane the "Red Headed Club" thought him worthy of their membership "by virtue of the color of his hair and in recognition of his services to this, our glorious country. . . ."

The "Valley of the Three Forks o' the Wolf," where Alvin York was born and lives, which has been the home of his ancestors for more than a hundred years, is a level fertile valley that is almost a rectangle in form. Three mountains rising on the north and south and west enclose it, while to the east four mountains jumble together, forming the fourth side. It seems that each of these is striving for a place by the valley. . . .

One can be in the center of Pall Mall and not know it, for the residents live in farm houses that dot the valley and in cabins on the mountainsides. The little church, which sits by the road with no homes near it, is the geographical as well as the religious center of the community—it is the heart of Pall Mall. . . .

Across the spring branch, up the mountainside in a clump of honeysuckle and roses and apple trees is the home to which Sergeant York returned.

It is a two-room cabin. The boxing is of rough boards as are the unplaned narrow strips of batting covering the cracks. There is a chimney at one end and in one room is a fireplace. The kitchen is a "lean-to" and the only porch is on the rear, the width of the kitchen-dining room. The porch is for service and work, railed partly with a board for a shelf, which holds the water-bucket, the tin wash basin and burdens brought in from the farm.

Parts of the walls of the two rooms are papered with newspapers and catalog pages; the rough rafters run above. The uncovered floor is of wide boards, worn smooth in service, chinked to keep out the blasts of winter. . . .

The house has been painted by Poverty; but the home is warmed and lit by a mountain mother's love. The front stoop is a wooden ladder with flat steps but the entrance to the home is an arbor of honey suckle and roses.

On summer nights the York boys sat on that stoop and sang, and their voices floated on the moonbeams out over the valley. The little mother "pottered" about, with ever a smile on her face for her boys. They were happy.

It was from this home that Alvin went to war, and it was to it he returned. . . .

Alvin York came from a line of ancestors who were cane-cutters and Indian fighters. The earliest ancestor of whom he has knowledge was a "Long Hunter," who with a rifle upon his shoulder strode into the Valley of the Wolf and homesteaded the river bottom-lands. Here his people lived far from the traveled paths. Marooned in their mountain fastnesses, they clung to the customs and the traditions of the past. Their life was simple, and their sports quaint. They held shooting-matches on the mountainside, enjoyed "log-rollings" and "corn-huskings." Strong in their loves and in their hates, they feared God, but feared no man. The Civil War swept over the valley and left splotches of blood.

Friends of Sergeant York, knowing that the history of his people was rich in story, and that the public was waiting, wanting to know more of the man the German army could not run, nor make surrender—and instead had to come to him—urged that his story be told.

He had been mustered out of the army and come back to the valley wanting to pick up again the dropped thread of his former life. He was striving earnestly and prayerfully to blot from recurrent memory that October morning scene on "York's Hill" in France. . . .

When home again, Alvin wanted no especial deference shown him. He wished to be again just one of them, to swing himself upon the counter at the general store and talk with them as of old.

He had much to tell from his experience, but always it was of other incidents than the one that made him famous.

Months passed. He lived in that mountain cabin with his little mother, whose counsel has ever influenced him, and yet not once did he mention to her that he had a fight in the Forest of Argonne.

His consent was gained for the publication of the story of his people, but it was with the pronounced stipulation that "it be told right."

Weeks afterward—for I had gone to live awhile among his people—the two of us were sitting upon the rugged rock, facing to the cliff above the York spring, talking about the fight in France.

He told of it hesitatingly, modestly. Some of the parts was simply the confirmation of assembled data; much of it, denial of published rumor and conjecture—before the story came out as a whole.

I asked the meaning of his statement that he would not "mind the publication if the story were done right."

"Well," he said with his mountain drawl, "I don't want you bearing down too much on that killing part. Tell it without so much of that!"

A rock was picked up and hurled down the mountain.

I then understood why the little mother was "jes' a-waiting till Alvin gits ready to talk." I understood why the son did not wish to be the one to bring into his mother's mind the picture of that hour in France when men were falling before his gun. I saw the reason he had for always courteously avoiding talking of the scene with anyone.

"But," and he turned with that smile that wins him friends, "I just can't help chuckling at that German major. I sure had him bluffed."

According to the code of mountain conversation there followed a silence. Another rock bounded off the sapling down the cliff.

"You should have seen the major," he resumed, "move on down that hill whenever I pulled down on him with that old Colt. 'Goose-step it', I think they call it. He was so little! His back so straight! And all huffed up over the way he had to mind me."

I had watched the rocks as they went down the cliff and it seemed nearly every one of them bounced off the same limb. I commented on the accuracy of his eye.

"Aw! I wasn't throwing at that sapling, but at—that—leaf."

He straightened up and threw more carefully; and the leaf floated down to the waters of the York spring.

Down by the spring I met the little mother bringing a tin bucket to the stone milk-house which nature had built. Her slender, drooping figure, capped by the sunbonnet she always wore, reached

just to the shoulder of her son, as he placed his arm protectingly about her.

I asked if she were not proud of that boy of hers.

"Yes," she answered, with pride in every line of her sweet though wrinkled face, "I am proud of all of them—all of my eight boys!"

The Cat Took the Kosher Meat

Jacob A. Riis, 1903

Jacob A. Riis came to the United States from Denmark as a young man in 1870. He worked as a police reporter for the New York Tribune newspaper. Riis had a deep concern and compassion for the poor of New York City, many of whom were immigrants like himself. He was dedicated to making their lives better. He wrote many articles and books and took many photographs to raise awareness of the living conditions of the poor. Theodore Roosevelt called him "New York's most useful citizen." The following story about Jewish immigrants is from a collection of true stories entitled Children of the Tenements. *"Kosher" means food that is acceptable to eat according to Jewish dietary laws. "Hoidenish" refers to a girl who is saucy and boisterous.*

The tenement No. 76 Madison Street had been for some time scandalized by the hoidenish ways of Rose Baruch, the little cloak maker on the top floor. Rose was seventeen, and boarded with her mother in the Pincus family. But for her harum-scarum ways she might, in the opinion of the tenement, be a nice girl and some day a good wife; but these were unbearable.

For the tenement is a great working hive in which nothing has value unless exchangeable for gold. Rose's animal spirits, which long hours and low wages had no power to curb, were exchangeable only for wrath in the tenement. Her noisy feet on the stairs when she came home woke up all the tenants. . . . Rose was so Americanized, they said impatiently among themselves, that nothing could be done with her.

Perhaps they were mistaken. Perhaps Rose's stout refusal to be subdued even by the tenement was their hope, as it was her capital. Perhaps her spiteful tread upon the stairs heralded the coming protest of the free-born American against slavery, industrial or otherwise, in which their day of deliverance was dawning. It may be so. They didn't see it. How should they? They were not Americanized; not yet.

However that might be, Rose came to the end that was to be expected. The judgment of the tenement was, for the time, borne out by experience. This was the way of it.

Rose's mother had bought several pounds of kosher meat and put it into the ice-box—that is to say, on the window-sill of their fifth-floor flat. Other ice-box these East Side sweaters' tenements have none. And it does well enough in cold weather, unless the cat gets around, or, as it happened in this case, it slides off and falls down. Rose's breakfast and dinner disappeared down the air-shaft, seventy feet or more, at 10.30 p.m.

There was a family consultation as to what should be done. It was late, and everybody was in bed, but Rose declared herself equal to the rousing of the tenants in the first floor rear, through whose window she could climb into the shaft for the meat. She had done it before for a nickel. Enough said. An expedition set out at once from the top floor to recover the meat. Mrs. Baruch, Rose, and Jake, the boarder, went in a body.

Arrived before the Knauff family's flat on the ground floor, they opened proceedings by a vigorous attack on the door. The Knauffs woke up in a fright, believing that the house was full of burglars. They were stirring to barricade the door, when they recognized Rose's voice and were calmed. Let in, the expedition explained matters, and was grudgingly allowed to take a look out of the window in the air-shaft. Yes! there was the meat, as yet safe from rats. The thing was to get it.

The boarder tried first, but crawled back frightened. He couldn't reach it. Rose jerked him impatiently away.

"Leggo!" she said. "I can do it. I was there wunst. You're no good."

And she bent over the window-sill, reaching down until her toes barely touched the floor, when all of a sudden, before they could grab her skirts, over she went, heels over head, down the shaft, and disappeared.

The shrieks of the Knauffs, of Mrs. Baruch, and of Jake, the boarder, were echoed from below. Rose's voice rose in pain and in bitter lamentation from the bottom of the shaft. She had fallen fully fifteen feet, and in the fall had hurt her back badly, if, indeed, she had not injured herself beyond repair. Her cries suggested nothing less. They filled the tenement, rising to every floor and appealing at every bedroom window.

In a minute the whole building was astir from cellar to roof. A dozen heads were thrust out of every window, and answering wails carried messages of helpless sympathy to the once so unpopular Rose. Upon this concert of sorrow the police broke in with anxious inquiry as to what was the matter.

When they found out, a second relief expedition was organized. It reached Rose through the basement coal-bin, and she was carried out and sent to the Gouverneur Hospital. There she lies, unable to move, and the tenement wonders what is amiss that it has lost its old spirits. . . .

The cat took the kosher meat.

Canyons of the Colorado

John Wesley Powell, 1895

John Wesley Powell was a scientist who worked with the Smithsonian Institution. He was one of the first white explorers of the Grand Canyon, leading a party of ten in 1869. In 1895 Powell published a book about the expedition, which included his diary and dozens of photographs and drawings of the landscape they explored and the Native Americans they met. This portion of the diary records the decision by three members to leave the rest of the party. Evidently these three explorers were soon afterwards killed by Native Americans in the region.

August 27 . . . After supper Captain Howland asks to have a talk with me. We walk up the little creek a short distance, and I soon find that his object is to remonstrate against my determination to proceed. He thinks that we had better abandon the river here. Talking with him, I learn that he, his brother, and William Dunn have determined to go no farther in the boats. So we return to camp. Nothing is said to the other men.

For the last two days our course has not been plotted. I sit down and do this now, for the purpose of finding where we are by dead reckoning. It is a clear night, and I take out the sextant to make observation for latitude, and I find that the astronomic determination agrees very nearly with that of the plot—quite as closely as might be expected from a meridian observation on a planet. In a direct line, we must be about 45 miles from the mouth of the Rio Virgen. If we can reach that point, we know that there are settlements up that river about 20 miles. This 45 miles in a direct line will probably be 80 or 90 by the meandering line of the river. But then we know that there is comparatively open country for many miles above the mouth of the Virgen, which is our point of destination.

As soon as I determine all this, I spread my plot on the sand and wake Howland, who is sleeping down by the river, and show him where I suppose we are, and where several Mormon settlements are situated.

We have another short talk about the morrow, and he lies down again; but for me there is no sleep. All night long I pace up and down a little path, on a few yards of sand beach, along by the river. Is it wise to go on? I go to the boats again to look at our rations. I feel satisfied that we can get over the danger immediately before us; what there may be below I know not. From our outlook yesterday on the cliffs, the canyon seemed to make another great bend to the south, and this, from our experience heretofore, means more and higher granite walls. I am not sure that we can climb out of the canyon here, and, if at the top of the wall, I know enough of the country to be certain that it is a desert of rock and sand between this and the nearest Mormon town, which, on the most direct line, must be 75 miles away. True, the late rains have been favorable to us, should we go out, for the probabilities are that we shall find water still standing in holes; and at one time I almost conclude to leave the river. But for years I have been contemplating this trip. To leave the exploration unfinished, to say that there is a part of the canyon which I cannot explore, having already nearly accomplished it, is more than I am willing to acknowledge, and I determine to go on.

I wake my brother and tell him of Howland's determination, and he promises to stay with me; then I call up Hawkins, the cook, and he makes a like promise; then Sumner and Bradley and Hall, and they all agree to go on.

August 28.—At last daylight comes and we have breakfast without a word being said about the future. The meal is as solemn as a funeral. After breakfast I ask the three men if they still think it best to leave us. The elder Howland thinks it is, and Dunn agrees with him. The younger Howland tries to persuade them to go on with the party; failing in which, he decides to go with his brother.

Then we cross the river. The small boat is very much disabled and unseaworthy. With the loss of hands, consequent on the departure of the three men, we shall not be able to run all of the boats; so I decide to leave my *Emma Dean*.

Two rifles and a shotgun are given to the men who are going out. I ask them to help themselves to the rations and take what they think to be a fair share. This they refuse to do, saying they have no fear but that they can get something to eat; but Billy, the cook, has a pan of biscuits prepared for dinner, and these he leaves on a rock.

Before starting, we take from the boat our barometers, fossils, the minerals, and some ammunition and leave them on the rocks. We are going over this place as light as possible. The three men help us lift our boats over a rock 25 or 30 feet high and let them down again over the first fall, and now we are all ready to start. The last thing before leaving, I write a letter to my wife and give it to Howland. Sumner gives him his watch, directing that it be sent to his sister should he not be heard from again. The records of the expedition have been kept in duplicate. One set of these is given to Howland; and now we are ready. For the last time they entreat us not to go on, and tell us that it is madness to set out in this place; that we can never get safely through it; and, further, that the river turns again to the south into the granite, and a few miles of such rapids and falls will exhaust our entire stock of rations, and then it will be too late to climb out. Some tears are shed; it is rather a solemn parting; each party thinks the other is taking the dangerous course.

My old boat left, I go on board of the *Maid of the Canyon*. The three men climb a crag that overhangs the river to watch us off. The *Maid of the Canyon* pushes out. We glide rapidly along the foot of the wall, just grazing one great rock, then pull out a little into the chute of the second fall and plunge over it. The open compartment is filled when we strike the first wave below, but we cut through it, and then the men pull with all their power toward the left wall and swing clear of the dangerous rock below all right. We are scarcely a minute in running it, and find that, although it looked bad from above, we have passed many places that were worse. The other boat follows without more difficulty. We land at the first practicable point below, and fire our guns, as a signal to the men above that we have come over in safety. Here we remain a couple of hours, hoping that they will take the smaller boat and follow us. We are behind a curve in the canyon and cannot see up to where we left them, and so we wait until their coming seems hopeless, and then push on.

Harding Appoints Taft

July 1, 1921

President William Howard Taft nominated Edward Douglas White as Chief Justice of the U.S. Supreme Court in 1910. In 1921, when Warren G. Harding was serving as President, Chief Justice White died. Harding nominated William Howard Taft to fill the position of Chief Justice on June 30, 1921, and Taft was confirmed by the Senate on the same day. This appointment was the fulfillment of a lifetime dream for Taft. This article appeared in the New York Tribune *newspaper the day after Taft's appointment and confirmation. Taft served until February 3, 1930. He died on March 8 of that year.*

NEW YORK TRIBUNE   JULY 1, 1921

HARDING APPOINTS TAFT

Harding Appoints Taft Chief Justice; Senate Confirms Him, 61 to 4
From The Tribune's *Washington Bureau*

WASHINGTON, June 30—Former President William Howard Taft was today named Chief Justice of the United States by President Harding. The nomination was sent to the Sentate at 4 o'clock this afternoon and announced at the White House shortly after that time.

Later the Senate confirmed the nomination by a vote of 61 to 4 on a roll call. The nomination was considered in executive session, and was not referred to committee. . . .

Mr. Taft by the appointment achieves the greatest ambition of his life—to sit on the bench of the Supreme Court as Chief Justice of the Unites States. His close friends say that to the former President the dignity of the Chief Justiceship always held a greater glamour than did the office of President.

Rumors of the naming of Mr. Taft have been rife here for some time, and it was indicated at the White House today in connection with making public the announcement that President Harding has been irritated at the widespread publicity naming Mr. Taft prior to the announcement. . . . President Harding has made no attempt to conceal his pleasure at making

WILLIAM HOWARD TAFT

what he regards as the most excellent appointment that could be made. In discussing the appointment with the correspondents he showed gratification at being able to name the former President to the post.

President Harding has always been a great admirer of Mr. Taft and his record as a jurist particularly . .

Friends of former President Taft here point to the coincidence occuring whereby Mr. Taft succeeds in the Chief Justiceship the man whom he as President made Chief Justice, and whom he valued highly as a lawyer and a friend. Prior to the death of Chief Justice White it was reported that the venerable Southerner contemplated retiring from the bench in order that his friend Taft might subsequently be elevated. . . .

MONTREAL, June 30—Former President William Howard Taft issued the following statement here tonight after learning of his appointment as Chief Justice of the United States and of the confirmation of the nomination by the Senate:

"I am profoundly grateful to the President for the confidence he has thus shown that I can discharge the important duties of the exalted office. I sincerely hope and pray that I may be able to show that his confidence has not been misplaced. I highly appreciate the immediate confirmation by the Senate.

"It has been the amibtion of my life to be Chief Justice, but now that it is gratified I tremble to think whether I can worthily fill the position and be useful to the country. . . .

"I shall have in the near future to resign my professorship of Federal constitutional law at Yale, the presidency of the League to Enforce Peace and my position as occasional editor on the staff of *The Public Ledger* of Philadelphia."

W. H. Taft

Made in America

1903-1921

These newspaper advertisements proudly describe some of the products made by Americans in America's many factories. Sources: Colgate's: New York Tribune, Dec. 8, 1921; Maytag: Tacoma Times, Jan. 29, 1918; Heinz: Evening Public Ledger (Philadelphia), May 26, 1921; Fussell's: Washington Times, Nov. 30, 1903; Hershey's: University Missourian, Nov. 12, 1912; Palmolive: New York Tribune, Oct. 15, 1911; Quaker: The San Francisco Call, Jan. 21, 1912.

Colgate's

Lovely Gifts for Christmas
At Your Favorite Store

There is a Colgate article to answer every problem on your gift list—a fragrant perfume or exquisitely scented soap for every feminine whim, shaving articles de luxe for the masculine puzzles, talcs for the new pink-and-white babies, "Petite Purfumes" for budding girlhood, and the perfect dentifrice to top every Christmas stocking. Make this a Colgate Christmas—subtract from the anxiety of the giver, add to the pleasure of the recipient, multiply the Christmas cheer of both—and divide the cost in two!

It Costs 2c Per Hour
to Do Your Washing
With a Maytag Washer

A Maytag Electric Washing Machine and the city's cheap electric power make it possible to have your washing done at home at a cost of 2 cents per hour. The Maytag is the only electric washer using the "Dolly" wheel. This wheel rubs the clothes back and forth against the corrugated sides of the tub, removing the dirt by the old and efficient washboard method. The use of chemicals and very strong soaps is unnecessary. It also runs the wringer and is equipped with pulley wheels for running a sewing machine or other home appliance. The Maytag is the lowest priced and most efficient electric washing machine on the market. Our salespeople will be glad to demonstrate it at any time. Price $75.00.
Sold on Easy Payment Terms.

Ah! that Tomato Sauce!
Heinz Oven Baked Beans
With Tomato Sauce

Yes, you detect it at once—that delicious flavor and tang of Heinz famous Tomato Sauce. It is made of choice, fresh, sun-ripened tomatoes, perfectly spiced and seasoned and used exclusively in the spotless Heinz kitchens. But in the supreme goodness of Heinz Baked Beans is the blending of this distinctive taste with the *real bean* flavor that oven baking gives. The Heinz method of actually baking in dry heat ovens retains the food value of beans as well as the flavor. These things mean *food economy*.

Heinz Oven Baked Beans

are all ready to eat—hot or cold.

The Only Automobile in Detroit

Henry Ford, 1922

There was a time when Detroit had only one automibile, and it belonged to Henry Ford. The following excerpt is from Henry Ford's autobiography My Life and Work, *published in 1922.*

My "gasoline buggy" was the first and for a long time the only automobile in Detroit. It was considered to be something of a nuisance, for it made a racket and it scared horses. Also it blocked traffic. For if I stopped my machine anywhere in town a crowd was around it before I could start up again. If I left it alone even for a minute some inquisitive person always tried to run it. Finally, I had to carry a chain and chain it to a lamp post whenever I left it anywhere. And then there was trouble with the police. I do not know quite why, for my impression is that there were no speed-limit laws in those days. Anyway, I had to get a special permit from the mayor and thus for a time enjoyed the distinction of being the only licensed chauffeur in America. I ran that machine about one thousand miles through 1895 and 1896 and then sold it to Charles Ainsley of Detroit for two hundred dollars. That was my first sale. I had built the car not to sell but only to experiment with. I wanted to start another car. Ainsley wanted to buy. I could use the money and we had no trouble in agreeing upon a price.

It was not at all my idea to make cars in any such petty fashion. I was looking ahead to production, but before that could come I had to have something to produce. It does not pay to hurry. I started a second car in 1896; it was much like the first but a little lighter. It also had the belt drive which I did not give up until some time later; the belts were all right excepting in hot weather. That is why I later adopted gears. I learned a great deal from that car. Others in this country and abroad were building cars by that time, and in 1895 I heard that a Benz car from Germany was on exhibition in Macy's store in New York. I traveled down to look at it but it had no features that seemed worthwhile. It also had the belt drive, but it was much heavier than my car. I was working for lightness; the foreign makers have never seemed to appreciate what light weight means. I built three cars in all in my home shop and all of them ran for years in Detroit. I still have the first car; I bought it back a few years later from a man to whom Mr. Ainsley had sold it. I paid one hundred dollars for it.

During all this time I kept my position with the electric company and gradually advanced to chief engineer at a salary of one hundred and twenty-five dollars a month. But my gas-engine experiments were no more popular with the president of the company than my first mechanical leanings were with my father. It was not that my employer objected to experiments—only to experiments with a gas engine. I can still hear him say: "Electricity, yes, that's the coming thing. But gas—no."

. . . The Edison Company offered me the general superintendency of the company but only on condition that I would give up my gas engine and devote myself to something really useful. I had to choose between my job and my automobile. I chose the automobile, or rather I gave up the job—there was really nothing in the way of a choice. For already I knew that the car was bound to be a success. I quit my job on August 15, 1899, and went into the automobile business.

Steadfast as These Ancient Hills

Calvin Coolidge, 1927

On August 10, 1927, President Calvin Coolidge spoke at the dedication of the site where carving was about to begin on the "Shrine of Democracy" at Mount Rushmore in South Dakota's Black Hills.

We have come here to dedicate a cornerstone that was laid by the hand of the Almighty. On this towering wall of Rushmore, in the heart of the Black Hills, is to be inscribed a memorial which will represent some of the outstanding features of four of our Presidents, laid on by the hand of a great artist in sculpture. This memorial will crown the height of land between the Rocky Mountains and the Atlantic seaboard, where coming generations may view it for all time.

It is but natural that such a design should begin with George Washington, for with him begins that which is truly characteristic of America. He represents our independence, our Constitution, our liberty. He formed the highest aspirations that were entertained by any people into the permanent institutions of our Government. He stands as the foremost disciple of ordered liberty, a statesman with an inspired vision who is not outranked by any mortal greatness.

Next to him will come Thomas Jefferson, whose wisdom insured that the Government which Washington had formed should be entrusted to the administration of the people. He emphasized the element of self-government which had been enshrined in American institutions in such a way

as to demonstrate that it was practical and would be permanent. In him, likewise, embodied the spirit of expansion. Recognizing the destiny of this Country, he added to its territory. By removing the possibility of any powerful opposition from a neighboring state, he gave new guaranties to the rule of the people.

After our country had been established, enlarged from sea to sea, and was dedicated to popular government, the next great task was to demonstrate the permanency of our Union and to extend the principle of freedom to all inhabitants of our land. The master of this supreme accomplishment was Abraham Lincoln. Above all other national figures, he holds the love of his fellow countrymen. The work which Washington and Jefferson began, he extended to its logical conclusion.

That the principles for which these three men stood might be still more firmly established, destiny raised up Theodore Roosevelt. To political freedom he strove to add economic freedom. By building the Panama Canal he brought into closer relationship the east and the west and realized the vision that inspired Columbus in his search for a new passage to the Orient.

The union of these four Presidents carved on the face of the everlasting hills of South Dakota will constitute a distinctly national monument. It will be decidedly American in its conception, in its magnitude, in its meaning and altogether worthy of our Country. No one can look upon it understandingly without realizing that it is a picture of hope fulfilled.

Its location will be significant. Here in the heart of the continent, on the side of a mountain which probably no white man had ever beheld in the days of Washington, in territory which was acquired by the action of Jefferson, which remained an unbroken wilderness beyond the days of Lincoln, which was especially beloved by Roosevelt, the people of the future will see history and art combined to portray the spirit of patriotism. They will know that the figure of these Presidents has been placed here because by following the truth they built for eternity. The fundamental principles which they represented have been wrought into the very being of our Country. They are steadfast as these ancient hills. . . .

Marveling at the Mysteries

William Jennings Bryan, 1922

William Jennings Bryan was one of the most famous, gifted, and popular orators in American history. He was a staunch defender of God and the Bible, and he dedicated his life to sharing and promoting truth. This excerpt is from a lecture entitled, "In the Beginning—God," part of a series Bryan gave at Union Theological Seminary in Virginia in 1922.

. . . We encourage children to raise vegetables; a little child can learn how to raise vegetables, but no grown person understands the mystery that is wrapped up in every vegetable that grows. Let me illustrate: I am fond of radishes; my good wife knows it and keeps me supplied with them when she can. I eat radishes in the morning; I eat radishes at noon; I eat radishes at night; I eat radishes between meals; I like radishes. I plant radish seed—put the little seed into the ground, and go out in a few days and find a full grown radish. The top is green, the body of the root is white and almost transparent, and around it I sometimes find a delicate pink or red. Whose hand caught the hues of a summer sunset and wrapped them around the radish's root down there in the darkness in the ground? I cannot understand a radish; can you? If one refused to eat anything until he could understand the mystery of its growth, he would die of starvation; but mystery does not bother us in the dining-room,—it is only in the church that mystery seems to give us trouble. . . .

Sometimes I go into a community and find a young man who has come in from the country and obtained a smattering of knowledge; then his head swells and he begins to swagger around and say that an intelligent man like himself cannot afford to have anything to do with anything that he cannot understand. Poor boy, he will be surprised to find out how few things he will be able to deal with if he adopts that rule. I feel like suggesting to him that the next time he goes home to show himself off to his parents on the farm he address himself to the first mystery that ever came under his observation, and has not yet been solved, notwithstanding the wonderful progress made by our agricultural colleges. Let him find out, if he can, why it is that a black cow can eat green grass and then give white milk with yellow butter in it? Will the mystery disturb him? No. He will enjoy the milk and the butter without worrying about the mystery in them.

And so we might take any vegetable or fruit. The blush upon the peach is in striking contrast to the serried walls of the seed within; who will explain the mystery of the apple, the queen of the orchard, or the nut with its meat, its shell, and its outer covering? Who taught the tomato vine to fling its flaming many-mansioned fruit before the gaze of the passer-by, while the potato modestly conceals its priceless gifts within the bosom of the earth?

. . . If among my readers any one has been presumptuous enough to attempt to confine the power and purpose of God by man's puny understanding, let me persuade him to abandon this absurd position by the use of an illustration which I once found in a watermelon. I was passing through Columbus, Ohio, some years ago and stopped to eat in the restaurant in the depot. My attention was called to a slice of watermelon, and I ordered it and ate it. I was so pleased with the melon that I asked the waiter to dry some of the seeds that I might take them home and plant them in my garden. That night a thought came into my mind—I would use that watermelon as an illustration. So, the next morning when I reached Chicago, I had enough seeds weighed to learn that it would take about five thousand watermelon seeds to weigh a pound, and I estimated that the watermelon weighed about forty pounds. Then I applied mathematics to the watermelon. A few weeks before some one, I knew not who, had planted a little watermelon seed in the ground. Under the influence of sunshine and shower that little seed had taken off its coat and gone to work; it had gathered from somewhere two hundred thousand times its own weight, and forced that enormous weight through a tiny stem and built a watermelon. On the outside it had put a covering of green, within that a rind of white and within the white a core of red, and then it had scattered through the red core little seeds, each one capable of doing the same work over again. What architect drew the plan? Where did that little watermelon seed get its tremendous strength? Where did it find its flavouring extract and its colouring matter? How did it build a watermelon? Until you can explain a watermelon, do not be too sure that you can set limits to the power of the Almighty, or tell just what He would do, or how He would do it. The most learned man in the world cannot explain a watermelon, but the most ignorant man can eat a watermelon, and enjoy it. God has given us the things that we need, and He has given us the knowledge necessary to use those things: the truth that He has revealed to us is infinitely more important for our welfare than it would be to understand the mysteries that He has seen fit to conceal from us. So it is with religion. If you ask me whether I understand everything in the Bible, I frankly answer, No. I understand some things to-day that I did not understand ten years ago and, if I live ten years longer, I trust that some things will be clear that are now obscure. But there is something more important than understanding everything in the Bible; it is this: If we will embody in our lives that which we do understand we will be kept so busy doing good that we will not have time to worry about the things that we do not understand.

Fireside Chat: On Drought Conditions

Franklin D. Roosevelt, 1936

Franklin D. Roosevelt was President of the United States during two of the country's most difficult periods: the Great Depression and World War II. Right after he was inaugurated in 1933, Roosevelt began a series of speeches to the American people he called "fireside chats." These were broadcast over the radio so that most Americans could listen to their President in their own homes. Roosevelt used these "chats" to help increase confidence and dispel fear, and to convince Americans that his many new programs and policies were good steps for the country. On September 6, 1936, he spoke to the American people about drought conditions in the Great Plains.

I have been on a journey of husbandry. I went primarily to see at first hand conditions in the drought states; to see how effectively Federal and local authorities are taking care of pressing problems of relief and also how they are to work together to defend the people of this country against the effects of future droughts.

I saw drought devastation in nine states. I talked with families who had lost their wheat crop, lost their corn crop, lost their livestock, lost the water in their well, lost their garden and come through to the end of the summer without one dollar of cash resources, facing a winter without feed or food— facing a planting season without seed to put in the ground.

That was the extreme case, but there are thousands and thousands of families on western farms who share the same difficulties.

I saw cattlemen who because of lack of grass or lack of winter feed have been compelled to sell all but their breeding stock and will need help to carry even these through the coming winter. I saw livestock kept alive only because water had been brought to them long distances in tank cars. I saw other farm families who have not lost everything but who, because they have made only partial crops, must have some form of help if they are to continue farming next spring.

I shall never forget the fields of wheat so blasted by heat that they cannot be harvested. I shall never forget field after field of corn stunted, earless and stripped of leaves, for what the sun left the grasshoppers took. I saw brown pastures which would not keep a cow on fifty acres.

Yet I would not have you think for a single minute that there is permanent disaster in these drought regions, or that the picture I saw meant depopulating these areas. No cracked earth, no blistering sun, no burning wind, no grasshoppers, are a permanent match for the indomitable American farmers and stockmen and their wives and children who have carried on through desperate days, and inspire us with their self-reliance, their tenacity and their courage. It was their fathers' task to make homes; it is their task to keep those homes; it is our task to help them with their fight.

First let me talk for a minute about this autumn and the coming winter. We have the option, in the case of families who need actual subsistence, of putting them on the dole or putting them to work. They do not want to go on the dole and they are one thousand percent right. We agree, therefore, that we must put them to work for a decent wage, and when we reach that decision we kill two birds with one stone, because these families will earn enough by working, not only to subsist themselves, but to buy food for their stock, and seed for next year's planting. Into this scheme of things there fit of course the government lending agencies which next year, as in the past, will help with production loans. . . .

Spending like this is not waste. It would spell future waste if we did not spend for such things now. These emergency work projects provide money to buy food and clothing for the winter; they keep the livestock on the farm; they provide seed for a new crop, and, best of all, they will conserve soil and water in the future in those areas most frequently hit by drought.

If, for example, in some local area the water table continues to drop and the topsoil to blow away, the land values will disappear with the water and the soil. People on the farms will drift into the nearby cities; the cities will have no farm trade and the workers in the city factories and stores will have no jobs. Property values in the cities will decline. If, on the other hand, the farms within that area remain as farms with better water supply and no erosion, the farm population will stay on the land and prosper and the nearby cities will prosper too. Property values will increase instead of disappearing. That is why it is worth our while as a nation to spend money in order to save money.

I have, however, used the argument in relation only to a small area—it holds good in its effect on the nation as a whole. Every state in the drought area is now doing and always will do business with every state outside it. The very existence of the men and women working in the clothing factories of New York, making clothes worn by farmers and their families; of the workers in the steel mills in Pittsburgh, in the automobile factories of Detroit, and in the harvester factories of Illinois, depend upon the farmers' ability to purchase the commodities they produce. In the same way it is the purchasing power of the workers in these factories in the cities that enables them and their wives and children to eat more beef, more pork, more wheat, more corn, more fruit and more dairy products, and to buy more clothing made from cotton, wool and leather. In a physical and a property sense, as well as in a spiritual sense, we are members one of another. . . .

A Nation-Wide System of Parks

United States Department of the Interior, 1939

The National Park Service, which operates within the United States Department of the Interior, made several short documentaries in the 1930s about the work of the Civilian Conservation Corps (CCC). The government used the still-novel media of film to show actual CCC workers on the job and in camp and to showcase the work of the CCC from Maine to California. The following excerpts are from the narration of the 16-minute film made in 1939, "A Nation-Wide System of Parks."

In 1933, the chief concern of the American government was to break the back of a bad depression. Among the conditions to be remedied were two President Roosevelt recognized at once: employment for hundreds of thousands of young men and war veterans was imperative; havoc wrought by soil erosion had long since shown the necessity of the immediate restoration, conservation, and further development of the country's natural resources. As one  solution for both problems, the organization and work of the Civilian Conservation Corps was undertaken, and in two years, through this unique plan, both problems were well on their way toward solution as great aids to economic recovery. The saving of natural resources was conservation pure and simple.

One important phase of the development of these resources was more than that. It was the making of a nationwide system of recreational areas, smaller more numerous state parks – closer to the people, more easily accessible for their use – supplementing the magnificent national parks.

Conservation work, in all its many phases, is being done in these state park areas from one end of the country to the other. Better facilities for forest firefighting are being provided through the building of truck trails, fire lanes, and observation towers, and the stringing of communication lines. Speed is imperative in fighting forest fires – quick discovery, the quick spreading of the alarm, and roads to reach the scene of action. Dead trees and tangled dry undergrowth are being cleared from the forest where necessary to prevent the starting of fires. . . .

An interesting state park in Georgia surrounds the one-time home of Alexander Stevens, Vice President of the Confederacy. Long ago, the memory of this outstanding southern statesman was honored by the erection of a statue on his home estate. Now the mansion, with its slave quarters and outbuildings, is being restored, and the grounds are being made more attractive to visitors. Strict attention is being paid to details; reproductions of the hand-wrought hardware originally used are being made by Conservation Corps enrollees under skilled direction. . . .

The government's rehabilitation program is transferring citizens from localities in which they have been finding it difficult to make a living into more desirable surroundings. . . . In the functioning of the Civilian Conservation Corps plan, however, there is another and even more interesting form of rehabilitation. Among hundreds of thousands of young men and war veterans enrolled, there have been many unable to read or write. Others, whose schooling has been interrupted, were found to be slipping in the matter of education and morale. The important job of mentally rehabilitating this extremely valuable cross section of the manpower of the country has been entrusted to the Office of Education, Department of the Interior. Competent instructors in

Conservation Corps camps conduct classes in many of the educational branches. The boys are given the opportunity to go to school just as they might have done years ago.

In addition, there are many practical manual training courses intended to prepare the enrollees for happier and more remunerative [better-paying] work when their association with the Corps has ended. Many of the Conservation Corps camps communicate with each other over shortwave radio sets for both transmission and reception, which the boys themselves have made.

Do the enrollees welcome these opportunities? Well, a field report not long ago disclosed that in a single Conservation Corps camp within a single month, five enrollees, in their joy at knowing for the first time how to use them, spent a big share of their $5 cash allowances for fountain pens.

. . . In the Conservation Corps development of state parks is found a perfect blending of conservation and recreation. Besides protecting and saving land and timber and wildlife, this phase of the program develops recreation areas for people who have not had them before. . . .

Hiking and bridle trails wind through the parks. Each of these trails being constructed by the Conservation Corps in state parks in 42 states is carefully placed by expert park planners so the natural growth of the area will be harmed as little as possible and yet so points of interest can be reached. Splendid views few men have seen because the peaks were inaccessible now open up as these trails lead hikers to the mountaintops.

Racing brooks and deep streams are spanned by rustic bridges of good design. They are built by skilled labor and Conservation Corps enrollees according to plans of graduate engineers and architects. Though thousands gather in the parks to enjoy these new recreational facilities, the old parking problem is no bother; adequate spaces have been provided. . . .

Probably the most attractive feature of a typical state park is the cabin community, located in one of the area's desirable spots and open to visitors who want to spend a night or a week. State park Conservation Corps companies cover the country and work through all the seasons. These snug cabins in Pueblo State Park in Colorado are going up despite the winter snow. Recreation buildings and picnic shelters are state park essentials. This one stands on the moss-draped banks of the black Edisto, one of South Carolina's loveliest Lowcountry streams. . . .

Building trails, cutting fire lanes, and protecting and improving timber and land make the conservation work program essentially one requiring well-directed massed manpower. But on the construction projects, skilled labor is necessary. Carpenters, bricklayers, plumbers, and electricians are hired from the community in which the camp is located. These men work on the park jobs with the Conservation Corps boys as helpers. Not only does this furnish employment for skilled labor and get the job well done, but it provides the enrollees with excellent opportunities to learn trades. Splitting handmade shingles is a colorful task. The tools for splitting the blocks are ingenious, as are also the appliances devised for holding the shingles during the finishing processes. And almost every camp has its own village blacksmith, plying his fascinating and still useful trade.

So it is all these factors that join forces in this unique phase of the recovery program: a Federal aid project to save and enjoy a country, to keep nature unsullied and unspoiled wherever possible as a healing retreat from the increasing difficulties of modern life. A project directed by that government agency which has given the world the American national parks: the National Park Service of the United States Department of the Interior.

The Fog in San Francisco

Almira Bailey, 1921

Almira Bailey loved her hometown of San Francisco. She wrote poetic descriptions of life in the city in Vignettes of San Francisco, *published in 1921. At that time, residents of San Francisco and the surrounding towns depended on a ferry to travel across the beautiful Golden Gate. The world-famous Golden Gate Bridge has been part of the fog-covered scenery of San Francisco since 1937.*

Sunsets in the desert, spring in New England, black-green oaks lying on tawny hills in Marin County, fields of cotton on red soil in Georgia, surf on the rocks of Maine, moonlight on Mobile Bay, and the way the fog comes upon San Francisco on summer afternoons.

Sometimes when all its hills lie sparkling in the sunshine and children play on the sidewalks, young fellows whistle, business autos go zippity-zip around the corners, and the whole city is out of doors or hanging out of the windows, then suddenly in great billows the fog comes rolling in through the Golden Gate, and between the hills right up the streets into the city.

Then immediately all is changed and everything is nearer and more intimate and nothing of the city is left but the street you're on. Then you hurry home for supper and home seems good and sometimes you even light a little fire in the grate.

Still it is not a cold fog, it is not a wet fog, it is never an unkind fog. It comes swiftly, but very gently, and lays its cool, dainty hand on your face lovingly. Hands are so different, sticky or wet or clammy or hot, but the hand of the San Francisco fog is the hand of a kind nurse on a tired head. The rain is a beautiful thing too, but the fog has another significance. It is the "small rain" that Moses spoke of, "My doctrine shall drop as the rain, my speech shall distill as the dew, as the small rain upon the tender herb, and as the showers upon the grass." [Deuteronomy 32:2]

It is very beautiful, too. My, but I've seen fogs that were ugly, and heard the fisherman say "She's pretty thick tonight." San Francisco fog is not like that, but like great billows of a bride's veil. Then in the morning when the sun comes it chases the bride and her veil out so fast, and they go out to sea together, sunshine and fog.

The other morning I awakened very early and there in the square of my window was a hard, black cube against a white background. I lay there and blinked and wondered where that telephone pole had come from, which like Jack's beanstalk, had grown there overnight. Then I saw that the fog had shut out the whole world and brought that pole close, and made it seem big and formidable and ugly.

The fog makes some people lose their perspective, and for others it only wraps with a great kindness the whole world and blots out all ugliness. But upon everyone . . . this San Francisco fog lays its gentle hand lovingly and with an ineffable kindness.

The Beauties of the State of Washington

Harry F. Giles, 1915

In 1915 the State of Washington Bureau of Statistics and Immigration published Beauties of the State of Washington, *a "book for tourists." Following is the section about the Olympic Peninsula.*

Lying between Hood Canal and the Pacific Ocean and extending from the Strait of Juan de Fuca southward toward the Chehalis river valley is the vast Olympic Peninsula, whose resources and wonders are probably less known than almost any other section of the world. The central portion constitutes one great forest reserve within which is the Olympic National Monument set apart by the government for the enjoyment of nature lovers. The population is distributed among the cities and towns situated on the level lands skirting the waterfront. This Monument contains the most rugged mountains, the deepest canyons, the most turbulent rivers and the thickest forests in the state.

The Peninsula is now reached both by steamer and automobile. Highways lead well up into the foothills from the cities of Port Angeles, Sequim, Port Townsend, Quilcene, Shelton, Aberdeen, Hoquiam, and Hood Canal points, and passable trails thread their way to the summits beyond. It is easy to surprise both deer and elk, confident of safety from the approach of man. Numerous flowering parks display seas of gorgeous colors which make the region famous for its beauty.

It also serves as a huge treasure chest. Billions of feet of choicest timber remain uncut; valuable ore veins and a vast lake of petroleum are buried within its depths; land well suited for agriculture girdles the entire peninsula; and the neighboring waters yield liberal quantities of fish.

Certain beauty spots in the mountains have been supplemented with the conveniences and luxuries of modern invention. Among these are Sol Duc Springs, at the headwaters of the Sol Duc river, where a little palace has been lifted into the mountains, Government Hot Springs, and Lake Crescent, all reached from Port Angeles; Lake Cushman, approached from Hoodsport; and Lake Quiniault, north of Grays Harbor. A visit to any of these resorts or any part of the peninsula will satisfy the most extravagant expectations of tourist and mountaineer.

D-Day Message

Dwight D. Eisenhower, 1944

Dwight D. Eisenhower began his distinguished military career when he entered West Point in 1911. He went on to be one of the most important figures in World War II, assuming responsibility as the Supreme Commander, Allied Expeditionary Forces, in December 1943. He was primarily responsible for the decision for the Allied forces to invade Europe on June 6, 1944. He wrote this letter to be given to the individual members of the Allied forces who would be involved in the heroic invasion. The document pictured at bottom shows Eisenhower's letter as the soldiers received it.

Supreme Headquarters
Allied Expeditionary Force

Soldiers, Sailors and Airmen of the Allied Expeditionary Force!

You are about to embark upon the Great Crusade, toward which we have striven these many months. The eyes of the world are upon you. The hopes and prayers of liberty-loving people everwhere march with you. In company with our brave Allies and brothers-in-arms on other Fronts, you will bring about the destruction of the German war machine, the elimination of Nazi tyranny over the oppressed peoples of Europe, and security for ourselves in a free world.

Your task will not be an easy one. Your enemy is well-trained, well-equipped and battle-hardened. He will fight savagely.

But this is the year 1944! Much has happened since the Nazi triumphs of 1940-41. The United Nations have inflicted upon the Germans great defeats, in open battle, man-to-man. Our air offensive has seriously reduced their strength in the air and their capacity to wage war on the ground. Our Home Fronts have given us an overwhelming superiority in weapons and munitions of war, and placed at our disposal great reserves of trained fighting men. The tide has turned! The free men of the world are marching together to Victory!

I have full confidence in your courage, devotion to duty and skill in battle. We will accept nothing less that full Victory!

Good Luck! And let us all beseech the blessing of Almighty God upon this great and noble undertaking.

Dwight D. Eisenhower

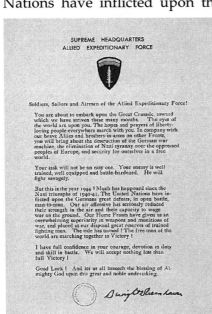

Fireside Chat: On the Declaration of War with Japan

Franklin D. Roosevelt, 1941

On December 9, 1941, two days after the Japanese attack on Pearl Harbor, President Franklin D. Roosevelt addressed the American people over the radio from the Oval Office at the White House. He used the method that had become familiar to the American people: a "fireside chat." Roosevelt explained the background of the war America had just entered, told what to expect, gave warnings and instructions, and assured his audience that America was fighting to win.

My Fellow Americans:

The sudden criminal attacks perpetrated by the Japanese in the Pacific provide the climax of a decade of international immorality.

Powerful and resourceful gangsters have banded together to make war upon the whole human race. Their challenge has now been flung at the United States of America. The Japanese have treacherously violated the longstanding peace between us. Many American soldiers and sailors have been killed by enemy action. American ships have been sunk; American airplanes have been destroyed.

The Congress and the people of the United States have accepted that challenge.

Together with other free peoples, we are now fighting to maintain our right to live among our world neighbors in freedom, in common decency, without fear of assault. . . .

"We'll have lots to eat this winter, won't we Mother?"

Grow your own
Can your own

WANT *ACTION?*

join
U·S·Marine Corps!

We are now in this war. We are all in it—all the way. Every single man, woman and child is a partner in the most tremendous undertaking of our American history. We must share together the bad news and the good news, the defeats and the victories—the changing fortunes of war.

So far, the news has been all bad. We have suffered a serious setback in Hawaii. Our forces in the Philippines, which include the brave people of that Commonwealth, are taking punishment, but are defending themselves vigorously. The reports from Guam and Wake and Midway Islands are still confused, but we must be prepared for the announcement that all these three outposts have been seized.

The casualty lists of these first few days will undoubtedly be large. I deeply feel the anxiety of all of the families of the men in our armed forces and the relatives of people in cities which have been bombed. I can only give them my solemn promise that they will get news just as quickly as possible. . . .

Now a word about the recent past and the future. A year and a half has elapsed since the fall of France, when the whole world first realized the mechanized might which the Axis nations had been building up for so many years. America has used that year and a half to great advantage.

DON'T BE A Sucker!

KEEP YOUR MOUTH SHUT

**For Baby's Future
BUY WAR BONDS**

Knowing that the attack might reach us in all too short a time, we immediately began greatly to increase our industrial strength and our capacity to meet the demands of modern warfare.

Precious months were gained by sending vast quantities of our war material to the nations of the world still able to resist Axis aggression. Our policy rested on the fundamental truth that the defense of any country resisting Hitler or Japan was in the long run the defense of our own country. That policy has been justified. It has given us time, invaluable time, to build our American assembly lines of production.

Assembly lines are now in operation. Others are being rushed to completion. A steady stream of tanks and planes, of guns and ships and shells and equipment—that is what these eighteen months have given us.

But it is all only a beginning of what still has to be done. We must be set to face a long war against crafty and powerful bandits. The attack at Pearl Harbor can be repeated at any one of many points, points in both oceans and along both our coast lines and against all the rest of the Hemisphere.

It will not only be a long war, it will be a hard war. That is the basis on which we now lay all our plans. That is the yardstick by which we measure what we shall need and demand; money, materials, doubled and quadrupled production—ever-increasing.

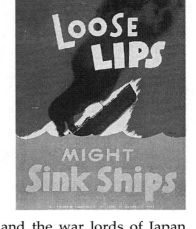

LOOSE LIPS MIGHT Sink Ships

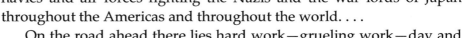

KEEP 'EM ROLLING!

The production must be not only for our own Army and Navy and air forces. It must reinforce the other armies and navies and air forces fighting the Nazis and the war lords of Japan throughout the Americas and throughout the world. . . .

On the road ahead there lies hard work—grueling work—day and night, every hour and every minute.

I was about to add that ahead there lies sacrifice for all of us.

But it is not correct to use that word. The United States does not consider it a sacrifice to do all one can, to give one's best to our nation, when the nation is fighting for its existence and its future life.

It is not a sacrifice for any man, old or young, to be in the Army or the Navy of the United States. Rather it is a privilege.

It is not a sacrifice for the industrialist or the wage earner, the farmer or the shopkeeper, the trainman or the doctor, to pay more taxes, to buy more bonds, to forego extra profits, to work longer or harder at the task for which he is best fitted. Rather it is a privilege.

It is not a sacrifice to do without many things to which we are accustomed if the national defense calls for doing without it.

A review this morning leads me to the conclusion that at present we shall not have to curtail the normal use of articles of food. There is enough food today for all of us and enough left over to send to those who are fighting on the same side with us.

But there will be a clear and definite shortage of metals for many kinds of civilian use, for the very good reason that in our increased

LICK THE PLATTER CLEAN

Don't Waste FOOD

program we shall need for war purposes more than half of that portion of the principal metals which during the past year have gone into articles for civilian use. Yes, we shall have to give up many things entirely.

And I am sure that the people in every part of the nation are prepared in their individual living to win this war. I am sure that they will cheerfully help to pay a large part of its financial cost while it goes on. I am sure they will cheerfully give up those material things that they are asked to give up.

And I am sure that they will retain all those great spiritual things without which we cannot win through. . . .

The true goal we seek is far above and beyond the ugly field of battle. When we resort to force, as now we must, we are determined that this force shall be directed toward ultimate good as well as against immediate evil. We Americans are not destroyers—we are builders.

We are now in the midst of a war, not for conquest, not for vengeance, but for a world in which this nation, and all that this nation represents, will be safe for our children. We expect to eliminate the danger from Japan, but it would serve us ill if we accomplished that and found that the rest of the world was dominated by Hitler and Mussolini.

So we are going to win the war and we are going to win the peace that follows.

And in the difficult hours of this day—through dark days that may be yet to come—we will know that the vast majority of the members of the human race are on our side. Many of them are fighting with us. All of them are praying for us. But, in representing our cause, we represent theirs as well—our hope and their hope for liberty under God.

Code-Talkers

Clayton B. Vogel, 1942

World War I veteran Philip Johnston grew up as the son of a missionary to the Navajo tribe. As one of the few non-Navajo speakers of the complex, unwritten Navajo language, he knew it would make an excellent "code" for transmitting secret military information during World War II. He offered to help the militray train Navajo speakers to transmit messages. The Navajo "code talkers" became a successful part of the operations of the Unites States Marine Corps. Their code was never broken by the enemy. The program remained highly classified until 1968, so the men involved came home from the war sworn to secrecy and received no special recognition. In 2001 the first 29 Navajo men enlisted as code talkers were awarded the Congressional Gold Medal. Following is a letter written in 1942, as the project was first under consideration, describing the initial demonstration Philip Johnston made to the United States Marine Corps and including a recommendation that Navajo code talkers be enlisted. Vogel, the general who wrote the letter, spelled the name of the tribe "Navaho." The photographs on the next page show the swearing-in of the first Navajo code-talker recruits and two of the Marine code-talkers in action.

HEADQUARTERS
AMPHIBIOUS FORCE, PACIFIC FLEET,
CAMP ELLIOTT, SAN DIEGO, CALIFORNIA

March 6, 1942
From: The Commanding General.
To: The Commandant, U.S. Marine Corps.

Subject: Enlistment of Navaho Indians.

Enclosures: (A) Brochure by Mr. Philip Johnston, with maps.
               (B) Messages used in demonstration.

1. Mr. Philip Johnston of Los Angeles recently offered his sevices to this force to demonstrate the use of Indians for the transmission of messages by telephone and voice-radio. His offer was accepted and the demonstration was held for the Commanding General and his staff.

2. The demonstration was interesting and successful. Messages were transmitted and received almost verbatim. In conducting the demonstration messages were written by a member of the staff and handed to the Indian; he would transmit the message in his tribal dialect and the Indian on the other end would write them down in English. The text of messages as written and received are enclosed. The Indians do not have many military terms in their dialect so it was necessary to give them a few minutes, before the demonstration, to improvise words for dive-bombing, anti-tank gun, etc.

3. Mr. Johnston stated that the Navaho is the only tribe in the United States that has not been infested with German students during the past twenty years. These Germans, studying the various tribal dialects under the guise of art students, anthropologists, etc., have undoubtedly attained a good working knowledge of all tribal dialects except Navaho. For this reason the Navaho is the

only tribe available offering complete security for the type of work under consideration. It is noted in Mr. Johnston's article (enclosed) that the Navaho is the largest tribe but the lowest in literacy. He stated, however, that 1,000—if that many were needed—could be found with the necessary qualifications. It should also be noted that the Navaho tribal dialect is completely unintelligible to all other tribes and all other people, with the possible exception of as many as 28 Americans who have made a study of the dialect. This dialect is thus equivalent to a secret code to the enemy, and admirably suited for rapid, secure communcation.

4. It is therefore recommended that an effort be made to enlist 200 Navaho Indians for this force. In addition to linguistic qualifications in English and their tribal dialect they should have the physical qualifications necessary for messengers.

Clayton B. Vogel

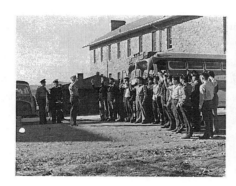 

Press Release

Eleanor Roosevelt, 1945

Eleanor Roosevelt wrote the following letter to the new President, Harry Truman, just four days after her husband, Franklin D. Roosevelt, died on April 12, 1945. The letter was sent out as a press release for publication in newspapers. The photographs show citizens of Washington, D.C., after hearing the news of President Roosevelt's death and lining the streets to view his funeral procession.

April 16, 1945

My dear Mr. President:

There have been many thousands of letters, telegrams and cards sent to me and my children which have brought great comfort and consolation to all of us. This outpouring of affectionate thought has touched us all deeply and we wish it were possible to thank each and every one individually.

My children and I feel in view of the fact that we are faced with a paper shortage and are asked not to use paper when it can be avoided, that all we can do is to express our appreciation collectively. We would therefore consider it a great favor if you would be kind enough to express our gratitude for us.

Sincerely yours,
Eleanor Roosevelt

Great Our Joint Rejoicings Here

Mary E. Anderson, 1865

In January 1863, Rufus Anderson, accompanied by his wife and daughter, traveled by boat from New York to Panama, from there to San Francisco, and from there to Hawaii. Anderson was Secretary of the American Board of Commissioners for Foreign Missions and represented the organization as he visited natives, foreigners living in Hawaii, and congregations of recently-converted Hawaiian Christians. Anderson and his family returned to New York in September. In 1865 Rufus' daughter Mary published Scenes in the Hawaiian Islands and California, *her memories of their remarkable journey. She composed the book as if she were telling the stories to her nieces and nephews in daily installments before tea time, which is why she refers to her parents as "grandma" and "grandpa."*

On Saturday, April 11, we left Kaawaloa, after a very pleasant visit of two weeks, starting about nine o'clock on our twelve miles ride to Kailua. Mr. Paris's family and Grandma were in a carriage, which some friends had given Mrs. P., and Grandpa and I were on horseback. I had my horse Bonaparte. The road was good most of the way; no carriage had ever traveled the whole length of it before. Part of the way was down the mountain, and when about half-way to the foot, a part of the carriage broke. We all dismounted and took a lunch, then, with some leather, Mr. Paris bound up the broken place firmly, and we went on our way rejoicing that no worse thing had befallen us; for we were far away from any house, and had still half of our journey to perform, and this being the only carriage on that part of the island, no native knew how to repair it. On reaching the seashore, we passed through a grove of coconut trees. Here we drank some delicious coconut milk, and quite a group of natives gathered about us, and shook hands. The Hawaiians as a race are very fond of shaking hands. As the shake of the hand, saying "aloha," love to you, was often our only mode of expressing our interest, we were very particular to do it.

After leaving the grove, the path lay between two stone walls, so near together that it seemed impossible for the carriage to go through. Our native friends said among themselves "pilikia!" trouble; for there was no other road for the carriage. But the carriage did pass, the wheels just grazing the stones. How glad we were, and the natives exclaimed, "maikai!" good.

We saw a great deal of rough hard lava, called "pahoihoi," and prickly pear-trees grew in abundance . . . .

We were amused at the excitement of many of the natives about the carriage. A great number of them had never seen one before. Whole families turned out, men, women, and children, just as people in our own land once did to see a railroad car, or as they do now to see a caravan with elephants and camels. Horses and mules all along the road became unmanageable. They would turn and look, with dilated nostrils and head erect, while trembling in every limb, till the carriage almost reached them, then they would break from their fastenings and gallop off, neighing with fear. Then they would turn and look till we nearly reached them again, when they darted away as before.

We reached the house of Mr. Thurston, at Kailua, about three o'clock in the afternoon. . . . Several natives called to see us, and a venerable deacon sent us two fowls, some very fine watermelons, and sweet potatoes. The melons were delicious, the soil of this part of the islands being well adapted to them. Watermelons are even sent to the San Francisco market.

The next day was Sabbath, the 12th of April, the forty-third anniversary of the missionaries first landing on these islands, which occurred on this very spot. We were interested in the fact that we should happen to be there at that time.

We went to the stone church, a venerable edifice built in the old style,—the pulpit and galleries being very high. Perhaps a thousand natives were present, and they paid remarkable attention to all that was said. After service, we shook hands with a large portion of the audience. Most of the people came on horseback, and there must have been as many as five hundred horses tied outside the church.

It was too far for us to go home before the afternoon service; so we spent the time in visiting the graves of mission families near the church. In the afternoon we partook of the communion with the congregation. Every thing was conducted with great propriety. A native evangelist has had the care of this church since Mr. T. left, and they have well sustained their church and prayer-meetings, with very little outside aid from missionaries.

We expected the steamer to call for us at any time after midnight, and so slept with one eye and one ear open. About twenty donkeys were in a pasture near us, and were braying all night long. We had little refreshing sleep, and were glad to see the smoke of the Kilauea as she came round a point in the distance at six o'clock in the morning. We wended our way to the beach, and amused ourselves by watching little native children playing in the water, and by picking up shells, until the boat came to take us on board the steamer, when we bade our friends good-by. As there was no wharf, a native took us up one by one and carried us to the boat. It seemed so funny at first for us grown people to be taken up like children; but we got accustomed to it, the men lifting us easily, and placing us in the boat as dry and comfortable as possible. By three o'clock in the afternoon we

were off to Honoipu, where we were to disembark. This is the landing for Kohala. Mr. Bond met us, and a kind German was there with his wagon to take Grandma and the baggage to Mr. B.'s house. The rest of us went on horseback. Before Grandpa mounted his horse, the natives gathered about him, and asked by an interpreter how old he was. They said, "his face and his form was young, but his hair was old." They expected to see an old decrepit man, and

were quite surprised to find him so fresh and vigorous. . . .

The trade-wind swept across that part of the island with great force. It really seemed as if we would be blown off our horses, and I was glad that my hat-strings were sewed on tightly. After a while, a sudden shower came up, lasting about five minutes; but the wind soon dried us. Another and heavier one making its appearance in the distance, we turned off the road to go a shorter way. Mr. Bond was mounted on a large white mule; as we were galloping hastily along over the grassy field, his mule stumbled, and over they went. All we could see was the mule's four feet in the air. Fortunately, Mr. Bond was not under the animal, as we feared, but rose from the soft grass a few feet ahead uninjured. The shower came steadily on, and we were obliged to take refuge in a native hut. The natives ran out, took off our saddles, and tied our horses for us, so that we might escape the shower. They were always ready to do a kind act for us. As I sat in the hut with two women and a pretty little native girl about three years old, I longed to be able to talk with them in their own language; but after each of us had said "aloha," we could only sit and look at each other.

Grandma and Mrs. Bond with her children were waiting on the piazza to meet us as we rode up. But there is the tea-bell, so we must wait until to-morrow to hear about Kohala.

. . . "We are ready to hear about that queer-named place now, aunty," said Alice at my elbow as I sat writing in my room.

Oh, yes, about Kohala.

Every thing at Mr. Bond's was the pink of neatness. . . . The garden looked beautifully, with some rose-bushes twenty-five feet in circumference, and scarlet geraniums perhaps fifteen feet. It does one good just to look at them, after seeing only our little dwarf shrubs at home. Kanoa and his wife, the good Hawaiian missionaries to Micronesia, came with their little baby to bid us good-by.

We had mangoes for the first time at Mr. Bond's, which were delicious. In shape they are like a pear, only flatter, with the large end growing next the stem. I can not describe the taste, it is unlike anything we have. The seed is very large, being nearly two thirds the size of the fruit. Fresh figs, too, we tried for the first time, and to our surprise liked them. We had some papayas, which grow on trees; the fruit tastes like a musk-melon, and pies made of them are very much like squash-pies.

Sabbath morning it cleared up about eleven, so that we could go to church. Notwithstanding the weather, a goodly congregation assembled, and listened to Grandpa with great respect and attention. After meeting, as usual, they all wanted to shake hands with us. As I was going down the aisle, thinking I had shaken hands with all, I heard some one call "keika mahine, keika mahine" [daughter, daughter], and looking round, there was an old man standing up on a seat with his hand stretched out to shake hands. Of course I must gratify him. Fortunately for us, Monday, April 20, was a pleasant day, and we started about nine o'clock for Waimea across the mountain. Grandma rode about twelve miles in Mr. Christianson's wagon, and then as the wagon-road ended, she went the remainder of the way on horseback. The rest of us were in the saddle all the way. How the wind did blow! It seemed as if I should be carried out of my saddle bodily; but we rode on over fields and barren wastes, and through steep and rocky gulches. . . . As we were riding, on the summit of a hill, or mountain as we should call it, a beautiful scene opened before us. High above us the fleecy clouds parted, and we caught a glimpse of what seemed like "the promised land." There stood the peak of a lofty mountain covered with newly-fallen snow, shining white and beautiful in the sun's clear beams. It seemed too high up, too pure and fair in its framework of clouds, to belong to earth. This was the summit of Mauna Kea, and we shall not soon forget that vision of beauty. It seemed as if angels might flit over its snowy sides without any danger of soiling their pure white garments. We arrived at Mr. Lyons's about five, and were cordially met by Mrs. L. and her daughter.

On Wednesday, we attended a meeting at Mr. Lyons's church. The house was filled with nicely-dressed natives. Grandpa and Mr. L. sat in front of the pulpit. At the back of the church was a large choir of men and women, who sung well and with animation, beating time with their hands.

Soon after we entered, they sung an original hymn by a native named Lyana. . . . Mr. Bingham, one of the first missionaries to the islands, has given us this translation:

> Wonderful that love sincere!
>   Great our joint rejoicings here,
> For the stranger guest we see;
>   Cordial welcome, friend, to thee.
>
> Sailing far to reach our homes,
>   From America he comes;
> Lo! in peace he enters here;
>   Welcome to our hearts sincere.
>
> Now on this delightful day,
>   We, in love, unite to pray:
> Here beneath our temple spire,
>   We our welcome give thee, sire.
>
> Jointly chanting, now rejoice;
>   Brethren, all unite your voice;
> Husbands, wives, and little ones,
>   Greet this friend with grateful tones.
>
> This is he who hither sends
>   These true missionary friends,
> To enlighten our dark mind;
>   Thanks and love to one so kind.
>
> Let us then all rise and sing,
>   And our grateful succor bring;
> For our sire our love to prove,—
>   Love, goodwill, unceasing love.

Time for Action

Harry Truman, 1946

One of the many crises Harry Truman faced as President was the desperate food situation abroad after World War II. Millions of people on the edge of starvation in war-ravaged countries looked to the United States for rescue. Harry Truman (pictured at top right) called upon former President Herbert Hoover (pictured at bottom left) for help. Hoover had valuable experience from his role in saving Europe from starvation after World War I. As Truman's honorary chairman of the Famine Emergency Committee, the 71-year-old Hoover traveled to starving nations to assess the situation and to countries with surplus food to seek assistance. Truman and Hoover worked together successfully to avert disaster and in the process forged a close friendship. The following speech by Truman was broadcast on April 19, 1946, by American radio networks and by shortwave radio around the world.

Good Evening:

It is my duty to join my voice with the voices of humanity everywhere in behalf of the starving millions of human beings all over the world. We have a high responsibility, as Americans, to go to their rescue.

I appointed the Famine Emergency Committee to make sure that we do all we can to help starving people. We are particularly grateful to former President Hoover for undertaking a survey of the situation in Europe. The messages he has sent back have driven home again and again the desperate plight of the people over there. We cannot doubt that at this moment, many people in the famine-stricken homes of Europe and Asia are dying of hunger.

America is faced with a solemn obligation. Long ago we promised to do our full part. Now we cannot ignore the cry of hungry children. Surely we will not turn our backs on the millions of human beings begging for just a crust of bread. The warm heart of America will respond to the greatest threat of mass starvation in the history of mankind.

We would not be Americans if we did not wish to share our comparative plenty with suffering people. I am sure I speak for every American when I say the United States is determined to do everything in its power to relieve the famine of half the world.

The United States Government is taking strong measures to export during the first half of this year a million tons of wheat a month for the starving masses of Asia and Europe. Our reserve stocks of wheat are low. We are going to whittle that reserve even further.

America cannot remain healthy and happy in the same world where millions of human beings are starving. A sound world order can never be built upon a foundation of human misery.

I am glad here and now to renew an appeal which I made the other day. I said then that we would all be better off, physically and spiritually, if we ate less. And then on two days a week let us reduce our food consumption to that of the average person in the hungry lands.

Once again I appeal to all Americans to sacrifice so that others may live. Millions will surely die unless we eat less. Again I strongly urge all Americans to save bread and to conserve oils and fats. These are the most essential weapons at our disposal to fight famine abroad. Every slice of bread, every ounce of fat and oil saved by your voluntary sacrifice, will help keep starving people alive.

By our combined effort, we will reduce starvation and, with God's help, we will avert the worst of this plague of famine that follows in the wake of war. I ask every American now to pledge himself to share.

The time for talk has passed. The time for action is here.

Letter to Bess

Harry Truman, 1947

Over a period of nearly fifty years, Harry Truman wrote hundreds of letters to his beloved wife Bess. He wrote this one during his first term as President. The photograph shows Harry and Bess Truman on the porch of their Independence, Missouri, home in 1953, the year Truman left the White House. "The Muehlebach" Truman mentions is a famous hotel in Kansas City, Missouri. "The baby" refers to Harry and Bess' daughter Margaret, who was then 23 years old.

September 30, 1947

Dear Bess - Yesterday was one of the most hectic of days as I told you. I'm not sure what has been my worst day. But here is a situation frought with terrible consequences. Suppose, for instance, that Italy should fold up and that Tito then would march into the Po Valley. All the Mediterranean coast of France then is open to Russian occupation and the iron curtain comes to Bordeaux, Callais, Antwerp, and the Hague. We withdraw from Greece and Turkey and *prepare for war*. It just must not happen. But here I am confronted with a violently opposition Congress whose committees with few exceptions are living in 1890: is not representative of the country's thinking at all. But I've a job and it must be done—win, lose or draw.

Sent letters to Taber, Bridges, Vandenburg, and Eaton requesting them to call their committees together as soon as possible. Had my food committee together and will make a radio speech Sunday. To feed France and Italy this winter will cost 580 millions, the Marshall Plan 16½ billions. But you know in October and November 1945 I cancelled 63 billions in appropriations, 55 billions at one crack. Our war cost that year was set at 105 billions. The 16½ is for a four year period and is for *peace*. A Russian war would cost us 400 billions and untold lives, mostly civilian. So I want to do what I can. I shouldn't write you this stuff but you should know what I've been facing since Potsdam. . . .

Hope you have a nice time, a good party at the Muehlebach. I'm sure you will. I haven't resumed my walks yet but will in a day or two. Too much to read. Gen. Bradley made a report to me today on his European trip and he remarked on my having had to make more momentous decisions than nearly any other president. He's right, and I hope most of 'em have been right.

Edward Arnold came in to see me this afternoon and brought me wonderful pictures of all the Presidents. He told me and the office force some good stories about Sam Goldwyn, Harry Warner, and Syros Skourus, imitating them in their manners and voice. It gave me sore sides from laughing.

Tell the baby I'll write her soon. Hope Frank doesn't get another boil.

Lots of love,
Harry

Letter to Eleanor Roosevelt

Harry Truman, 1945

When Franklin D. Roosevelt died on April 12, 1945, his wife Eleanor was not sure what her new role would be. She told a reporter, "The story is over." However, many people had ideas and suggestions for her and wanted her help in causes and campaigns. In December 1945, President Harry Truman appointed Eleanor Roosevelt a United States delegate to the "United Nations Organization," which was still being developed. She accepted the appointment and used her position for many years to continue to campaign for humanitarian causes. Harry Truman wrote this letter by hand on White House stationery. The photographs below show Eleanor Roosevelt in her role as delegate to the United Nations.

December 17, '45

Dear Mrs. Roosevelt,

Replying to yours about your proposed trip to Russia. I think you can go ahead with your arrangements for the trip in March, if you like, without interfering with the meetings of the United Nations Organization.

The first meeting will be sometime in January and should not last over thirty days. It will be an organization meeting and will decide on the location in the United States, etc.

The next meeting will not come until the latter part of April which will give plenty of time for your trip. Hope you have a happy and pleasant one.

I was highly pleased when you accepted the UNO appointment. I shall send the names down as soon as the House acts.

Hope you have a lovely Christmas.

Most sincerely,
Harry Truman

Mrs. Truman and I are looking forward to seeing you on the 7th of January. Hope your family are all in good health and can be with you for Christmas.

Don'ts for Tourists

H. C. Ostermann, 1916

The Lincoln Highway, the first road to connect America from coast-to-coast, was the brainchild of automobile enthusiast Carl Fisher. Fisher introduced his idea in 1912 and soon had many supporters. The Lincoln Highway Association was formed in 1913. A cross-country road was a novel idea in 1913, when automobiles were still a new-fangled arrival on the scene. America's roads had been designed for foot, horse, and wagon travel, so motorists faced frustrating to impossible conditions. While driving cross-country is a commonplace event today, in the early 1900s it was a momentous undertaking. Lincoln Highway Association Field Scretary H. C. Ostermann wrote these tips for travelers in The Complete Official Road Guide of the Lincoln Highway, *published in 1916.*

There are a few don'ts which every tourist should store away in his mind for future use. They will come in handy some time during the coast-to-coast trip.

Don't wait until your gasoline is almost gone before filling up. There might be a delay, or it might not be obtainable at the next point you figured on. Always fill your tank at every point gasoline can be secured, no matter how little you have used from your previous supply.

Don't allow your water can to be other than full of fresh water, and fill it whenever you get a chance. You might spring a leak in your radiator, or burst a water hose.

Don't allow the car to be without food of some sort at any time west of Salt Lake City. You might break down out in the desert, and have to wait some time until the next tourist comes along.

Don't buy oil in bulk when it can be avoided. Buy it in the one gallon original cartons.

Don't fail to have warm clothing in the outfit. The high altitudes are cold, and the dry air is penetrating.

Don't carry loaded firearms in the car. Nothing of this kind is in the least necessary except for sport, anyhow.

Don't fail to put out your camp fire when leaving.

Don't forget the yellow goggles. In driving west you face the sun all afternoon, and the glare of the western desert is hard on the eyes.

Don't forget the camphor ice [a type of moisturizer]. The dry air of the west will crack your lips and fingers without it.

Don't build a big fire for cooking. The smaller the better.

Don't ford water without first wading through it.

Don't drink alkali water. Serious cramps result.

Don't wear new shoes.

As a help to tourists making a coast-to-coast trip over the Lincoln Highway, and from a knowledge which has been dearly bought with experience, I offer a few suggestions and also a list of supplies which it has been found advisable to carry. These supplies largely depend upon the taste of the individual and the nature of the trip being made, but there are some things which should not be omitted from the outfit under any circumstances.

In case of a break down or delay, hunger or thirst are not pleasant companions, nor can a man work if his mouth is dry from dust and lack of water.

Camping directions will be useful when the party gets west of Omaha, Nebraska, the point where most people begin to camp, although it is not necessary to camp at all if you do not so desire.

No extra gasoline need be carried, although it is advisable to have an extra tank for use in case of emergency, such as a leak in your gas tank or a break in your gasoline connections.

Keep your tank filled as full as possible at all times. Fill it at each opportunity, no matter whether it is low or not. Then you will never be without it.

In sleeping on the ground, dig a trench or shallow indentation across the bed location for the hips. You will sleep much easier. Make it about one inch deep, with round edges about 8 inches wide, and the full width of the sleeping bag.

Put shoes, etc. under the edge of the sleeping bag, even in fair weather, as the dew is very heavy in the west. Several light blankets are warmer than one or two heavy ones. A cotton comfort with the blankets will keep out the wind.

The regular sleeping bag constructed for the purpose is the best thing to carry, if you intend to sleep out. These bags can be secured at any good sporting goods store, and will contain all the necessary blankets and quilts, with an outside waterproof covering.

Start early and stop before dark to select a camp site. If you wait until dark you may be unable to find a spot free from rocks.

Always camp on high ground—never by water on account of mosquitoes.

Casey at the Bat

Ernest Lawrence Thayer, 1888

Ernest Lawrence Thayer (1863-1940) first published this American classic anonymously in the San Francisco Examiner *newspaper on June 3, 1888. Thayer was a journalist who contributed a weekly ballad for the Sunday edition. "Casey at the Bat" became famous when comedian De Wolf Hopper recited it in New York City later that summer. It was a "home run" for Hopper, who went on to perform it over 10,000 times.*

The outlook wasn't brilliant for the Mudville nine that day;
    The score stood four to two with but one inning more to play.
And then when Cooney died at first, and Barrows did the same,
    A sickly silence fell upon the patrons of the game.

A straggling few got up to go in deep despair. The rest
    Clung to that hope which springs eternal in the human breast;
They thought if only Casey could but get a whack at that—
    We'd put up even money now with Casey at the bat.

But Flynn preceded Casey, as did also Jimmy Blake,
    And the former was a lulu and the latter was a cake;
So upon that stricken multitude grim melancholy sat,
    For there seemed but little chance of Casey's getting to the bat.

But Flynn let drive a single, to the wonderment of all,
    And Blake, the much despised, tore the cover off the ball;
And when the dust had lifted, and men saw what had occurred,
    There was Jimmy safe at second and Flynn a-hugging third.

Then from 5,000 throats and more there rose a lusty yell;
    It rumbled through the valley, it rattled in the dell;
It knocked upon the mountain and recoiled upon the flat,
    For Casey, mighty Casey, was advancing to the bat.

There was ease in Casey's manner as he stepped into his place;
  There was pride in Casey's bearing and a smile on Casey's face.
And when, responding to the cheers, he lightly doffed his hat,
  No stranger in the crowd could doubt 'twas Casey at the bat.

Ten thousand eyes were on him as he rubbed his hands with dirt;
  Five thousand tongues applauded when he wiped them on his shirt.
Then while the writhing pitcher ground the ball into his hip,
  Defiance gleamed in Casey's eye, a sneer curled Casey's lip.

And now the leather-covered sphere came hurtling through the air,
  And Casey stood a-watching it in haughty grandeur there.
Close by the sturdy batsman the ball unheeded sped—
  "That ain't my style," said Casey. "Strike one," the umpire said.

From the benches, black with people, there went up a muffled roar,
  Like the beating of the storm-waves on a stern and distant shore.
"Kill him! Kill the umpire!" shouted some one on the stand;
  And it's likely they'd have killed him had not Casey raised his hand.

With a smile of Christian charity great Casey's visage shone;
  He stilled the rising tumult; he bade the game go on;
He signaled to the pitcher, and once more the spheroid flew;
  But Casey still ignored it, and the umpire said, "Strike two."

"Fraud!" cried the maddened thousands, and echo answered fraud;
  But one scornful look from Casey and the audience was awed.
They saw his face grow stern and cold, they saw his muscles strain,
  And they knew that Casey wouldn't let that ball go by again.

The sneer is gone from Casey's lip, his teeth are clinched in hate;
  He pounds with cruel violence his bat upon the plate.
And now the pitcher holds the ball, and now he lets it go,
  And now the air is shattered by the force of Casey's blow.

Oh, somewhere in this favored land the sun is shining bright;
  The band is playing somewhere, and somewhere hearts are light,
And somewhere men are laughing, and somewhere children shout;
  But there is no joy in Mudville—mighty Casey has struck out.

Take Me Out to the Ball Game

Jack Norworth, 1908

This classic song is third behind "The Star-Spangled Banner" and "Happy Birthday" as the most easily recognized songs in America. Composer Albert von Tilzer and lyricist Jack Norworth, neither of whom had ever seen a baseball game, introduced the song in 1908. It enjoys enduring affection as America's "other" national anthem. "Take Me Out to the Ball Game" is sung at nearly every major league game during the "seventh-inning stretch." "Sou" in the fourth line refers to a coin. The baseball cards shown were produced in the 1880s.

Katie Casey was baseball mad.
　　Had the fever and had it bad;
Just to root for the home town crew,
　　Ev'ry sou Katie blew.
On a Saturday, her young beau
　　Called to see if she'd like to go,
To see a show but Miss Kate said,
　　"No, I'll tell you what you can do."

Take me out to the ball game,
　　Take me out with the crowd.
Buy me some peanuts and cracker jack,
　　I don't care if I never get back,
Let me root, root, root for the home team,
　　If they don't win it's a shame.
For it's one, two, three strikes, you're out,
　　At the old ball game.

Katie Casey saw all the games,
　　Knew the players by their first names;
Told the umpire he was wrong,
　　All along good and strong.
When the score was just two to two,
　　Katie Casey knew what to do,
Just to cheer up the boys she knew,
　　She made the gang sing this song:

Take me out to the ball game,
　　Take me out with the crowd.
Buy me some peanuts and cracker jack,
　　I don't care if I never get back,
Let me root, root, root for the home team,
　　If they don't win it's a shame.
For it's one, two, three strikes, you're out,
　　At the old ball game.

Spirit of Freedom

Jackie Robinson, 1958

When Jackie Robinson stepped onto the field with the Brooklyn Dodgers in 1947, he was not there just to play baseball. He was also taking a stand for civil rights for African Americans. After an exceptional ten-year career in professional baseball, Jackie Robinson entered the business world and continued to work for civil rights. He said, "I believe in the goodness of a free society. And I believe that society can remain good only as long as we are willing to fight for it—and to fight against whatever imperfections may exist." One part of his mission was keeping the cause before political leaders, exemplified in this letter he wrote to President Dwight D. Eisenhower in 1958.

The President
The White House
Washington, D.C.

May 13, 1958

My dear Mr. President:

I was sitting in the audience at the Summit Meeting of Negro Leaders yesterday when you said we must have patience. On hearing you say this, I felt like standing up and saying, "Oh no! Not again."

I respectfully remind you sir, that we have been the most patient of all people. When you said we must have self-respect, I wondered how we could have self-respect and remain patient considering the treatment accorded us through the years.

17 million Negroes cannot do as you suggest and wait for the hearts of men to change. We want to enjoy now the rights that we feel we are entitled to as Americans. This we cannot do unless we pursue aggressively goals which all other Americans achieved over 150 years ago.

As the chief executive of our nation, I respectfully suggest that you unwittingly crush the spirit of freedom in Negroes by constantly urging forbearance and give hope to those pro-segregation leaders like Governor Faubus who would take from us even those freedoms we now enjoy. Your own experience with Governor Faubus is proof enough that forbearance and not eventual integration is the goal the pro-segregation leaders seek.

In my view, an unequivocal statement backed up by action such as you demonstrated you could take last fall in dealing with Governor Faubus if it became necessary, would let it be known that America is determined to provide—in the near future—for Negroes—the freedoms we are entitled to under the Constitution.

Respectfully yours,
Jackie Robinson

My Hope and My Deep Faith

Dwight D. Eisenhower, 1954

President Dwight D. Eisenhower wrote this letter to an American woman named Marie Green.

June 14, 1954

Dear Mrs. Green,

I have heard of the tragic misfortunes that you have suffered during and since World War II. To lose a son is heart-breaking; to lose a son on a battlefield has a special tragedy of its own because of the inescapable conviction that man, long ago, should have found a way to eliminate such conflicts. You have my deepest and most sincere sympathy. I wonder if I may be bold enough to tell you a little bit about one of my most profound beliefs.

I abhor war as much as I know you do. But we in America cherish the freedom we have had throughout the 178 years of our existence as a nation; we cherish it above all else and we have never hesistated when necessary to fight to preserve it. In recent years there have risen fanatical individuals, possessed of greed and lust for power, who have managed for a time to threaten our security, our safety and our freedom. To stop these aggressors, America has had to make tremendous sacrifices, both as a nation and as individuals. We have succeeded in thwarting those who have attempted to destroy us; we always will.

Now, science has provided us with weapons of unprecedented power. But I know that if we are wise enough and strong enough and courageous enough, we can eventually—and in our lifetime—turn that force toward constructive efforts for the betterment of mankind everywhere, and not permit it to be used—at least exclusively—for mankind's destruction.

I feel impelled to express my belief that the sacrifices you and thousands of other mothers have made are bringing us—in a slow and painful process to be sure—but steadily bringing us to the place where man's freedom and personal dignity will forever be secure. That is my hope and my deep faith, and I pray that it is in some measure shared by you.

Sincerely,
Dwight D. Eisenhower

Pledge of Allegiance

1954

The first version of the pledge of allegiance, written by Francis Bellamy, was published in 1892 in a children's magazine called The Youth's Companion. *It was used as part of the 400th anniversary celebration of the arrival of Columbus. Though use of the pledge had long been common, the United States Congress did not officially recognize it until 1942, when it became part of the U.S. Flag Code. President Eisenhower approved a joint resolution of Congress to add the words "under God" to the pledge in 1954. On that occasion, he said, "In this way we are reaffirming the transcendence of religious faith in America's heritage and future; in this way we shall constantly strengthen those spiritual weapons which forever will be our country's most powerful resource in peace and war."*

83RD UNITED STATES CONGRESS
2ND SESSION

Joint Resolution

To amend the pledge of allegiance to the flag of the United States of America.

Resolved by the Senate and House of Representatives of the United States of America in Congress assembled,

That section 7 of the joint resolution entitled "Joint resolution to codify and emphasize existing rules and customs pertaining to the display and use of the flag of the United States of America", approved June 22, 1942, as amended (36 U. S. C., sec. 172), is amended to read as follows:

"Sec. 7. The following is designated as the pledge of allegiance to the flag, 'I pledge allegiance to the flag of the United States of America and to the Republic for which it stands, one Nation under God, indivisible, with liberty and justice for all.' Such pledge should be rendered by standing with the right hand over the heart. However, civilians will always show full respect to the flag when the pledge is given by merely standing at attention, men removing the headdress. Persons in uniform shall render the military salute."

Approved June 14, 1954.

The Situation in Little Rock

Dwight D. Eisenhower, 1957

President Eisenhower addressed the American people by radio and television on September 24, 1957, to explain the situation in Little Rock, Arkansas, surrounding the integration of Little Rock Central High School. He had earlier that day issued the order to send Federal troops to Little Rock to uphold the law.

Good Evening, My Fellow Citizens: For a few minutes this evening I want to speak to you about the serious situation that has arisen in Little Rock. To make this talk I have come to the President's office in the White House. I could have spoken from Rhode Island, where I have been staying recently, but I felt that, in speaking from the house of Lincoln, of Jackson and of Wilson, my words would better convey both the sadness I feel in the action I was compelled today to take and the firmness with which I intend to pursue this course until the orders of the Federal Court at Little Rock can be executed without unlawful interference.

In that city, under the leadership of demagogic extremists, disorderly mobs have deliberately prevented the carrying out of proper orders from a Federal Court. Local authorities have not eliminated that violent opposition and, under the law, I yesterday issued a Proclamation calling upon the mob to disperse.

This morning the mob again gathered in front of the Central High School of Little Rock, obviously for the purpose of again preventing the carrying out of the Court's order relating to the admission of Negro children to that school.

Whenever normal agencies prove inadequate to the task and it becomes necessary for the Executive Branch of the Federal Government to use its powers and authority to uphold Federal Courts, the President's responsibility is inescapable.

In accordance with that responsibility, I have today issued an Executive Order directing the use of troops under Federal authority to aid in the execution of Federal law at Little Rock, Arkansas. This became necessary when my Proclamation of yesterday was not observed, and the obstruction of justice still continues.

It is important that the reasons for my action be understood by all our citizens.

As you know, the Supreme Court of the United States has decided that separate public educational facilities for the races are inherently unequal and therefore compulsory school segregation laws are unconstitutional.

Our personal opinions about the decision have no bearing on the matter of enforcement; the responsibility and authority of the Supreme Court to interpret the Constitution are very clear. Local Federal Courts were instructed by the Supreme Court to issue such orders and decrees as might be necessary to achieve admission to public schools without regard to race—and with all deliberate speed.

During the past several years, many communities in our Southern states have instituted public school plans for gradual progress in the enrollment and attendance of school children of all races in order to bring themselves into compliance with the law of the land.

They thus demonstrated to the world that we are a nation in which laws, not men, are supreme.

I regret to say that this truth—the cornerstone of our liberties—was not observed in this instance.

It was my hope that this localized situation would be brought under control by city and State authorities. If the use of local police powers had been sufficient, our traditional method of leaving the problems in those hands would have been pursued. But when large gatherings of obstructionists made it impossible for the decrees of the Court to be carried out, both the law and the national interest demanded that the President take action.

Here is the sequence of events in the development of the Little Rock school case.

In May of 1955, the Little Rock School Board approved a moderate plan for the gradual desegregation of the public schools in that city. It provided that a start toward integration would be made at the present term in the high school, and that the plan would be in full operation by 1963. Here I might say that in a number of communities in Arkansas integration in the schools has already started and without violence of any kind. Now this Little Rock plan was challenged in the courts by some who believed that the period of time as proposed in the plan was too long.

The United States Court at Little Rock, which has supervisory responsibility under the law for the plan of desegregation in the public schools, dismissed the challenge, thus approving a gradual rather than an abrupt change from the existing system. The court found that the school board had acted in good faith in planning for a public school system free from racial discrimination.

Since that time, the court has on three separate occasions issued orders directing that the plan be carried out. All persons were instructed to refrain from interfering with the efforts of the school board to comply with the law.

Proper and sensible observance of the law then demanded the respectful obedience which the nation has a right to expect from all its people. This, unfortunately, has not been the case at Little Rock. Certain misguided persons, many of them imported into Little Rock by agitators, have insisted upon defying the law and have sought to bring it into disrepute. The orders of the court have thus been frustrated.

The very basis of our individual rights and freedoms rests upon the certainty that the President and the Executive Branch of Government will support and insure the carrying out of the decisions of the Federal Courts, even, when necessary with all the means at the President's command.

Unless the President did so, anarchy would result.

There would be no security for any except that which each one of us could provide for himself.

The interest of the nation in the proper fulfillment of the law's requirements cannot yield to opposition and demonstrations by some few persons.

Mob rule cannot be allowed to override the decisions of our courts.

Now, let me make it very clear that Federal troops are not being used to relieve local and state authorities of their primary duty to preserve the peace and order of the community. Nor are the troops there for the purpose of taking over the responsibility of the School Board and the other responsible local officials in running Central High School. The running of our school system and the maintenance of peace and order in each of our States are strictly local affairs and the Federal Government does not interfere except in a very few special cases and when requested by one of the several States. In the present case the troops are there, pursuant to law, solely for the purpose of preventing interference with the orders of the Court.

The proper use of the powers of the Executive Branch to enforce the orders of a Federal Court is limited to extraordinary and compelling circumstances. Manifestly, such an extreme situation has been created in Little Rock. This challenge must be met and with such measures as will preserve to the people as a whole their lawfully-protected rights in a climate permitting their free and fair exercise.

The overwhelming majority of our people in every section of the country are united in their respect for observance of the law—even in those cases where they may disagree with that law.

They deplore the call of extremists to violence.

The decision of the Supreme Court concerning school integration, of course, affects the South more seriously than it does other sections of the country. In that region I have many warm friends, some of them in the city of Little Rock. I have deemed it a great personal privilege to spend in our Southland tours of duty while in the military service and enjoyable recreational periods since that time.

So from intimate personal knowledge, I know that the overwhelming majority of the people in the South—including those of Arkansas and of Little Rock—are of good will, united in their efforts to preserve and respect the law even when they disagree with it.

They do not sympathize with mob rule. They, like the rest of our nation, have proved in two great wars their readiness to sacrifice for America.

A foundation of our American way of life is our national respect for law.

In the South, as elsewhere, citizens are keenly aware of the tremendous disservice that has been done to the people of Arkansas in the eyes of the nation, and that has been done to the nation in the eyes of the world.

At a time when we face grave situations abroad because of the hatred that Communism bears toward a system of government based on human rights, it would be difficult to exaggerate the harm that is being done to the prestige and influence, and indeed to the safety, of our nation and the world.

Our enemies are gloating over this incident and using it everywhere to misrepresent our whole nation. We are portrayed as a violator of those standards of conduct which the peoples of the world united to proclaim in the Charter of the United Nations. There they affirmed "faith in fundamental human rights" and "in the dignity and worth of the human person" and they did so "without distinction as to race, sex, language or religion."

And so, with deep confidence, I call upon the citizens of the State of Arkansas to assist in bringing to an immediate end all interference with the law and its processes. If resistance to the Federal Court orders ceases at once, the further presence of Federal troops will be unnecessary and the City of Little Rock will return to its normal habits of peace and order and a blot upon the fair name and high honor of our nation in the world will be removed.

Thus will be restored the image of America and of all its parts as one nation, indivisible, with liberty and justice for all. Good night, and thank you very much.

The Northern Lights

Hudson Stuck, 1914

Hudson Stuck was archdeacon of the Episcopal Church in Alaska. He traveled many thousands of miles by dogsled to visit mission stations and seek unreached native communities. In 1914 he published Ten Thousand Miles with a Dog Sled, *in which he described the landscape and climate of Alaska, native peoples and mission work among them, and his many Alaskan adventures. Following are his descriptions of two of the many times he observed the natural phenomenon known as the* northern lights *or* aurora borealis.

This was on the 6th of October, 1904, at Fairbanks, a little removed from the town itself. When first the heavens were noticed there was one clear bow of milky light stretching from the northern to the southern horizon, reflected in the broken surface of the river, and glistening on the ice cakes that swirled down with the swift current. Then the southern end of the bow began to twist on itself until it had produced a queer elongated corkscrew appearance half-way up to the zenith, while the northern end spread out and bellied from east to west. Then the whole display moved rapidly across the sky until it lay low and faint on the western horizon, and it seemed to be all over. But before one could turn to go indoors a new point of light appeared suddenly high up in the sky and burst like a pyrotechnic bomb into a thousand pear-shaped globules with a molten centre flung far out to north and south. Then began one of the most beautiful celestial exhibitions that the writer has ever seen. These globules stretched into ribbon streamers, dividing and subdividing until the whole sky was filled with them, and these ribbon streamers of greenish opalescent light curved constantly inward and outward upon themselves, with a quick jerking movement like the cracking of a whip, and every time the ribbons curved, their lower edges frayed out, and the fringe was prismatic. The pinks and mauves flashed as the ribbon curved and frayed—and were gone. There was no other color in the whole heavens save the milky greenish-white light, but every time the streamers thrashed back and forth their under edges fringed into the glowing tints of mother-of-pearl. Presently, the whole display faded out until it was gone. But, as we turned again to seek the warmth of the house, all at once tiny fingers of light appeared all over the upper sky, like the flashing of spicules of alum under a microscope when a solution has dried to the point of crystallisation, and stretched up and down, lengthening and lengthening to the horizon, and gathering themselves together at the zenith into a crown. Three times this was repeated; each time the light faded gradually but completely from the sky and flashed out again instantaneously. . . .

The next to be described . . . was the most striking and beautiful manifestation of the Northern Lights the writer has ever seen. It was that rare and lovely thing—a colored aurora—all of one rich deep tint.

It was on the 11th of March, 1907, on the Chandalar River, a day's march above the gap by which that stream enters the Yukon Flats and five days north of Fort Yukon. A new "strike" had been made on the Chandalar, and a new town, "Caro," established;—abandoned since. All day long we had been troubled and hindered by overflow water on the ice, saturating the snow, an unpleasant feature for which this stream is noted; and when night fell and we thought we ought to be approaching the town, it seemed yet unaccountably far off. At last, in the darkness, we came to a creek that we decided must surely be Flat Creek, near the mouth of which the new settlement stood; and at the same time we came to overflow water so deep that it covered both ice and snow and looked dangerous. So the dogs were halted while the Indian boy went ahead cautiously to see if the town were not just around the bend, and the writer sat down, tired, on the sled. While sitting there, all at once, from the top of the mountainous bluff that marked the mouth of the creek, a clear red light sprang up and spread out across the sky, dyeing the snow and gleaming in the water, lighting up all the river valley from mountain to mountain with a most beautiful carmine [red] of the utmost intensity and depth. In wave after wave it came, growing brighter and brighter, as though some gigantic hand on that mountain top were flinging out the liquid radiance into the night. There was no suggestion of any other color, it was all pure carmine, and it seemed to accumulate in mid-air until all the landscape was bathed in its effulgence. And then it gradually died away. The native boy was gone just half an hour. It began about five minutes after he left and ended about five minutes before he returned, so that its whole duration was twenty minutes. There had been no aurora at all before; there was nothing after, for his quest had been fruitless, and, since we would not venture that water in the dark, we made our camp on the bank and were thus two hours or more yet in the open. The boy had stopped to look at it himself, "long time," as he said, and declared it was the only red aurora he had ever seen in his twenty-odd years' life. It was a very rare and beautiful sight, and it was hard to resist that impression of a gigantic hand flinging liquid red fire from the mountain top into the sky. Its source seemed no higher than the mountain top—seemed to be the mountain top itself—and its extent seemed confined within the river valley.

The Exciting Adventure of Space

John F. Kennedy, 1961

On May 25, 1961, President John F. Kennedy made a speech to a joint session of Congress which he called a "Special Message to the Congress on Urgent National Needs." The following section of the speech has become legendary. Kennedy made a bold challenge to the American people and their government: put a man on the moon by the end of the 1960s. Though Kennedy tragically did not live to see it happen, America accepted the challenge and landed astronauts Neil Armstrong and Buzz Aldrin on the moon on July 20, 1969.

. . . Finally, if we are to win the battle that is now going on around the world between freedom and tyranny, the dramatic achievements in space which occurred in recent weeks should have made clear to us all, as did the Sputnik in 1957, the impact of this adventure on the minds of men everywhere, who are attempting to make a determination of which road they should take. Since early in my term, our efforts in space have been under review. With the advice of the Vice President, who is Chairman of the National Space Council, we have examined where we are strong and where we are not, where we may succeed and where we may not. Now it is time to take longer strides—time for a great new American enterprise—time for this nation to take a clearly leading role in space achievement, which in many ways may hold the key to our future on earth.

I believe we possess all the resources and talents necessary. But the facts of the matter are that we have never made the national decisions or marshalled the national resources required for such leadership. We have never specified long-range goals on an urgent time schedule, or managed our resources and our time so as to insure their fulfillment.

Recognizing the head start obtained by the Soviets with their large rocket engines, which gives them many months of leadtime, and recognizing the likelihood that they will exploit this lead for some time to come in still more impressive successes, we nevertheless are required to make new efforts on our own. For while we cannot guarantee that we shall one day be first, we can guarantee that any failure to make this effort will make us last. We take an additional risk by making it in full view of the world, but as shown by the feat of astronaut Shepard, this very risk enhances our stature when we are successful. But this is not merely a race. Space is open to us now; and our eagerness to share its meaning is not governed by the efforts of others. We go into space because whatever mankind must undertake, free men must fully share.

I therefore ask the Congress, above and beyond the increases I have earlier requested for space activities, to provide the funds which are needed to meet the following national goals:

First, I believe that this nation should commit itself to achieving the goal, before this decade is out, of landing a man on the moon and returning him safely to the earth. No single space project in this period will be more impressive to mankind, or more important for the long-range exploration of space; and none will be so difficult or expensive to accomplish. We propose to accelerate the development of the appropriate lunar space craft. We propose to develop alternate liquid and solid fuel boosters, much larger than any now being developed, until certain which is superior. We propose additional funds for other engine development and for unmanned explorations— explorations which are particularly important for one purpose which this nation will never overlook: the survival of the man who first makes this daring flight. But in a very real sense, it will not be one man going to the moon—if we make this judgment affirmatively, it will be an entire nation. For all of us must work to put him there.

Secondly, an additional 23 million dollars, together with 7 million dollars already available, will accelerate development of the Rover nuclear rocket. This gives promise of some day providing a means for even more exciting and ambitious exploration of space, perhaps beyond the moon, perhaps to the very end of the solar system itself.

Third, an additional 50 million dollars will make the most of our present leadership, by accelerating the use of space satellites for world-wide communications.

Fourth, an additional 75 million dollars—of which 53 million dollars is for the Weather Bureau—will help give us at the earliest possible time a satellite system for world-wide weather observation.

Let it be clear—and this is a judgment which the Members of the Congress must finally make—let it be clear that I am asking the Congress and the country to accept a firm commitment to a new course of action, a course which will last for many years and carry very heavy costs: 531 million dollars in fiscal '62—an estimated seven to nine billion dollars additional over the next five years. If we are to go only half way, or reduce our sights in the face of difficulty, in my judgment it would be better not to go at all.

Now this is a choice which this country must make, and I am confident that under the leadership of the Space Committees of the Congress, and the Appropriating Committees, that you will consider the matter carefully.

It is a most important decision that we make as a nation. But all of you have lived through the last four years and have seen the significance of space and the adventures in space, and no one can predict with certainty what the ultimate meaning will be of mastery of space.

I believe we should go to the moon. But I think every citizen of this country as well as the Members of the Congress should consider the matter carefully in making their judgment, to which we have given attention over many weeks and months, because it is a heavy burden, and there is no sense in agreeing or desiring that the United States take an affirmative position in outer space, unless we are prepared to do the work and bear the burdens to make it successful. If we are not, we should decide today and this year.

This decision demands a major national commitment of scientific and technical manpower, materiel and facilities, and the possibility of their diversion from other important activities where they are already thinly spread. It means a degree of dedication, organization and discipline which have not always characterized our research and development efforts. It means we cannot afford undue work stoppages, inflated costs of material or talent, wasteful interagency rivalries, or a high turnover of key personnel.

New objectives and new money cannot solve these problems. They could in fact, aggravate them further—unless every scientist, every engineer, every serviceman, every technician, contractor, and civil servant gives his personal pledge that this nation will move forward, with the full speed of freedom, in the exciting adventure of space.

Immense Flocks

Howard Stansbury, 1855

In 1849 Howard Stansbury, captain of the Corps of Topographical Engineers of the U.S. Army, was ordered to lead an expedition to explore the little-known Great Salt Lake of Utah. Stansbury published his report in 1855 as An Expedition to the Valley of the Great Salt Lake of Utah. *These excerpts are some of his observations of the Great Salt Lake's bird population.*

. . . The Salt Lake, which lay about half a mile to the eastward, was covered by immense flocks of wild geese and ducks, among which many swans were seen, being distinguishable by their size and the whiteness of their plumage. I had seen large flocks of these birds before, in various parts of our country, and especially upon the Potomac, but never did I behold any thing like the immense numbers here congregated together. Thousands of acres, as far as the eye could reach, seemed literally covered with them, presenting a scene of busy, animated cheerfulness, in most graceful contrast with the dreary, silent solitude by which we were immediately surrounded. . . .

The whole neck and the shores on both of the little bays were occupied by immense flocks of pelicans and gulls, disturbed now for the first time, probably, by the intrusion of man. They literally darkened the air as they rose upon the wing, and, hovering over our heads, caused the surrounding rocks to re-echo with their discordant screams. The ground was thickly strewn with their nests, of which there must have been some thousands. Numerous young, unfledged pelicans were found in the nests on the ground, and hundreds half-grown, huddled together in groups near the water, while the old ones retired to a long line of sand-beach on the southern side of the bay, where they stood drawn up, like Prussian soldiers, in ranks of three or four feet deep, for hours together, apparently without motion.

A full-grown one was surprised and captured by the men, just as he was rising from the ground, and hurried in triumph to the beach. He was very indignant at the unceremonious manner in which he was treated, and snapped furiously with his long bill to the right and left at everybody that came near him. . . .

In a ramble around the shores of the island, I came across a venerable-looking old pelican, very large and fat, which allowed me to approach him without attempting to escape. Surprised at his apparent tameness, we examined him more closely, and found that it was owing to his being perfectly blind; for he proved to be very pugnacious, snapping fiercely, but vaguely, on each side, in search of his enemies, whom he could hear, but could not see. As he was totally helpless, he must have subsisted on the charity of his neighbors, and his sleek and comfortable condition showed that, like beggars in more civilized communities, he had "fared sumptuously every day." The food of these birds consists entirely of fish, which they must necessarily obtain either from Bear River, from the Weber, the Jordan, or from the warm springs on the eastern side of Spring Valley, at all of which places they were observed fishing for food. The nearest of these points is more than thirty miles distant, making necessary a flight of at least sixty miles to procure and transport food for the sustenance of their young. Immense numbers of the young birds are huddled together in groups about the islands, under the charge of a grave-looking nurse or keeper, who, all the time

that we were there, was relieved from guard at intervals, as regularly as a sentinel. The goslings are an awkward, ungainly mass of fat, covered with a fine and exceedingly thick down of a light color.

. . . Rounding the north point of Antelope Island, we called at the little islet to which we had given the name of Egg Island, to look after our old friends, the gulls and pelicans. The former had hatched out their eggs, and the island was full of little, half-fledged younglings, who fled at our approach, and hid themselves under the first stone they could find. We caught several of them, and amused ourslves by putting them into the water, when they immediately followed the instinct of their natures, and paddled away with their little black feet most assiduously. One poor fellow, about four inches long, driven by the extemity of his fear, took to the water of his own accord, when he was swept out by the current to the distance of two or three hundred yards, and seemed quite bewildered by the novelty of his situation. As soon as he was discovered by the old birds, who hovered over our heads by thousands, watching our proceedings with great anxiety and noise, one—the parent, we judged, by its greater solicitude—lighted down by his side, and was soon joined by half a dozen others, who began guiding the little navigator to the shore, flying a little way before him, and again alighting, the mother swimming beside him, and evidently encouraging him in this his first adventure upon the water. The little fellow seemed perfectly to understand what was meant, and when we sailed away, was advancing rapidly under the convoy of his friends, and was within a few yards of the shore, which he doubtless reached in safety.

The young herons had grown, since our last visit, to nearly their full size, although they were not sufficiently feathered to fly. They, too, fled as fast as they could, and "cached" themselves in the recesses of the rocks. When closely pursued, however, they would turn and fight most fiercely, striking furiously with their long sharp bills as well as with their claws, screaming all the while with a shrill, discordant, and angry note. Those that were too small to leave the nest were equally pugnacious, standing on the defensive with a watchful and determined eye, which evinced any thing but a disposition to succumb, if attacked. A large number of young cormorants were also seen, who exhibited the same combative spirit when hard pressed; but the greater portion of them

ran from the nest to the water, where they gave instant evidence of the peculiar instinct belonging to the species, by desperate attempts to dive, and thus conceal themselves beneath the water. This they were unable to do, owing, I suppose, partly to the great density of the water, and partly to their want of strength. The stench was very offensive, from the great quantity of fish brought by the parent birds for the support of their very numerous progeny.

I Will Sing the Wondrous Story

Francis H. Rowley, 1886

This long-beloved American hymn was written in 1886 by Baptist minister Francis H. Rowley of Massachusetts. George Beverly Shea chose to sing it at Billy Graham's first evangelistic meeting in Charlotte, North Carolina, in 1947. Billy Graham's parents were in the audience. His mother especially liked the song and often requested that George Beverly Shea sing it. The photo shows young Billy Graham preaching at a Youth for Christ rally.

I will sing the wondrous story
    Of the Christ Who died for me.
How He left His home in glory
    For the cross of Calvary.

Chorus
Yes, I'll sing the wondrous story
    Of the Christ Who died for me,
Sing it with the saints in glory,
    Gathered by the crystal sea.

I was lost, but Jesus found me,
    Found the sheep that went astray,
Threw His loving arms around me,
    Drew me back into His way. *(Chorus)*

I was bruised, but Jesus healed me,
    Faint was I from many a fall,
Sight was gone, and fears possessed me,
    But He freed me from them all. *(Chorus)*

Days of darkness still come o'er me,
    Sorrow's path I often tread,
But His presence still is with me;
    By His guiding hand I'm led. *(Chorus)*

He will keep me till the river
    Rolls its waters at my feet;
Then He'll bear me safely over,
    Where the loved ones I shall meet. *(Chorus)*

Unchanging Principles

Jimmy Carter, 1977

Jimmy Carter, born in Plains, Georgia, in 1924, moved quickly up the political ladder to become a surprise presidential candidate and surprise winner of the 1976 presidential election. Following is his Inaugural Address of January 20, 1977. His swearing-in is pictured below.

For myself and for our Nation, I want to thank my predecessor for all he has done to heal our land.

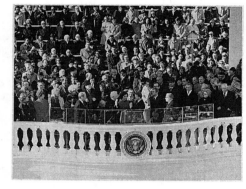

In this outward and physical ceremony, we attest once again to the inner and spiritual strength of our Nation. As my high school teacher, Miss Julia Coleman, used to say, "We must adjust to changing times and still hold to unchanging principles."

Here before me is the Bible used in the inauguration of our first President, in 1789, and I have just taken the oath of office on the Bible my mother gave me just a few years ago, opened to a timeless admonition from the ancient prophet Micah: "He hath showed thee, O man, what is good; and what doth the Lord require of thee, but to do justly, and to love mercy, and to walk humbly with thy God."

This inauguration ceremony marks a new beginning, a new dedication within our Government, and a new spirit among us all. A President may sense and proclaim that new spirit, but only a people can provide it.

Two centuries ago, our Nation's birth was a milestone in the long quest for freedom. But the bold and brilliant dream which excited the founders of this Nation still awaits its consummation. I have no new dream to set forth today, but rather urge a fresh faith in the old dream.

Ours was the first society openly to define itself in terms of both spirituality and human liberty. It is that unique self-definition which has given us an exceptional appeal, but it also imposes on us a special obligation to take on those moral duties which, when assumed, seem invariably to be in our own best interests.

You have given me a great responsibility—to stay close to you, to be worthy of you, and to exemplify what you are. Let us create together a new national spirit of unity and trust. Your strength can compensate for my weakness, and your wisdom can help to minimize my mistakes.

Let us learn together and laugh together and work together and pray together, confident that in the end we will triumph together in the right.

The American dream endures. We must once again have full faith in our country—and in one another. I believe America can be better. We can be even stronger than before.

Let our recent mistakes bring a resurgent commitment to the basic principles of our Nation, for we know that if we despise our own government, we have no future. We recall in special times when we have stood briefly, but magnificently, united. In those times no prize was beyond our grasp.

But we cannot dwell upon remembered glory. We cannot afford to drift. We reject the prospect of failure or mediocrity or an inferior quality of life for any person. Our Government must at the same time be both competent and compassionate.

We have already found a high degree of personal liberty, and we are now struggling to enhance equality of opportunity. Our commitment to human rights must be absolute, our laws fair, our national beauty preserved; the powerful must not persecute the weak, and human dignity must be enhanced.

We have learned that more is not necessarily better, that even our great Nation has its recognized limits, and that we can neither answer all questions nor solve all problems. We cannot afford to do everything, nor can we afford to lack boldness as we meet the future. So, together, in a spirit of individual sacrifice for the common good, we must simply do our best.

Our Nation can be strong abroad only if it is strong at home. And we know that the best way to enhance freedom in other lands is to demonstrate here that our democratic system is worthy of emulation.

To be true to ourselves, we must be true to others. We will not behave in foreign places so as to violate our rules and standards here at home, for we know that the trust which our Nation earns is essential to our strength.

The world itself is now dominated by a new spirit. Peoples more numerous and more politically aware are craving, and now demanding, their place in the sun—not just for the benefit of their own physical condition, but for basic human rights.

The passion for freedom is on the rise. Tapping this new spirit, there can be no nobler nor more ambitious task for America to undertake on this day of a new beginning than to help shape a just and peaceful world that is truly humane.

We are a strong nation, and we will maintain strength so sufficient that it need not be proven in combat—a quiet strength based not merely on the size of an arsenal but on the nobility of ideas.

We will be ever vigilant and never vulnerable, and we will fight our wars against poverty, ignorance, and injustice, for those are the enemies against which our forces can be honorably marshaled.

We are a proudly idealistic nation, but let no one confuse our idealism with weakness.

Because we are free, we can never be indifferent to the fate of freedom elsewhere. Our moral sense dictates a clear-cut preference for those societies which share with us an abiding respect for individual human rights. We do not seek to intimidate, but it is clear that a world which others can dominate with impunity would be inhospitable to decency and a threat to the well-being of all people.

The world is still engaged in a massive armaments race designed to ensure continuing equivalent strength among potential adversaries. We pledge perseverance and wisdom in our efforts to limit the world's armaments to those necessary for each nation's own domestic safety. And we will move this year a step toward our ultimate goal—the elimination of all nuclear weapons from this Earth. We urge all other people to join us, for success can mean life instead of death.

Within us, the people of the United States, there is evident a serious and purposeful rekindling of confidence. And I join in the hope that when my time as your President has ended, people might say this about our Nation:

—that we had remembered the words of Micah and renewed our search for humility, mercy, and justice;

—that we had torn down the barriers that separated those of different race and region and religion, and where there had been mistrust, built unity, with a respect for diversity;

—that we had found productive work for those able to perform it;

—that we had strengthened the American family, which is the basis of our society;

—that we had ensured respect for the law and equal treatment under the law, for the weak and the powerful, for the rich and the poor; and

—that we had enabled our people to be proud of their own Government once again.

I would hope that the nations of the world might say that we had built a lasting peace, based not on weapons of war but on international policies which reflect our own most precious values.

These are not just my goals—and they will not be my accomplishments—but the affirmation of our Nation's continuing moral strength and our belief in an undiminished, ever-expanding American dream. Thank you very much.

One Small Step

Richard Nixon and Neil Armstrong, 1969

At 11:49 p.m. on July 20, 1969, President Richard Nixon had a telephone conversation from the White House with Apollo 11 astronauts Neil Armstrong and Buzz Aldrin Jr., stationed at Tranquility Base on the moon. This historic moment was captured in the photograph below. The President's daily record for July 20 recorded this as a long-distance telephone call.

President Nixon: Neil and Buzz, I am talking to you by telephone from the Oval Room at the White House, and this certainly has to be the most historic telephone call ever made from the White House.

I just can't tell you how proud we all are of what you have done. For every American this has to be the proudest day of our lives, and for people all over the world I am sure that they, too, join with Americans in recognizing what an immense feat this is.

Because of what you have done the heavens have become a part of man's world, and as you talk to us from the Sea of Tranquility, it inspires us to redouble our efforts to bring peace and tranquility to earth.

For one priceless moment in the whole history of man all the people on this earth are truly one—one in their pride in what you have done and one in our prayers that you will return safely to earth.

Neil Armstrong: Thank you, Mr. President. It is a great honor and privilege for us to be here representing not only the United States, but men of peaceable nations, men with an interest and a curiosity, and men with a vision for the future. It is an honor for us to be able to participate here today.

President Nixon: Thank you very much, and I look forward, all of us look forward, to seeing you on the *Hornet* on Thursday.

Neil Armstrong: Thank you. We look forward to that very much, sir.

The Story of the Navel Orange

Ella M. Sexton, 1902

Ella M. Sexton wrote Stories of California *in 1902 chiefly "to interest the children of California in the beautiful land of their birth, to unfold to them the life and occurrences of bygone days, and to lead them to note and to enjoy their fortunate surroundings." She included this chapter on the history of one of America's favorite fruits and one of California's many profitable agricultural products. The 1882 postcard below showcases the celebrity status of California oranges.*

Who has not enjoyed a juicy navel orange, while wondering at its peculiar shape and lack of troublesome seeds? Yet few people know that this particular variety has brought millions of dollars into our state and made orange growing our third greatest industry.

Read this story of the seedless orange, this "golden apple of California," which was first cultivated by Luther Tibbets, of Riverside, and learn how Southern California has profited by its navel orange crops.

Nearly thirty years ago Mr. Tibbets came from New York to this state and took up free government land near what is now the beautiful city of Riverside. He was one of the half-dozen pioneer fruit-growers of that region, and had noticed at the San Gabriel Mission how well orange trees grew there. His wife and daughter waited in Washington, D.C., until a home should be ready here for them, and they often sent Mr. Tibbets plants and seeds from the Department of Agriculture. To this Department and its gardens in Washington, many curious plants are forwarded from other countries for growing and experiment in the United States. New kinds of grain or fruits are carefully cultivated and watched by the Department, and from it farmers can always get seeds or cuttings to try on their own farms.

Mrs. Tibbets often visited the Department gardens, and in 1873 she wrote to her husband that she could get him some fine orange trees if he would promise the government to take great care of them and to keep them apart from other trees till they fruited. Of course he agreed to give them special attention, and therefore that December he received three small, rooted orange trees. A cow chewed up one of these, but for five years the others were watched and tended. Then sweet white blossoms appeared on each little tree, and afterwards two oranges, like hard green bullets at first. Finally, in January, 1879, Mr. Tibbets picked four large, well-flavored, golden oranges, the first seedless ones ever grown outside of Brazil.

From the hot swamps of the tropical country at Bahia the United States Consul had sent six cuttings of this peculiar orange to be planted in the Washington gardens. All died but the two at Riverside. In 1880 they bore half a bushel of fruit, and the new seedless oranges were talked of throughout Southern California. The other orange growers had been cultivating "seedlings," trees which bore smaller fruit, with many bitter seeds and a thick skin. Many of these growers now cut

back their seedlings to bare limbs, and grafted the new orange on these branches. This is called "budding," and is done by cutting off a thin slip of bark with a tiny folded-up leaf-bud on it, inserting the graft in the branch to be budded and securing it there with wax to keep the air out. The little bud drinks in sap from the tree stem, and grows and blossoms true to its own mother tree.

There were few orange groves then, but soon nearly all were budded to the new kind, seventy-five acres being so changed on the Baldwin Ranch; and when these trees began to bear, some five years afterwards, people were much excited over the seedless fruit.

Such high prices were paid for these oranges at first, that orange growing boomed all over Southern California. People thought their fortunes were made when they set out a few acres of small budded trees they had paid a dollar or more apiece for. Whole towns sprang up in dry treeless valleys where only cattle and sheep had pastured, and land worth only twenty-five dollars an acre before the orange excitement, sold quickly for eight hundred and a thousand when planted with trees. The towns of Pomona, Redlands, Monrovia, and others in the orange localities were unknown before 1885, and grew to several thousand population in a few years. Everybody talked of the great profit in orange growing, and people who had nurseries of young trees grown from navel buds made fortunes.

At this day thousands of acres of seedless oranges are in full bearing and no one buys the old kinds. Hundreds of car-loads of the seedlings are not even picked, and ninety per cent of the eighteen thousand car-loads which make the season's orange crop are navel oranges. Over forty-five millions of dollars are now invested in the growing and marketing of this remarkable fruit.

At Riverside, the home of the orange, the two original Washington navel trees still stand. Mr. Tibbets guarded them for years, had them fenced with high latticework, and seldom allowed any one to touch them. He refused ten thousand dollars for them, since for months he sold hundreds of dollars' worth of buds from these parent trees. These two trees and their large family have caused thousands of people to come to the state, and have built up Southern California wonderfully.

Every Human Life is Precious

George H. W. Bush, 1990

President George H. W. Bush wrote this letter to his children as America prepared to take action against Iraq in Operation Desert Storm. The photograph shows the extended Bush family in 1992.

December 31, 1990

Dear George, Jeb, Neil, Marvin, Doro,

I am writing this letter on the last day of 1990.

First, I can't begin to tell you how great it was to have you here at Camp David. I loved the games (the Marines are still smarting over their 1 and 2 record), I loved Christmas Day, marred only by the absence of Sam and Ellie. I loved the movies—some of 'em—I loved the laughs. Most of all, I loved seeing you together. We are a family blessed; and Christmas simply reinforced all that.

I hope I didn't seem moody. I tried not to.

When I came into this job I vowed I would never wring my hands and talk about "the loneliest job in the world" or wring my hands about the "pressures of the trials."

Having said that, I *have* been concerned about what lies ahead. There is no 'loneliness,' though, because I am backed by a first-rate team of knowledgeable and committed people. No President has been more blessed in this regard.

I have thought long and hard about what might have to be done. As I write this letter at year's end, there is still some hope that Iraq's dictator will pull out of Kuwait. I vary on this. Sometimes I think he might, at others I think he simply is too unrealisitc—too ignorant of what he might face. I have the peace of mind that comes from knowing that we have tried hard for peace. We have gone to the UN; we have formed an historic coalition; there have been diplomatic initiatives from country after country. And so here we are a scant 16 days from a very important date—the date set by the UN for his total compliance with all UN resolutions including getting out of Kuwait—totally.

I guess what I want you to know as a father is this:

Every human life is precious. When the question is asked, "How many lives are you willing to sacrifice," it tears at my heart. The answer, of course, is none—none at all. We have waited to give sanctions a chance, we have moved a tremendous force so as to reduce the risk to every American soldier if force has to be used, but the question of loss of life still lingers and plagues the heart. My mind goes back to history:

How many lives might have been saved if appeasement had given way to force earlier on in the late '30's or earliest '40's? How many Jews might have been spared the gas chambers, or how many Polish patriots might be alive today? I look at today's crisis as "good" vs. "evil." Yes, it is that clear.

I know my stance must cause you a little grief from time to time; and this hurts me; but here at 'years-end' I just wanted you to know that I feel:

- Every human life is precious . . . the little Iraqi kids' too.

- Principle must be adhered to—Saddam cannot profit in any way at all from his aggression and from his brutalizing the people of Kuwait.

- And sometimes in life you have to act as you think best—you can't compromise, you can't give in, even if your critics are loud and numerous.

So, dear kids, batten down the hatches.

Senator Inouye of Hawaii told me, "Mr. President, do what you have to do. If it is quick and successful everyone can take the credit. If it is drawn out, then be prepared for some in Congress to file impeachment papers against you." That's what he said, and he's 100% correct.

And so I shall say a few more prayers, mainly for our kids in the Gulf, and I shall do what must be done, and I shall be strengthened every day by our family love which lifts me up every single day of my life. I am the luckiest dad in the whole wide world. I love you. Happy New Year and may God bless every one of you and all in your family.

Devotedly,
Dad

A National Loss

Ronald Reagan, 1986

On January 28, 1986, at about 11:40 a.m., 73 seconds after take-off, a leak in one of the solid rocket boosters ignited the main fuel tank of the space shuttle Challenger, *causing the shuttle to explode. The seven astronauts aboard died. That evening, from the Oval Office of the White House, President Ronald Regan addressed the nation in a television and radio broadcast with these words of comfort.*

Ladies and gentlemen, I'd planned to speak to you tonight to report on the state of the Union, but the events of earlier today have led me to change those plans. Today is a day for mourning and remembering. Nancy and I are pained to the core by the tragedy of the shuttle *Challenger*. We know we share this pain with all of the people of our country. This is truly a national loss.

Nineteen years ago, almost to the day, we lost three astronauts in a terrible accident on the ground. But we've never lost an astronaut in flight; we've never had a tragedy like this. And perhaps we've forgotten the courage it took for the crew of the shuttle. But they, the Challenger Seven, were aware of the dangers, but overcame them and did their jobs brilliantly. We mourn seven heroes: Michael Smith, Dick Scobee, Judith Resnik, Ronald McNair, Ellison Onizuka, Gregory Jarvis, and Christa McAuliffe. We mourn their loss as a nation together.

For the families of the seven, we cannot bear, as you do, the full impact of this tragedy. But we feel the loss, and we're thinking about you so very much. Your loved ones were daring and brave, and they had that special grace, that special spirit that says, "Give me a challenge, and I'll meet it with joy." They had a hunger to explore the universe and discover its truths. They wished to serve, and they did. They served all of us. We've grown used to wonders in this century. It's hard to dazzle us. But for 25 years the United States space program has been doing just that. We've grown used to the idea of space, and perhaps we forget that we've only just begun. We're still pioneers. They, the members of the *Challenger* crew, were pioneers.

And I want to say something to the schoolchildren of America who were watching the live coverage of the shuttle's takeoff. I know it is hard to understand, but sometimes painful things like this happen. It's all part of the process of exploration and discovery. It's all part of taking a chance and expanding man's horizons. The future doesn't belong to the fainthearted; it belongs to the brave. The *Challenger* crew was pulling us into the future, and we'll continue to follow them.

I've always had great faith in and respect for our space program, and what happened today does nothing to diminish it. We don't hide our space program. We don't keep secrets and cover things up. We do it all up front and in public. That's the way freedom is, and we wouldn't change it for a minute. We'll continue our quest in space. There will be more shuttle flights and more shuttle crews and, yes, more volunteers, more civilians, more teachers in space. Nothing ends here; our hopes and our journeys continue. I want to add that I wish I could talk to every man and woman who works for NASA or who worked on this mission and tell them: "Your dedication and professionalism have moved and impressed us for decades. And we know of your anguish. We share it."

There's a coincidence today. On this day 390 years ago, the great explorer Sir Francis Drake died aboard ship off the coast of Panama. In his lifetime the great frontiers were the oceans, and an historian later said, "He lived by the sea, died on it, and was buried in it." Well, today we can say of the *Challenger* crew: Their dedication was, like Drake's, complete.

The crew of the space shuttle *Challenger* honored us by the manner in which they lived their lives. We will never forget them, nor the last time we saw them, this morning, as they prepared for their journey and waved goodbye and "slipped the surly bonds of earth" to "touch the face of God."

Bunny Brown and His Sister Sue Keeping Store

Laura Lee Hope, 1922

Laura Lee Hope was listed as the author of scores of children's books in the 20th century, but she is not a real person. In the early 1900s, author Edward Stratemeyer (1862-1930) found his niche in the huge untapped market for children's books in America. His brilliant marketing scheme was to produce fiction series to keep young readers coming back to the bookstore. He was soon unable to keep up with all the writing himself and gathered a team of ghost-writers (writers who do not have their name attached to their work) to churn out books. Each series was given an author pseudonym that represented one or multiple authors. After Stratemeyer's death, his two daughters continued their father's successful business. Some of the most famous series of the Stratemeyer Syndicate are The Bobbsey Twins, Nancy Drew, *and* The Hardy Boys. *The* Bunny Brown and His Sister Sue *series had 20 titles. This excerpt from the installment published in 1922 reveals the way Americans shopped before self-service became the norm.*

"Here, Bunny! Here, Sue!" called Mrs. Brown, one bright, sunny morning. "Where are you?"

"We're coming, Mother!" answered Bunny. . . .

Then they ran to their mother, who was waiting for them on the back steps.

"What do you want, Mother?" asked Sue.

"Is it time to eat?" is what Bunny Brown asked. Bunny, like many children, was always ready for this.

"No, it isn't time for lunch," laughed Mrs. Brown. "But I want you to bring some things from the store so Mary can get lunch ready. And this is a chance for you to help your friend Mrs. Golden."

"What do you mean—help her?" asked Bunny. "Is daddy going to give her some money out of his bank so she can pay the cross man?"

"I don't know about that," replied Mrs. Brown. "But I mean you can help her now by getting some groceries from her. The more we buy and the more other families buy, the more money she will make, and then she can pay her bills."

"That's so!" exclaimed Bunny. "I'm going to ask all the fellows to buy their things of Mrs. Golden instead of going to Gordon's."

"And I'll ask the girls!" exclaimed Sue.

"We mustn't desert Mr. Gordon altogether," said Mrs. Brown. "He wants to do business, too. But Mrs. Golden needs our trade most, I guess, so get these things of her. I've written them down on a paper so you'll not forget, and as there are a number of them you had better take a basket, Bunny. . . ."

Together Bunny and Sue went around the corner to the little grocery and notion store. . . . Slowly Bunny read the little notice on the front door. It said: "Please come to the side door." Wonderingly the children went along the path to the side door, for the grocery of Mrs. Golden was in an old-fashioned house which had been built over so she could sell things in it. The side door was almost closed, but, though open a small crack, Bunny and Sue did not want to push it open further and go in. Instead they knocked.

"Yes? What is it? Who's there?" called the voice of Mrs. Golden. It was a weak, quavering old voice. . . .

"Are you very sick?" asked Sue.

"Cause if you are I'll go for the doctor," offered Bunny.

"Oh, no, thank you, my dears, I'm not ill enough for that," answered Mrs. Golden. "Just a bad sick-headache. I'll be better tomorrow. But I couldn't keep the store open today."

"That's too bad," said Bunny. "We came to get some things," and he took out the list his mother had written for him.

"Well, I want to sell things, but I am too ill to get up and wait on you," said the storekeeper. "I put that sign in the front door so if any wholesale wagons came to leave stuff they could find me. But, really, I don't feel able to get up."

Then Bunny had an idea.

"Couldn't Sue and I wait on ourselves?" he asked eagerly. "We want to get these things here, and if you told me where to find them—though I know where to find some myself—and if you told me how much they were, I could pay you, and it would be all right. I have the money."

"Yes, you might do that," said Mrs. Golden. "It would be fine if you could. Now let me see what you want, and then see if you can get it from the shelves."

"I can climb like anything!" said Bunny gleefully.

"Well, don't fall!" cautioned Mrs. Golden. Together, with the help of their friend, Bunny and Sue picked out from the closed store the things their mother had written on the list for them to get. Mrs. Golden told them where certain groceries were kept, and the price.

"Why, you are regular little storekeepers!" declared Mrs. Golden, trying not to think of her aching head. "You have waited on yourselves as well as I could have done."

"I wish we could wait on some regular customers!" boldly exclaimed Bunny.

"Wouldn't it be fun!" laughed Sue. . . .

Mrs. Golden thought it over for a minute. Really, with her head aching as it did, she was in almost too much pain to think, but she felt that something must be done. She needed all the money she could take in, and if customers were turned away from her store, because the door was closed, she would lose trade. . . .

"Couldn't we tend store for you—a little while?" asked Bunny again, as he saw Mrs. Golden thinking, as his mother sometimes thought, when he or Sue asked her if they might do something.

"We could ask you where things are that we don't know about," added Sue, "and we wouldn't talk loud or make a noise. . . ."

"Very well," said Mrs. Golden. "You may keep store for me, Bunny and Sue."

"Goodie!" exclaimed Sue, clapping her hands. Then she happened to remember that she must not make too much noise, and she grew quieter.

"I'll open the front door and take down the sign," said Bunny. "We'll wait on the customers for you, Mrs. Golden."

Bunny felt quite like a grown man as he removed the card and turned the lock in the front door, swinging it open. The shades had been pulled down over the show windows, and Bunny and Sue now ran these up. . . .

"You go to sleep now, Mrs. Golden," said Sue, going on tiptoe to the rear room, to look at the old woman lying on the couch. "You go to sleep. Bunny and I will tend store."

Then she went back to Bunny, who sat on a stool behind the grocery counter. He had decided he would sell things from that side of the store, while Sue could wait on the dry-goods and notions side.

"All we want now is some customers," remarked the little boy.

"Yes," agreed Sue. "We want to sell things."

They waited some little time, for the corner store was not in a busy part of town. Several times, as footsteps were heard outside, Bunny and Sue hardly breathed, hoping some one would come in to buy. But each time they were disappointed.

Finally, however, just when they were about to give up, thinking they would have to go home, a woman came in and looked around, not at first seeing any one.

"What can I do for you to-day, lady?" asked Bunny Brown, as he had often heard Mr. Gordon say.

"Oh, are you tending store?" the lady asked. She was a stranger to Bunny and Sue.

"Yes'm, I and my sister—I mean my sister and I—are keeping store for Mrs. Golden. She's sick," said Bunny. "I can get you anything you want."

"All I want is a loaf of bread," the lady answered.

Bunny knew where to get this, and also the kind the lady wanted, as it was the same sort of loaf his mother often sent him for. He put it in a paper bag and took the money. The lady gave the right change, so Bunny did not have to trouble Mrs. Golden.

All this while Sue stood on her side of the store, rather anxiously waiting. She wished the customer would buy of her.

"You are rather small to be in a store, aren't you?" asked the lady, as she started to leave with the bread.

"Oh, we know lots about stores," said Bunny. "We often play keep one, but this is the first time we ever did it regular."

"I know how to keep store, too," said Sue, unable to keep still any longer. "Would you like some needles and thread?"

"Yes, now that you speak of it, I remember I do need some thread, my dear," the lady answered, with a smile. "Can you get me the kind I want?"

"I—I guess so," Sue answered, yet she was a bit doubtful, as there were so many things among the notions.

"Well, perhaps I can help you," said the lady. "I see the tray of spools of silk right behind you, and if you'll pull it out I'll pick the shade I want. I have a sample of dress goods here."

Sue had often been with her mother when Mrs. Brown matched sewing silk in this way, and the little girl pulled out the shallow drawer of small spools. She saw the sample and knew the lady needed red sewing silk; so she at once pulled out the right drawer. Then she helped the customer match her sample until she had what she wanted.

"How much is it?" asked the lady, taking out her purse.

Here was Sue's trouble—she did not know exactly, and she did not want to go ask Mrs. Golden, for the storekeeper might be sleeping. To call her might make her head suddenly ache worse.

"I generally pay ten cents a spool," said the customer, "and I suppose that's what it is here. If it's any more I can stop in the next time I pass. That is, unless you can find out for sure."

"Oh, I guess ten cents is all right," said Sue, and she found out later that it was. Then the lady left with her bread and thread. The children had waited on their first customer all alone.

In the next hour, during which the children remained in the store, they waited on several customers, and did it very well, too, not having to ask Mrs. Golden about anything, for which they were glad. Of course the things they sold were simple articles, easy to find, and of such small price that the men or women who bought them had the right change all ready.

Once a boy came in, and you should have seen how surprised he was when Bunny waited on him. He was Tommy Shadder, a boy Bunny knew slightly.

"Huh! you workin' here?" asked Tommy, as he took the sugar Bunny put in a bag, not having spilled very much.

"Sure, I'm working here!" declared Bunny. "That is, for a while," he added, for he knew he would soon have to go home.

"Huh!" said Tommy again, as he went out. "Huh!"

A Time for Healing

William J. Clinton, 1995

On April 30, 1995, around 20,000 people gathered in the Oklahoma state fairgrounds for the "A Time for Healing" prayer and memorial service following the Oklahoma City bombing on April 19. In addition to President Bill Clinton, Billy Graham addressed the assembled mourners. The photograph below shows the Oklahoma City National Memorial, dedicated by President William J. Clinton on April 19, 2000, the fifth anniversary of the terrorist attack.

Thank you very much. Governor Keating and Mrs. Keating, Reverend Graham, to the families of those who have been lost and wounded, to the people of Oklahoma City who have endured so much, and the people of this wonderful State, to all of you who are here as our fellow Americans.

I am honored to be here today to represent the American people. But I have to tell you that Hillary and I also come as parents, as husband and wife, as people who were your neighbors for some of the best years of our lives.

Today our Nation joins with you in grief. We mourn with you. We share your hope against hope that some may still survive. We thank all those who have worked so heroically to save lives and to solve this crime, those here in Oklahoma and those who are all across this great land and many who left their own lives to come here to work hand in hand with you.

We pledge to do all we can to help you heal the injured, to rebuild this city, and to bring to justice those who did this evil.

This terrible sin took the lives of our American family . . . citizens in the building going about their daily business and many there who served the rest of us, who worked to help the elderly and the disabled, who worked to support our farmers and our veterans, who worked to enforce our laws and to protect us. Let us say clearly, they served us well, and we are grateful. But for so many of you they were also neighbors and friends. You saw them at church or the PTA meetings, at the civic clubs, at the ball park. You know them in ways that all the rest of America could not.

And to all the members of the families here present who have suffered loss, though we share your grief, your pain is unimaginable, and we know that. We cannot undo it. That is God's work.

Our words seem small beside the loss you have endured. But I found a few I wanted to share today. I've received a lot of letters in these last terrible days. One stood out because it came from a young widow and a mother of three whose own husband was murdered with over 200 other Americans when Pan Am 103 was shot down. Here is what that woman said I should say to you today: "The anger you feel is valid, but you must not allow yourselves to be consumed by it. The hurt you feel must not be allowed to turn into hate but instead into the search for justice. The loss you feel must not paralyze your own lives. Instead, you must try to pay tribute to your loved ones by continuing to do all the things they left undone, thus ensuring they did not die in vain." Wise words from one who also knows.

You have lost too much, but you have not lost everything. And you have certainly not lost America, for we will stand with you for as many tomorrows as it takes.

If ever we needed evidence of that, I could only recall the words of Governor and Mrs. Keating. If anybody thinks that Americans are mostly mean and selfish, they ought to come to Oklahoma. If anybody thinks Americans have lost the capacity for love and caring and courage, they ought to come to Oklahoma.

To all my fellow Americans beyond this hall, I say, one thing we owe those who have sacrificed is the duty to purge ourselves of the dark forces which gave rise to this evil. They are forces that threaten our common peace, our freedom, our way of life.

Let us teach our children that the God of comfort is also the God of righteousness. Those who trouble their own house will inherit the wind. Justice will prevail.

Let us let our own children know that we will stand against the forces of fear. When there is talk of hatred, let us stand up and talk against it. When there is talk of violence, let us stand up and talk against it. In the face of death, let us honor life. As St. Paul admonished us, let us not be overcome by evil, but overcome evil with good.

[T]his morning before we got on the plane to come here, at the White House, we planted [a] tree in honor of the children of Oklahoma. It was a dogwood with its wonderful spring flower and its deep, enduring roots. It embodies the lesson of the Psalms: that the life of a good person is like a tree whose leaf does not wither.

My fellow Americans, a tree takes a long time to grow and wounds take a long time to heal. But we must begin. Those who are lost now belong to God. Someday we will be with them. But until that happens, their legacy must be our lives.

Thank you all, and God bless you.

Home

Edgar A. Guest, 1916

"Home," the most famous poem of one of America's most beloved poets, Edgar A. Guest (1881-1959), is presented here in honor of the work of Habitat for Humanity International, begun by Millard and Linda Fuller in 1976, which has built over 350,000 homes for and with families of every state and around the world.

It takes a heap o' livin' in a house t' make it home,
    A heap o' sun an' shadder, an' ye sometimes have t' roam
Afore ye really 'preciate the things ye lef' behind,
    An' hunger fer 'em somehow, with 'em allus on yer mind.
It don't make any differunce how rich ye get t' be,
    How much yer chairs an' tables cost, how great yer luxury;
It ain't home t' ye, though it be the palace of a king,
    Until somehow yer soul is sort o' wrapped round everything.

Home ain't a place that gold can buy or get up in a minute;
    Afore it's home there's got t' be a heap o' livin' in it;
Within the walls there's got t' be some babies born, and then
    Right there ye've got t' bring 'em up t' women good, an' men;
And gradjerly, as time goes on, ye find ye wouldn't part
    With anything they ever used—they've grown into yer heart:
The old high chairs, the playthings, too, the little shoes they wore
    Ye hoard; an' if ye could ye'd keep the thumbmarks on the door.

Ye've got t' weep t' make it home, ye've got t' sit an' sigh
    An' watch beside a loved one's bed, an' know that Death is nigh;
An' in the stillness o' the night t' see Death's angel come,
    An' close the eyes o' her that smiled, an' leave her sweet voice dumb.
Fer these are scenes that grip the heart, an' when yer tears are dried,
    Ye find the home is dearer than it was, an' sanctified;
An' tuggin' at ye always are the pleasant memories
    O' her that was an' is no more—ye can't escape from these.

Ye've got t' sing an' dance fer years, ye've got t' romp an' play,
    An' learn t' love the things ye have by usin' 'em each day;
Even the roses 'round the porch must blossom year by year
    Afore they 'come a part o' ye, suggestin' someone dear
Who used t' love 'em long ago, an' trained 'em jes' t' run
    The way they do, so's they would get the early mornin' sun;
Ye've got t' love each brick an' stone from cellar up t' dome:
    It takes a heap o' livin' in a house t' make it home.

Righteous Fundamentals

Wesley Notgrass, 1933

Wesley Notgrass (1915-2007), grandfather of the editor, wrote this essay for his senior English class at age 18 in 1933. This was long before the modern homeschooling movement began to impact many American families, but then as now, children needed godly teaching and examples at home.

It is a well known fact that one's training at home determines what one is to be in the future. Good citizenship, like charity, begins at home. It is at home that the individual gains the moral ideals that he may carry with him through life. It is here that he obtains his first lessons in obedience, loyalty, and respect, and the way that he is taught these things may make him or may cause his downfall.

No matter which one, or how many members, earn the living in the home, each member should feel the responsibility for the success or failure of the rest.

It is certain that the home is an important place in the community, but too few people fully realize the real value of a home. Many regard it only as a place to eat and sleep, and are not satisfied with living in the same house for a great length of time, but are continually looking forward to moving somewhere else. Some do not live in a house long enough to really love it.

The home life of today is different from that of yesterday. Back in the days when mother was a girl, there were not as many things to draw the young people from the homes as there are today, and thus the young people were content to remain at home. But now the young people are attracted by the movies, dance halls, etc., and think that they cannot have a good time if they remain at home.

Future home life has been pictured as being torn up by divorce, economic burdens, and the increase of ease and luxury, and the virtues that can only be taught at home are being destroyed.

All the homes are not going to the "bow-wows," and we should be thankful that there are thousands that are not. The things that can only be learned at mother's knee are still being placed into the hearts of many growing children, and many marriages are partnerships.

Sunday schools, schools, and churches are wonderful institutions, but the righteous fundamentals will have to be firmly fixed in the mind of the child at home.

Freedom and Fear At War

George W. Bush, 2001

President George W. Bush delivered this "Address To a Joint Session of Congress and the American People" from the House Chamber in the United States Capitol on September 20, 2001, nine days after the terrorist attacks of September 11, 2001.

Mr. Speaker, Mr. President Pro Tempore, members of Congress, and fellow Americans, in the normal course of events, presidents come to this chamber to report on the state of the union. Tonight, no such report is needed; it has already been delivered by the American people.

We have seen it in the courage of passengers who rushed terrorists to save others on the ground. Passengers like an exceptional man named Todd Beamer. And would you please help me welcome his wife Lisa Beamer here tonight?

We have seen the state of our union in the endurance of rescuers working past exhaustion. We've seen the unfurling of flags, the lighting of candles, the giving of blood, the saying of prayers in English, Hebrew and Arabic. We have seen the decency of a loving and giving people who have made the grief of strangers their own.

My fellow citizens, for the last nine days, the entire world has seen for itself the state of our Union, and it is strong.

Tonight, we are a country awakened to danger and called to defend freedom. Our grief has turned to anger and anger to resolution. Whether we bring our enemies to justice or bring justice to our enemies, justice will be done.

I thank the Congress for its leadership at such an important time. All of America was touched on the evening of the tragedy to see Republicans and Democrats joined together on the steps of this Capitol singing "God Bless America."

And you did more than sing. You acted, by delivering $40 billion to rebuild our communities and meet the needs of our military. Speaker Hastert, Minority Leader Gephardt, Majority Leader Daschle and Senator Lott, I thank you for your friendship, for your leadership and for your service to our country.

And on behalf of the American people, I thank the world for its outpouring of support.

America will never forget the sounds of our national anthem playing at Buckingham Palace, on the streets of Paris and at Berlin's Brandenburg Gate.

We will not forget South Korean children gathering to pray outside our embassy in Seoul, or the prayers of sympathy offered at a mosque in Cairo. We will not forget moments of silence and days of mourning in Australia and Africa and Latin America.

Nor will we forget the citizens of 80 other nations who died with our own. Dozens of Pakistanis, more than 130 Israelis, more than 250 citizens of India, men and women from El Salvador, Iran, Mexico and Japan, and hundreds of British citizens.

America has no truer friend than Great Britain. Once again, we are joined together in a great cause. I'm so honored the British prime minister had crossed an ocean to show his unity with America. Thank you for coming, friend.

On September the 11th, enemies of freedom committed an act of war against our country. Americans have known wars, but for the past 136 years they have been wars on foreign soil, except for one Sunday in 1941. Americans have known the casualties of war, but not at the center of a great city on a peaceful morning. Americans have known surprise attacks, but never before on thousands of civilians. All of this was brought upon us in a single day, and night fell on a different world, a world where freedom itself is under attack.

. . . We will direct every resource at our command—every means of diplomacy, every tool of intelligence, every instrument of law enforcement, every financial influence, and every necessary weapon of war—to the destruction and to the defeat of the global terror network.

. . . And tonight a few miles from the damaged Pentagon, I have a message for our military: Be ready. I have called the armed forces to alert, and there is a reason. The hour is coming when America will act, and you will make us proud. This is not, however, just America's fight. And what is at stake is not just America's freedom. This is the world's fight. This is civilization's fight. This is the fight of all who believe in progress and pluralism, tolerance and freedom.

We ask every nation to join us. We will ask and we will need the help of police forces, intelligence services and banking systems around the world. The United States is grateful that many nations and many international organizations have already responded with sympathy and with support—nations from Latin America to Asia to Africa to Europe to the Islamic world. Perhaps the NATO charter reflects best the attitude of the world: An attack on one is an attack on all. The civilized world is rallying to America's side.

They understand that if this terror goes unpunished, their own cities, their own citizens may be next. Terror unanswered can not only bring down buildings, it can threaten the stability of legitimate governments. And you know what? We're not going to allow it.

Americans are asking, "What is expected of us?"

I ask you to live your lives and hug your children. I know many citizens have fears tonight, and I ask you to be calm and resolute, even in the face of a continuing threat. I ask you to uphold the values of America and remember why so many have come here. We're in a fight for our principles, and our first responsibility is to live by them. No one should be singled out for unfair treatment or unkind words because of their ethnic background or religious faith. . . .

The thousands of FBI agents who are now at work in this investigation may need your cooperation, and I ask you to give it. I ask for your patience with the delays and inconveniences that may accompany tighter security and for your patience in what will be a long struggle.

I ask your continued participation and confidence in the American economy. Terrorists attacked a symbol of American prosperity; they did not touch its source.

America is successful because of the hard work and creativity and enterprise of our people. These were the true strengths of our economy before September 11, and they are our strengths today.

And finally, please continue praying for the victims of terror and their families, for those in uniform and for our great country. Prayer has comforted us in sorrow and will help strengthen us for the journey ahead.

Tonight I thank my fellow Americans for what you have already done and for what you will do.

And ladies and gentlemen of the Congress, I thank you, their representatives, for what you have already done and for what we will do together . . . .

After all that has just passed, all the lives taken and all the possibilities and hopes that died with them, it is natural to wonder if America's future is one of fear.

Some speak of an age of terror. I know there are struggles ahead and dangers to face. But this country will define our times, not be defined by them. As long as the United States of America is determined and strong, this will not be an age of terror. This will be an age of liberty here and across the world. Great harm has been done to us. We have suffered great loss. And in our grief and anger we have found our mission and our moment. Freedom and fear are at war. The advance of human freedom, the great achievement of our time and the great hope of every time, now depends on us. Our nation, this generation, will lift the dark threat of violence from our people and our future. We will rally the world to this cause by our efforts, by our courage. We will not tire, we will not falter, and we will not fail.

It is my hope that in the months and years ahead life will return almost to normal. We'll go back to our lives and routines and that is good. Even grief recedes with time and grace. But our resolve must not pass. Each of us will remember what happened that day and to whom it happened. We will remember the moment the news came, where we were and what we were doing. Some will remember an image of a fire or a story of rescue. Some will carry memories of a face and a voice gone forever.

And I will carry this. It is the police shield of a man named George Howard who died at the World Trade Center trying to save others. It was given to me by his mom, Arlene, as a proud memorial to her son. It is my reminder of lives that ended and a task that does not end. I will not forget the wound to our country and those who inflicted it. I will not yield, I will not rest, I will not relent in waging this struggle for freedom and security for the American people. The course of this conflict is not known, yet its outcome is certain. Freedom and fear, justice and cruelty, have always been at war, and we know that God is not neutral between them.

Fellow citizens, we'll meet violence with patient justice, assured of the rightness of our cause and confident of the victories to come. In all that lies before us, may God grant us wisdom and may he watch over the United States of America. Thank you.

Ascending Long's Peak

Isabella L. Bird, 1879

An adventurous Victorian lady named Isabella L. Bird traveled alone in the Rocky Mountains of Colorado during the autumn and early winter of 1873. She wrote letters to her sister describing her adventures and later published her accounts under the title A Lady's Life in the Rocky Mountains.

Long's Peak, "the American Matterhorn," as some call it, was ascended five years ago for the first time. I thought I should like to attempt it. . . . "Mountain Jim" came in, and said he would go up as guide, and the two youths who rode here with me from Longmount and I caught at the proposal. Mrs. Edwards at once baked bread for three days, steaks were cut from the steer which hangs up conveniently, and tea, sugar, and butter were benevolently added. Our picnic was not to be a luxurious or "well-found" one, for, in order to avoid the expense of a pack mule, we limited our luggage to what our saddle horses could carry. Behind my saddle I carried three pair of camping blankets and a quilt, which reached to my shoulders. My own boots were so much worn that it was painful to walk, even about the park, in them, so Evans had lent me a pair of his hunting boots, which hung to the horn of my saddle. The horses of the two young men were equally loaded, for we had to prepare for many degrees of frost. Jim was a shocking figure; he had on an old pair of high boots, with a baggy pair of old trousers made of deer hide, held on by an old scarf tucked into them; a leather shirt, with three or four ragged unbuttoned waistcoats over it; an old smashed wideawake [style of hat], from under which his tawny, neglected ringlets hung; and with his one eye, his one long spur, his knife in his belt, his revolver in his waistcoat pocket, his saddle covered with an old beaver skin, from which the paws hung down; his camping blankets behind him, his rifle laid across the saddle in front of him, and his axe, canteen, and other gear hanging to the horn, he was as awful-looking a ruffian as one could see. By way of contrast he rode a small Arab mare, of exquisite beauty, skittish, high spirited, gentle, but altogether too light for him, and he fretted her incessantly to make her display herself.

Heavily loaded as all our horses were, Jim started over the half-mile of level grass at a hard gallop, and then throwing his mare on her haunches, pulled up alongside of me, and with a grace of manner which soon made me forget his appearance, entered into a conversation which lasted for more than three hours, in spite of the manifold checks of fording streams, single file, abrupt ascents and descents, and other incidents of mountain travel. The ride was one series of glories and surprises, of "park" and glade, of lake and stream, of mountains on mountains, culminating in the rent pinnacles of Long's Peak, which looked yet grander and ghastlier as we crossed an attendant mountain 11,000 feet high. The slanting sun added fresh beauty every hour. There were dark pines against a lemon sky, gray peaks reddening and etherealizing, gorges of deep and infinite blue, floods of golden glory pouring through canyons of enormous depth, an atmosphere of

absolute purity, an occasional foreground of cottonwood and aspen flaunting in red and gold to intensify the blue gloom of the pines, the trickle and murmur of streams fringed with icicles, the strange sound of gusts moving among the pine tops—sights and sounds not of the lower earth, but of the solitary, beast-haunted, frozen upper altitudes. From the dry, buff grass of Estes Park we turned off up a trail on the side of a pine-hung gorge, up a steep pine-clothed hill, down to a small valley, rich in fine, sun-cured hay about eighteen inches high, and enclosed by high mountains whose deepest hollow contains a lily-covered lake, fitly named "The Lake of the Lilies." Ah, how magical its beauty was, as it slept in silence, while there the dark pines were mirrored motionless in its pale gold, and here the great white lily cups and dark green leaves rested on amethyst-colored water!

From this we ascended into the purple gloom of great pine forests which clothe the skirts of the mountains up to a height of about 11,000 feet, and from their chill and solitary depths we had glimpses of golden atmosphere and rose-lit summits, not of "the land very far off," but of the land nearer now in all its grandeur, gaining in sublimity by nearness—glimpses, too, through a broken vista of purple gorges, of the illimitable Plains lying idealized in the late sunlight, their baked, brown expanse transfigured into the likeness of a sunset sea rolling infinitely in waves of misty gold.

We rode upwards through the gloom on a steep trail blazed through the forest, all my intellect concentrated on avoiding being dragged off my horse by impending branches, or having the blankets badly torn, as those of my companions were, by sharp dead limbs, between which there was hardly room to pass—the horses breathless, and requiring to stop every few yards, though their riders, except myself, were afoot. The gloom of the dense, ancient, silent forest is to me awe-inspiring. On such an evening it is soundless, except for the branches creaking in the soft wind, the frequent snap of decayed timber, and a murmur in the pine tops as of a not distant waterfall, all tending to produce eeriness and a sadness "hardly akin to pain." There no lumberer's axe has ever rung. The trees die when they have attained their prime, and stand there, dead and bare, till the fierce mountain winds lay them prostrate. The pines grew smaller and more sparse as we ascended, and the last stragglers wore a tortured, warring look. The timber line was passed, but yet a little higher a slope of mountain meadow dipped to the south-west towards a bright stream trickling under ice and icicles, and there a grove of the beautiful silver spruce marked our camping ground. The trees were in miniature, but so exquisitely arranged that one might well ask what artist's hand had planted them, scattering them here, clumping them there, and training their slim spires towards heaven. Hereafter, when I call up memories of the glorious, the view from this camping ground will come up. Looking east, gorges opened to the distant Plains, then fading into purple gray. Mountains with pine-clothed skirts rose in ranges, or, solitary, uplifted their gray summits, while close behind, but nearly 3,000 feet above us, towered the bald white crest of Long's Peak, its huge precipices red with the light of a sun long lost to our eyes. Close to us, in the caverned side of the Peak, was snow that, owing to its position, is eternal. Soon the afterglow came on, and before it faded a big half-moon hung out of the heavens, shining through the silver blue foliage of the pines on the frigid background of snow, and turning the whole into fairyland . . . .

Unsaddling and picketing the horses securely, making the beds of pine shoots, and dragging up logs for fuel, warmed us all. Jim built up a great fire, and before long we were all sitting around it at supper. It didn't matter much that we had to drink our tea out of the battered meat tins in which it was boiled, and eat strips of beef reeking with pine smoke without plates or forks. . . .

That night I made the acquaintance of [Jim's] dog "Ring," said to be the best hunting dog in Colorado, with the body and legs of a collie, but a head approaching that of a mastiff, a noble face with a wistful human expression, and the most truthful eyes I ever saw in an animal. His master loves him if he loves anything, but in his savage moods ill-treats him. Ring's devotion never swerves, and his truthful eyes are rarely taken off his master's face. He is almost human in his intelligence, and, unless he is told to do so, he never takes notice of any one but Jim. In a tone as if speaking to a human being, his master, pointing to me, said, "Ring, go to that lady, and don't leave her again tonight." Ring at once came to me, looked into my face, laid his head on my shoulder, and then lay down beside me with his head on my lap, but never taking his eyes from Jim's face.

The long shadows of the pines lay upon the frosted grass, an aurora leaped fitfully, and the moonlight, though intensely bright, was pale beside the red, leaping flames of our pine logs and their red glow on our gear, ourselves, and Ring's truthful face. One of the young men sang a Latin student's song and two Negro melodies; the other "Sweet Spirit, Hear My Prayer." Jim sang one of Moore's melodies in a singular falsetto, and all together sang, "The Star-Spangled Banner" and "The Red, White, and Blue." Then Jim recited a very clever poem of his own composition, and told some fearful Indian stories. A group of small silver spruces away from the fire was my sleeping place. . . . It was thickly strewn with young pine shoots, and these, when covered with a blanket, with an inverted saddle for a pillow, made a luxurious bed. The mercury at 9 p.m. was 12 degrees below the freezing point. Jim, after a last look at the horses, made a huge fire, and stretched himself out beside it, but Ring lay at my back to keep me warm. I could not sleep, but the night passed rapidly. I was anxious about the ascent, for gusts of ominous sound swept through the pines at intervals. Then wild animals howled, and Ring was perturbed in spirit about them. . . . But, above all, it was exciting to lie there, with no better shelter than a bower of pines, on a mountain 11,000 feet high, in the very heart of the Rocky Range, under twelve degrees of frost, hearing sounds of wolves, with shivering stars looking through the fragrant canopy, with arrowy pines for bed-posts, and for a night lamp the red flames of a camp-fire.

Day dawned long before the sun rose, pure and lemon colored. The rest were looking after the horses, when one of the students came running to tell me that I must come farther down the slope, for Jim said he had never seen such a sunrise. From the chill, gray Peak above, from the everlasting snows, from the silvered pines, down through mountain ranges with their depths of Tyrian purple, we looked to where the Plains lay cold, in blue-gray, like a morning sea against a far horizon. Suddenly, as a dazzling streak at first, but enlarging rapidly into a dazzling sphere, the sun wheeled above the grey line, a light and glory as when it was first created. Jim involuntarily and reverently uncovered his head, and exclaimed, "I believe there is a God!" . . . The gray of the Plains changed to purple, the sky was all one rose-red flush, on which vermilion cloud-streaks rested; the ghastly peaks gleamed like rubies, the earth and heavens were new created. Surely "the Most High dwelleth not in temples made with hands!"

Songs of Septimus Winner

Septimus Winner was born in Philadelphia in 1827. He was a prolific and popular composer, teacher, performer, and music publisher. His song "Listen to the Mockingbird" was wildly popular, selling millions of copies in the United States and Europe after its publication in 1856. He published the song under the pseudonym "Alice Hawthorne," which he used for many of his songs. In addition to his songs, Winner wrote over two hundred musical instruction books and thousands of arrangements for violin, piano, and other instruments. His well-loved hymn "Whispering Hope" was published in 1868, also under the pseudonum Alice Hawthorne.

Whispering Hope
1868

Soft as the voice of an angel,
   Breathing a lesson unheard,
Hope with a gentle persuasion
   Whispers her comforting word:
Wait till the darkness is over,
   Wait till the tempest is done,
Hope for the sunshine tomorrow,
   After the shower is gone.

Chorus
Whispering hope, oh how welcome thy voice,
Making my heart in its sorrow rejoice.

If, in the dusk of the twilight,
   Dim be the region afar,
Will not the deepening darkness
   Brighten the glimmering star?
Then when the night is upon us,
   Why should the heart sink away?
When the dark midnight is over,
   Watch for the breaking of day. *(Chorus)*

Hope, as an anchor so steadfast,
   Rends the dark veil for the soul,
Whither the Master has entered,
   Robbing the grave of its goal.
Come then, O come, glad fruition,
   Come to my sad weary heart;
Come, O Thou blest hope of glory,
   Never, O never depart. *(Chorus)*

Listen to the Mockingbird
1856

I'm dreaming now of Hally,
    Sweet Hally, sweet Hally;
I'm dreaming now of Hally,
    For the thought of her is one that never dies.
She's sleeping in the valley,
    The valley, the valley;
She's sleeping in the valley,
    And the mockingbird is singing where she lies.

Chorus
Listen to the mockingbird,
Listen to the mockingbird,
    The mockingbird still singing o'er her grave.
Listen to the mockingbird,
Listen to the mockingbird,
    Still singing where the weeping willows wave.

Ah! Well I yet remember,
    Remember, remember,
Ah! Well I yet remember,
    When we gather'd in the cotton side by side.

'Twas in the mild September,
    September, September,
'Twas in the mild September,
    And the mockingbird singing far and wide. *(Chorus)*

When the charms of spring awaken,
    Awaken, awaken,
When the charms of spring awaken,
    And the mockingbird is singing on the bough,
I feel like one forsaken,
    Forsaken, forsaken,
I feel like one forsaken,
    Since my Hally is no longer with me now. *(Chorus)*

Songs of the Carter Family

The Carter Family is known as the "First Family of Country Music." The trio was comprised of husband and wife A. P. and Sara Carter and her cousin Maybelle Carter, who was married to A. P.'s brother Ezra. They made their first recordings in Bristol, Tennessee, in 1927. Their repertoire centered around traditional "hillbilly" music, which was a national hit during the Great Depression. Below are two of the songs they made popular.

Will the Circle Be Unbroken?
Ada R. Habershon, 1907

There are loved ones in the glory,
   Whose dear forms you often miss;
When you close your earthly story,
   Will you join them in their bliss?

Chorus
Will the circle be unbroken
   By and by, by and by?
In a better home awaiting
   In the sky, in the sky?

In the joyous days of childhood,
   Oft they told of wondrous love,
Pointed to the dying Savior
   Now they dwell with Him above. *(Chorus)*

You remember songs of heaven
   Which you sang with childish voice,
Do you love the hymns they taught you,
   Or are songs of earth your choice? *(Chorus)*

You can picture happy gatherings
   Round the fireside long ago,
And you think of tearful partings,
   When they left you here below: *(Chorus)*

One by one their seats were emptied,
   One by one they went away;
Here the circle has been broken—
   Will it be complete one day? *(Chorus)*

Keep On the Sunny Side of Life

Ada R. Blenkhorn, 1899

There's a dark and a troubled side of life;
　　There's a bright and a sunny side, too;
Though we meet with the darkness and strife,
　　The sunny side we also may view.

Chorus
Keep on the sunny side,
Always on the sunny side
　　Keep on the sunny side of life;
It will help us ev'ry day,
It will brighten all the way,
　　If we keep on the sunny side of life.

Though the storm in its fury break today,
　　Crushing hopes that we cherished so dear,
Storm and cloud will in time pass away,
　　The sun again will shine bright and clear. (*Chorus*)

Let us greet with a song of hope each day,
　　Though the moments be cloudy or fair;
Let us trust in our Savior, alway,
　　Who keepeth ev'ry one in his care. (*Chorus*)

The Glorious Fourth

Historically, a grand oration on the Fourth of July was as essential as the picnics and fireworks. Towns large and small gathered to hear a famous orator or a local politician remind them of the blessings of Independence Day. The first selection is an excerpt from John Adams' famous letter to his wife Abigail predicting future celebrations of America's birthday. The following selections are excerpts from Independence Day orations from a few famous Americans.

July 3, 1776

. . . I am apt to believe that it will be celebrated, by succeeding Generations, as the great anniversary Festival. It ought to be commemorated, as the Day of Deliverance, by solemn Acts of Devotion to God Almighty. It ought to be solemnized with Pomp and Parade, with Shews, Games, Sports, Guns, Bells, Bonfires and Illuminations from one End of this Continent to the other from this Time forward forever more.

You will think me transported with Enthusiasm but I am not.—I am well aware of the Toil and Blood and Treasure, that it will cost Us to maintain this Declaration, and support and defend these States.—Yet through all the Gloom I can see the Rays of ravishing Light and Glory. I can see that the End is more than worth all the Means. And that Posterity will tryumph in that Days Transaction, even altho We should rue it, which I trust in God We shall not.

From a speech delivered by Daniel Webster on July 4, 1851, at the laying of the cornerstone of an addition to the U.S. Capitol.

Fellow-Citizens: I congratulate you, I give you joy, on the return of this Anniversary . . . . Hail! All hail! I see before and around me a mass of faces, glowing with cheerfulness and patriotic pride. I see thousands of eyes, turned towards other eyes, all sparkling with gratification and delight. This is the New World! This is America! This is Washington! And this the Capitol of the United States! And where else, among the Nations, can the sea of government be surrounded, on any day of any year, by those who have more reason to rejoice in the blessings which they possess? Nowhere, fellow-citizens; assuredly, nowhere. Let us, then, meet this rising sun with joy and thanksgiving!

From a speech by Frederick Douglass given in Rochester, New York, on July 5, 1852: "The Meaning of July Fourth for the Negro."

. . . This, for the purpose of this celebration, is the 4th of July. It is the birthday of your National Independence, and of your political freedom. This, to you, is what the Passover was to the emancipated people of God. It carries your minds back to the day, and to the act of your great deliverance; and to the signs, and to the wonders, associated with that act, and that day. This celebration also marks the beginning of another year of your national life; and reminds you that the Republic of America is now 76 years old. I am glad, fellow-citizens, that your nation is so young. Seventy-six years, though a good old age for a man, is but a mere speck in the life of a nation. Three score years and ten is the allotted time for individual men; but nations number their years by thousands. According to this fact, you are, even now, only in the beginning of your national career, still lingering in the period of childhood. I repeat, I am glad this is so. There is hope in the thought, and hope is much needed, under the dark clouds which lower above the horizon. The eye of the reformer is met with angry flashes, portending disastrous times; but his heart may well beat lighter at the thought that America is young, and that she is still in the impressible stage of her existence. May he not hope that high lessons of wisdom, of justice and of truth, will yet give direction to her destiny?

From a speech by Woodrow Wilson delivered at Gettysburg, Pennsylvania on July 4, 1913.

Here is the nation God has builded by our hands. What shall we do with it? Who stands ready to act again and always in the spirit of this day of reunion and hope and patriotic fervor? The day of our country's life has but broadened into morning. Do not put uniforms by. Put the harness of the present on. Lift your eyes to the great tracts of life yet to be conquered in the interest of righteous peace, of that prosperity which lies in a people's hearts and outlasts all wars and errors of men. Come, let us be comrades and soldiers yet to serve our fellow-men in quiet counsel, where the blare of trumpets is neither heard nor heeded and where the things are done which make blessed the nations of the world in peace and righteousness and love.

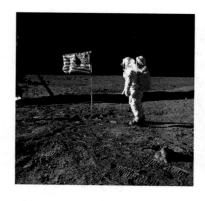

From a speech by John F. Kennedy given on July 4, 1946, as he campaigned for a seat in the United States Congress.

[T]he right of the individual against the State is the keystone of our Constitution. Each man is free. He is free in thought. He is free in expression. He is free in worship.

To us, who have been reared in the American tradition, these rights have become part of our very being. They have become so much a part of our being that most of us are prone to feel that they are rights universally recognized and universally exercised. But the sad fact is that this is not true. They were dearly won for us only a few short centuries ago and they were dearly preserved for us in the days just past. And there are large sections of the world today where these rights are denied as a matter of philosophy and as a matter of government. We cannot assume that the struggle is ended. It is never-ending. Eternal vigilance is the price of liberty. It was the price yesterday. It is the price today, and it will ever be the price. . . .

From an address given by Ronald Reagan on July 3, 1981.

. . . What makes our revolution unique and so exciting, then, is that it changed the very concept of government. Here was a new nation telling the world that it was conceived in liberty, that all men are created equal with God-given rights, and that power ultimately resides in "We the people."

We sometimes forget this great truth, and we never should, because putting people first has always been America's secret weapon. It's the way we've kept the spirit of our revolution alive—a spirit that drives us to dream and dare, and take great risks for a greater good. It's the spirit of Fulton and Ford, the Wright brothers and Lindbergh, and of all our astronauts. It's the spirit of Joe Louis, Babe Ruth, and a million others who may have been born poor, but who would not be denied their day in the sun.

Well, I'm convinced that we're getting that spirit back. The Nation is pulling together. We're looking to the future with new hope and confidence—and we know we can make America great again by putting the destiny of this Nation back in the hands of the people. And why shouldn't we? Because, after all, we are Americans.

As Dwight Eisenhower once said: "There is nothing wrong with America that the faith, love of freedom, intelligence and energy of her citizens cannot cure."

He was right. If we just stick together, and remain true to our ideals, we can be sure that America's greatest days lie ahead. Happy Fourth of July!

Sources

Books

1897 Sears, Roebuck & Co. Catalog, Fred. L. Israel, ed.

500 Best-Loved Song Lyrics, Ronald Herder, ed.

A Compilation of the Messages and Papers of the Presidents, James D. Richardson, ed.

A Heap O' Livin' by Edgar A. Guest

A Lady's Life in the Rocky Mountains by Isabella L. Bird

A New Version of the Psalms of David by Nicholas Brady and Nahum Tate

A Sermon Preached at The Quaker's Meeting House, in Gracechurch Street, London
    by William Penn

The Adventures of Colonel Daniel Boone by John Filson

Alaska Days with John Muir by Samuel Hall Young

The American Spelling Book by Noah Webster

An Expedition to the Valley of the Great Salt Lake of Utah by Howard Stansbury

Audubon and His Journals: The Missouri River Journal 1843 by John James Audubon

Autobiography of Andrew Carnegie

The Beauties of the State of Washington by Harry F. Giles

Bunny Brown and His Sister Sue Keeping Store by Laura Lee Hope

Canyons of the Colorado by John Wesley Powell

Children of the Tenements by Jacob A. Riis

The Complete Official Road Guide of the Lincoln Highway by H. C. Osterman

The Complete Works of Henry Wadsworth Longfellow

Discovery of Yellowstone Park by Nathaniel Pitt Langford

Early History of the Airplane by Orville and Wilbur Wright

The Experiences of a Bandmaster by John Philip Sousa

Foods That Will Win the War and How to Cook Them
    by C. Houston Goudiss and Alberta M. Goudiss

The Generall Historie of Virginia, New-England, and the Summer Isles by John Smith

Great Lakes Rhythm & Rhyme by Denise Rodgers

Hymns and Spiritual Songs by Isaac Watts

In His Image by William Jennings Bryan

Indian Child Life by Charles A. Eastman

Journal of Christopher Columbus, Clements R. Markham, ed.

Journals of Lewis and Clark, 1804-1806 by William Clark and Meriwether Lewis

Letters of a Woman Homesteader by Elinore Pruitt Stewart

Letters to His Children by Theodore Roosevelt, Joseph Bucklin Bishop, ed.

The Life of George Washington by Mason Locke Weems

Life on the Mississippi by Mark Twain

My Life and Work by Henry Ford

Myths and Legends of the Sioux by Mrs. Marie L. McLaughlin

The New England Primer, Paul Leicester Ford, ed.

Of Plimoth Plantation by William Bradford

One Man's Gold: The Letters and Journal of a Forty-Niner by Enos Christman,
    Florence Morrow Christman, ed.

Over There by Edgar A. Guest

Poor Richard's Almanack by Benjamin Franklin

Recollections and Letters of General Robert E. Lee by Captain Robert E. Lee

Reminiscences of My Life in Camp with the 33rd United States Colored Troops,
    Late 1st S.C. Volunteers by Susie King Taylor

Samuel F. B. Morse: His Letters and Journals in Two Volumes, Vol. 2, Edward Lind Morse, ed.

Scenes in the Hawaiian Islands and California by Mary E. Anderson

Sergeant York and His People by Sam K. Cowan

Songs of Faith and Praise, Alton H. Howard, ed.

Songs of the Civil War, Irwin Silber, ed.

The Songs of the Gold Rush, Richard A. Dwyer and Richard E. Lingenfelter, ed.

Speeches and Letters of Abraham Lincoln 1832-1865, Merwin Rose, ed.

Steamboatin' Days: Folk Songs of the River Packet Era by Mary Wheeler

Stories of California by Ella M. Sexton

Ten Thousand Miles with a Dog Sled by Hudson Stuck

The Treasury of American Prayer, James P. Moore, Jr., ed.

The Unwritten Literature of the Hopi by Hattie Greene Lockett

Vignettes of San Francisco by Almira Bailey

Works of John Adams by John Adams and Charles Francis Adams

The Yosemite by John Muir

Other Publications

"Fifth Annual Report of the Bureau of Ethnology to the Secretary of the Smithsonian Institution, 1883-84" by Washington Matthews

Denver Times

Evening Public Ledger (Philadelphia, Pennsylvania)

Globe (St. Paul, Minnesota)

Missouri Ruralist

New York Tribune

Sacramento Daily Record-Union

Tacoma Times (Tacoma, Washington)

The Evening Critic (Washington, D.C.)

The San Francisco Call

The Washington Times

University Missourian (Columbia, Missouri)

Virginia Gazette

Washington Post

Other Sources

Amaranth Publishing

American Presidency Project at the University of California, Santa Barbara

Ashbrook Center for Public Affairs at Ashland University

Chicago Historical Society

Chronicling America (Library of Congress)

Columbia University

Nethymnal.org

Dickinson College

Eisenhower Presidential Library and Museum

Flushing Monthly Meeting

Franklin D. Roosevelt Presidential Library and Museum

George Mason University

Grace Bedell Foundation

Harry S. Truman Presidential Library and Museum

John D. Rockefeller, Jr. Library at Colonial Williamsburg

John F. Kennedy Presidential Library and Museum

Library of Congress

Maine Historical Society

Massachusetts Historical Society

Other Sources, continued

Miller Center of Public Affairs at the
University of Virginia
National Archives and Records Administration
National Park Service
National Postal Museum
(Smithsonian Institution)
National Public Radio
Poetry Foundation
Public Broadcasting Service
Ronald Reagan Presidential Foundation
and Library
San José State University
SandHillCity.com
Smithsonian Institution
Texas State Library and Archives Commission
Thomas Jefferson Foundation
University of Missouri
University of Virginia Library
Virginia Polytechnic Institute and
State University

Image Credits

Selections as Assigned in Lessons of *America the Beautiful*

Selections in Alphabetical Order by Title

Selections in Alphabetical Order by Author

Selections in Chronological Order

Selections by Category

Poetry

Songs

Speeches

Index